Software
Development
with Ada

INTERNATIONAL COMPUTER SCIENCE SERIES

Consulting editors   **A D McGettrick**   University of Strathclyde
                        J van Leeuwen   University of Utrecht

OTHER TITLES IN THE SERIES

Software Development with Ada

Ian Sommerville
University of Lancaster

Ron Morrison
University of St Andrews

ADDISON-WESLEY
PUBLISHING
COMPANY

Wokingham, England · Reading, Massachusetts · Menlo Park, California
New York · Don Mills, Ontario · Amsterdam · Bonn · Sydney
Singapore · Tokyo · Madrid · Bogota · Santiago · San Juan

Cover graphic by kind permission of Digital Pictures, London.
Typeset by Wordsmiths Typesetting Ltd.
Printed and bound in Great Britain by R J Acford.

First printed 1987.

British Library Cataloguing in Publication Data

Software development with Ada.—
    (International computer science series).
    1. Computer software—Development   2. Ada
    (Computer program language)
    I. Title   II. Morrison, Ron   III. Series
    005.1'2   QA76.76.D47

    ISBN 0–201–14227–9

Library of Congress Cataloging in Publication Data

Sommerville, Ian.
    Software development with Ada.

    (International computer science series)
    Bibliography: p.
    Includes index.
    1. Computer software—Development.   2. Ada (Computer
program language)   I. Morrison, R. (Ronald), 1946 –
II. Title.   III. Series.
QA76.76.D47S67   1987   005.13'3   87–11553
ISBN 0–201–14227–9 (pbk.)

Preface

The construction of large, reliable software systems is a very expensive business. This is particularly true when they are embedded real-time systems, which are becoming more and more essential to the functioning of the economies of the developed countries. The programming language Ada was invented in an attempt to reduce such system costs, and this book is about the best ways to use Ada in building large software systems. The book is not an introduction to Ada but is concerned with software engineering and the use of Ada in developing large software systems.

Why this book was written

We believe that the effective use of Ada will make a dramatic difference to the cost and to the quality of real-time software systems. However, effective use of Ada does not simply imply learning the language itself; it also implies that the programmer has an understanding of the concepts which underlie the language facilities in Ada. Without this understanding, the software engineer will inevitably develop Ada programs that are really like programs in some other simpler language but which are expressed using Ada syntax.

Therefore, in this book, we discuss what we believe to be good software development practice and embody this discussion in Ada. Whilst Ada programs and examples pervade the book, what are really important are the concepts that these examples illustrate. So, this is not just a book about Ada, it is also a book about software engineering and practices which will lead to cheaper, more reliable, more maintainable software systems.

Who this book is for

This book is for readers who have some programming experience. Readers must be familiar with at least one high-level programming language such as Pascal, C or FORTRAN and should either be familiar with Ada or be in the process of learning Ada. This is not an Ada primer and we spend little time discussing the general syntax and semantics of the language. The book has been designed so that it may be used in conjunction with one of the many Ada primers now available. The book will be of use to software engineers who are working in industry, graduate students working in some aspect of software engineering and advanced undergraduate students who are learning Ada or who have completed a first course in the language.

What's in the book

It is about software systems design and programming. We start by introducing software engineering and the notion of a software life cycle. We then discuss the rationale for the development of Ada, the costs of software development and the influence Ada is likely to have on these software costs.

In Chapter 2, we discuss a topic that is of increasing importance, namely software engineering environments. A software engineering environment is a support system which assists with software development, and we look at different types of environment and assess their utility as software engineering environments. We pay particular attention to the APSE, an environment to support Ada program development. As well as discussing its good points, we also critically examine what features of that environment are likely to cause problems for environment developers.

Chapters 3–5 reflect our view of the activity of software design. Simplistically, we consider design to be a staged process in which the designer starts by identifying a system architecture and defines the interfaces between subsystems. The next stage is to specify the system in more detail, and the final stage is to express the system design as a set of algorithms that may be translated easily to an executable program. We illustrate the design process using a linking example of an electronic mail system.

Chapter 3 concentrates on the activity of high-level design. We discuss a technique for decomposing a system into subsystems that is based on different subsystem classes, and we spend some time discussing the design of subsystem interfaces. This discussion is continued in Chapter 4, where we describe some techniques for augmenting Ada programs with formal specifications of the semantics as well as the syntax of interfaces. In general, the topic of formal specification is too large to be discussed in a book like this so we concentrate on interface specification in this chapter.

Chapter 5 takes a more detailed look at design. We examine in some detail two design methodologies, namely top-down functional decomposition and object oriented design, and show how each of these may be used in Ada. In fact, we conclude that the best approach to large systems design is not to adopt a single methodology but to use different methodologies as appropriate for different parts of the system.

Chapters 6–11 look at Ada language features and how they may best be used in large systems implementation. Chapter 6 is a discussion of data typing in general and Ada's type facilities in particular. We discuss the factors that influence the design of language type systems and look at abstract data type implementation. In fact, the notion of abstract data types and their use pervades the book and it is clear that Ada support for this construct is probably the most significant language feature.

Chapter 7 discusses how effective programming style with Ada enhances the readability and maintainability of programs. We show how layout and style affect readability and discuss how types, subprograms and packages should be used. We also discuss the use of Ada's control structures and, in particular, how exceptions should be used.

Chapter 8 describes the features of Ada that are most useful in the construction of large software systems. We describe the incremental compilation facilities of Ada and its drawbacks, and we show how compilation units may be used in top-down program construction. We also look at name space management and the correct use of the Ada renaming and overloading facilities. Finally in this chapter, we discuss Ada generics and how these may be used to produce generalized packages and subprograms.

Chapters 9 and 10 look at parallel programming and the features of Ada that are used in real-time systems development. Chapter 9 is a comprehensive discussion of Ada's tasking facilities and how these may be used, and this is continued in Chapter 10 where we show how time-critical programs may be developed. We also discuss the implementation of interrupt-driven programs, the use of representation clauses and exceptions in real-time systems.

Chapter 11 tackles the topic of input/output. We explain the technique that the designers of Ada have adopted in their input/output model and discuss the difficult problems inherent in I/O design. We also show how Ada constructs may be used to isolate I/O facilities, thus leading to more maintainable programs.

Finally, Chapter 12 discusses portability and software reuse. We look at system dependencies that may arise and show how they can be managed. We also discuss the difficulties inherent in producing reusable software and suggest that this may be more difficult than was perhaps envisaged by Ada's designers.

All chapters conclude with a summary of the material covered and suggested further reading. An appendix which includes a number of examples and project suggestions is included for instructors or those using the book for self-study.

How to read the book

Readers who are already familiar with Ada should have no difficulty in reading the book from end to end. Naturally, however, such readers will normally dip into the book, selecting chapters of most interest. Readers who are learning Ada and are using this book in conjunction with an Ada primer might have some problems in understanding some of the examples in Chapters 3–5. These readers should look at Chapter 1 and then go on to Chapter 6 and the following chapters. After reading these chapters, the examples in the early part of the book should be straightforward.

Ian Sommerville
Ron Morrison

Contents

Chapter 1 Software Engineering

Although all computer programs have much in common, it is now recognized that the problems of developing large software systems are distinct from those that arise in the development of small computer programs. Typically, small programs implement well-defined objectives and, after implementation and testing, are not subject to a great deal of change. The programmer of these small systems usually understands the problem to be solved and can write the entire solution (program) in a relatively short time. For such programs, there is often no need for detailed specification and design documents to describe the system as a listing of the code is often all that is needed to understand it.

Some problems, however, are so complex that programs to solve these problems must be very large indeed. They may be made up of thousands or even millions of lines of code and cannot possibly be understood in detail or developed by a single person. They require large project teams for their implementation, and many documents are required to communicate the system requirements, specifications and design to the team members. In fact, the problems of developing a large software system are akin to those in any large engineering project such as the building of a new aircraft or power station. It is therefore appropriate to use the term 'software engineering' to describe the process of large software system construction.

Software engineering includes, but is broader than computer programming. It also embraces the analysis, specification, design, validation, documentation and maintenance of computer software systems. This distinction is brought out by Boehm (1979) who redefines the term 'software'. Rather than simply 'computer programs', he defines software to mean the computer programs plus all associated document- ation required to develop, operate and maintain these programs. Using this definition of software, Boehm goes on to define software engineering as follows:

> The practical application of scientific knowledge in the design and construction of computer programs and the associated documentation required to develop, operate and maintain them.

Boehm emphasizes that the term 'design' covers not just program design but also requirements design. Requirements design is the definition of the functions the system must provide and the constraints on the system's operation. He points out that the definition covers the complete software life cycle (discussed in the following section) and that the scientific knowledge base of software engineering is very small.

Software engineering is a new discipline. It was conceived in the late 1960s after the so-called software crisis was identified. This was the name given to the failure of software developers to build large systems which were required to run on the then-new third-generation computer hardware. The availability of powerful, relatively cheap hardware meant that it was possible to develop large software systems for complex applications. The problems in building these systems included massive cost overruns, delayed delivery, unreliability and software which was hard to use and maintain. In total, these problems made up the 'software crisis'.

Software engineering's childhood was in the 1970s. In response to the software crisis, new methods of software development evolved. The need for discipline and standardization rather than wizardry was recognized, and it was accepted that high-level programming languages were generally superior, in life cycle terms, to assembly languages for the implementation of machine-executable algorithms.

The 1970s saw the emergence of structured programming – a disciplined approach to computer program implementation. Design methodologies such as structured design (Constantine and Yourdon, 1979) and JSP (Jackson, 1975) and important ideas on data typing (Liskov and Zilles, 1974) were developed. The 1970s also saw the publication of several books on software management such as that by Brooks (1975). In these texts, good management was identified as the key to effective software engineering.

In spite of these important developments, the software crisis was not resolved. One reason for this was that new semiconductor technologies allowed very cheap computers to be built and this resulted in an explosion of new kinds of computer application. These new applications required programmers, generally recruited from other disciplines, who had had no exposure to software development methodologies. Sadly, they sometimes repeated the mistakes of their predecessors in the 1960s.

Another reason for the continuation of the software crisis was the fact that the tools which the software engineer had at his disposal were primitive in design and poorly engineered. Just as it is possible to build a major road using only hand tools and a large number of labourers, it is also possible to build software systems in this way. However, we can build better roads more cheaply by using fewer workers equipped with better, more powerful tools. It is therefore likely that the same applies to software systems and, by the late 1970s, the first basic software toolkits (Dolotta *et al.*, 1977) were being used for software production.

The general area of software tools is now one of the most important research areas in software engineering. The importance of tools and standards was realized by the major software customers and directly resulted in the creation of Ada as a standard programming language. Along with the language, the development of a standard Ada toolkit (more precisely, an environment), was also proposed. This is discussed in Chapter 2.

However, the most fundamental reason for the continuing software crisis is that programming methods and most existing software tools only address the implementation part of the software development process. They provide no assistance to the software specifier and only limited assistance to the software designer. Better methods, standards and tools will make software production more efficient. Until we understand and quantify the specification and design of software and build tools to support this process, the software crisis is unlikely to be completely resolved.

To continue our metaphor of software engineering as a growing and developing subject, it is now a healthy adolescent. The innocence of childhood has disappeared and we realize that there are rarely easy answers to the problems of software development. However, a great deal of investment of both money and effort is being made in software engineering, one sign of which is the programming language Ada.

Ada is a relatively new programming language which incorporates direct support for the programming methodologies of the 1970s. A tenet of Ada's design requirements was that the language should, as far as possible, force discipline on the programmer, and the language compiler should carry out as much checking as possible. Although Ada is far from perfect, it offers the opportunity for software engineers to build better systems by making use of the work of others. It is the first real software engineering standard and, by using Ada, we should be able to advance by standing on each other's shoulders rather than hobble around the same place because we are standing on each other's feet!

The aims of this chapter are to describe how Ada was conceived and developed and to discuss the role that Ada will play in the software life cycle. We examine the notion of a software life cycle and discuss how software costs are distributed across that life cycle. Given this life cycle model and associated cost distribution, it is possible to define what we consider to be a well-engineered computer system. In the final section of the chapter, we look at the specific effects that the use of Ada might have on the software life cycle and on life cycle costs.

1.1   The evolution of Ada

As discussed in the introduction to this chapter, software engineering came into being because the techniques used to develop small computer programs cannot usually be applied successfully to the building of large software systems. Many 'failed' software projects were military systems and the defence departments in all countries were (and still are) amongst the highest spenders on software systems.

In the UK the programming language Coral66 was adopted as a standard programming language for military systems, but in the United States chaos reigned. Although no one is really sure of the exact number, a study in 1974 showed that somewhere between 400 and 1500 different programming languages and language dialects were used in US Department of Defense (DoD) software projects. By far the largest percentage of DoD software costs was expended in building and maintaining embedded computer systems, and it was in this area that there was most diversity in programming languages and development support tools.

This diversity of programming languages reflected the variety of different computers in use, and many languages were targeted at a single type of computer system. Others were application-oriented higher level languages which were developed for a specific project and used only for that project.

Accordingly, in 1975, the notion of a single, common, high-level language specifically geared to the development of embedded computer systems was proposed. Although there are disadvantages in this approach (special applications-oriented languages can simplify the development of specific projects) the overall benefits of language standardization outweigh its disadvantages.

The benefits of standardization may be summarized as follows:

- Training costs are reduced because there is no need to learn a new language and environment for every new project.

- Software portability is increased so that the costs of moving software from one computer to another are minimized. This is particularly important given the current rate of hardware development which means computers become outdated in a very short time indeed.

- Software sharing is encouraged so that tools, techniques and software components developed during one project may be used on subsequent projects.

- Better communications between software engineers should exist in that a common programming language makes for a common understanding of concepts. Thus misunderstandings between software engineers are reduced.

- Training and conversion costs are reduced as, once trained, staff may move from project to project without the need to learn a new language.

In addition to these benefits which result from any common language, the use of a common language which directly supports methods based on structured programming, data abstraction, etc. seems likely to lead to better, more reliable software systems.

The US DoD set up a working group to study programming languages. This group included representatives from the Army, Navy and Air Force and had members from the UK, France and West Germany. Its remit was to identify requirements for embedded system programming languages, to evaluate existing languages against these requirements, and to recommend the adoption of one or a minimal set of programming languages for embedded systems projects.

First of all, a set of qualitative language requirements were established and refined. These were issued in documents which were given the names STRAWMAN, WOODENMAN and TINMAN (to imply hardening requirements). Basically, these documents identified a language whose features provided for a great deal of static compile-time checking, which incorporated structured control constructs, which had explicit facilities for parallel programming, etc. In short, the language should incorporate those developments in programming language research which took place in the early and mid 1970s.

The TINMAN document established fairly firm requirements for a common higher-order language and, using these requirements, 23 existing high-level languages were evaluated. All were found wanting in some way or another, but the evaluators concluded that it was technically feasible to design a programming language to meet the TINMAN requirements.

After further investigation of the economic costs and benefits of developing a new language, the DoD set up an international design competition for the language. Language evaluation had established that the acceptable bases for the language (called DoD-1 at this stage) were Algol68, Pascal or PL/1. All submitted designs had to be based on one of these languages.

Seventeen preliminary designs were submitted and four of these were chosen for further development. Each of these four languages used Pascal as a base language, although all of them were radically different from that language. After this development phase, two of the four languages were eliminated thus leaving two contenders in the design competition. Around about this time, initial discussions on programming environments to support DoD-1 were taking place. These discussions resulted in a set of requirements for the support environment described in Chapter 2.

In early 1979 the designs of the remaining two DoD-1 contenders were completed, and after a review lasting several months, one of them was chosen as a common high-level language for developing embedded computer systems. To the surprise of many, the language was not a US design, but was a European design by a team based at CII Honeywell-Bull in France. As it was hoped that the language would be used in non-military projects, the name DoD-1 was thought to be too militaristic. The language was renamed Ada. This name was chosen to honour the world's first computer programmer, Ada, Countess of Lovelace, who assisted Charles Babbage in the construction of his 'computing engines' in the nineteenth century.

Since 1979, the definition of Ada has been revised a number of times to iron out problems in the language design. To ensure standardization, the US DoD has forbidden subsets and supersets of the language and has established a compiler validation facility to check that implementations comply with the language definition. An ANSI standard for Ada was established in February 1983 and all the examples of Ada programs in this book were written to conform to that standard. At the time of writing several validated implementations of Ada are available and, by the late 1980s, Ada is likely to be in widespread use as a production programming language.

It is to the credit of the United States Department of Defense that the whole process of language requirements specification and review was carried out in public with inputs invited from the international computer science community. It is even more to its credit that chauvinistic considerations did not overrule technical considerations and that a language that was not designed in the USA was chosen because of its technical merits. The result of this is that Ada is now seen as an international language, not just an American idea, and it is almost certain that Ada will become the world standard language for embedded computer system programming.

1.2   The software life cycle

Like most biological and engineering systems, large software systems have an associated life cycle. During this life cycle, they are conceived, developed, used and, after becoming obsolete, they are finally discarded. In essence, the life cycle consists of a sequence of stages and the system moves through these stages by (it is hoped) systematic transformations of the representation of each stage. There are various opinions on what exactly these stages should be, but the most commonly adopted ('classical') model is that discussed here.

The classical software life cycle model is based on that of other large engineered systems and consists of a number of broad phases:

1. **Requirements analysis and definition**. During this phase, it is decided what the system should do.

2. **System design**. This phase consists of a translation of the system requirements into a software design. That is, the design phase involves deciding 'how' the requirements should be satisfied.

3. **Implementation**. This phase involves converting the system design

into an implementation in some programming language.

4. **Validation and testing**. During this phase, the system implementation is exercised with test data to ensure that the requirements are satisfied.

5. **Operation and maintenance**. This phase is usually the longest phase in the life cycle. The system is put into use and, as requirements and the system's environment change, the system is modified. At some stage, the system becomes obsolete either because of changing technologies, changing user needs or excessive maintenance costs.

This simple life cycle model can be broken down into more detailed stages as shown later in this section. The simple model also implies that the process is linear (Figure 1.1).

Figure 1.1   A linear software life cycle.

This linear model may be appropriate for small-to-medium scale hardware systems where, after delivery, system maintenance consists basically of replacing components that have worn out and that are not usually redesigned after they have gone into use.

For long-lived software systems (and for complex hardware systems such as aircraft) the linear life cycle model is not appropriate. It is usually impossible to provide completely specific requirements, and the requirements may not become clear until the system has been designed. System designs may not be implementable and design and requirements errors may not be discovered until system testing or until after the system has gone into use. After system delivery, new technology may become available and the system may have to be adapted to accomodate this. Some of the user's requirements may change and this may have to be reflected in the services provided by the system.

Rather than a linear model, therefore, it is more appropriate to look at the software life cycle as a graph. Each phase feeds information back into one or more earlier phases so that there is a constant repetition of life cycle stages. This is illustrated in Figure 1.2. Each phase feeds back information directly to the previous phase, which means that that phase must be modified. Furthermore, any one phase can feed back information to any other phase so that an error or omission can result in the repetition of all previous life cycle phases.

It is clear that a change that has to be made to the system after it has gone into use may affect any or all of the life cycle phases from

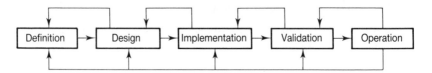

Figure 1.2   A cyclic life cycle model.

definition to testing and validation. For example, if a system coding error is discovered, this requires the implementation and testing phases to be re-entered. If a new peripheral device is to be incorporated, this may require some system redesign, implementation and testing. If a system user demands that the system should support some new requirement, this may involve repeating all of the software life cycle phases.

This model of the software life cycle is very broad and generalized. In practical software development projects, it must be broken down into smaller stages for the purposes of software management and to allow effective division of the work involved in producing the system.

Now let us look at each of the substages in this extended software development cycle. We describe these by considering each of the broad life cycle phases and by examining how each of these may be broken into substages.

1.2.1   Requirements analysis and definition

The first stage in the development of a software system is the definition phase during which the behaviour of the software system and its operational constraints are defined. For embedded systems, this stage is normally preceded by an overall systems definition which sets down what the complete (hardware and software) system must do and how functions are to be distributed between software and hardware.

The definition phase is normally made up of at least three substages:

- feasibility study
- requirements analysis
- requirements definition

The feasibility study establishes if it is feasible to construct the required software system and works from a broad statement of the overall goals of the project. The requirements analysis stage (sometimes called systems analysis) involves talking to users to establish what they require of the system. The resulting document might be a conceptual model of the system in a notation such as CORE, a proprietary requirements definition notation which is briefly described in Downes and Goldsack (1982) or in the form of a dataflow diagram (DeMarco, 1980). In some cases, this document might be combined with the requirements definition document described below.

After analysis, the precise system requirements must be established. This involves defining, as precisely as possible, the services that the system should provide and the constraints under which the system must operate. In addition, the requirements definition should define the external system entities and their relationships (broadly, system inputs and outputs). Thus if the system handles inputs from radars (say) and outputs to display screens, the precise form of the inputs and expected outputs should be set out in the requirements definition. Sometimes the detailed requirements document is termed a functional specification (FS), but we prefer to reserve this term for part of the activity of software design.

The most appropriate notation for requirements definition is probably some semi-formal structured natural language notation such as PSL/PSA (Teichrow and Hershey, 1976) or the so-called 'A7-method' (Heninger, 1980) where standard forms were used to describe inputs and associated outputs. Mathematically formal notations are not really appropriate during this phase because the requirements specification document must be read by both software developers and users.

1.2.2   System design

The next stage in the software life cycle is software design. During this stage a computational model is derived. The behaviour of this model must be that set out in the requirements specification, and the form must be such that it may be readily implemented in some programming language.

For large software systems, the process of software design involves several substages. During the early design stages, the system model is developed in outline and this is filled in as the design activity progresses. There are differing views, but the one we favour considers the design stage of the software life cycle to be made up of four substages:

- high-level design
- interface design
- design specification
- detailed or algorithmic design

During high-level design the system services are set out in the requirements definition and are allocated to particular subsystems. For example, all aspects of data collection might be gathered together into a 'data collection subsystem' responsible for collecting data from various sources. Alternatively, all systems associated with a particular device such as a radar might be gathered together into a 'radar subsystem'.

In large software systems, it is generally true that each first-stage subsystem is a large system in its own right. Therefore, different subsystems are normally designed in parallel by different design teams. In many cases, subsystems themselves are partitioned into sub-subsystems with the subsystem design carried out as if it was an independent system.

However, before design commences, it is vitally important that the interfaces between subsystems should be designed. This stage is critical as subsystem communication and integration depends on complete and consistent interfaces. Inadequately defined interfaces were one of the principal causes of many of the problems associated with the first large software systems. Because of this, it is helpful to use a formal notation for interface specification and to use software tools to check adherence to that specification.

In Chapter 3, we look at the process of partitioning a system into subsystems and present a graphical notation which shows subsystem relationships. We also describe, in that chapter, how Ada is useful for interface specifications in that its data abstraction facilities allow interfaces to be described without recourse to implementation details. However, Ada's facilities are only adequate for specifying the syntax of interfaces and the types passed across these interfaces. A more complete interface specification requires a definition of the interface semantics, and this is the topic covered in Chapter 4. There we make use of formal specification techniques to augment interface descriptions in Ada.

After interface design and specification, the next substage in the design process is to decompose each subsystem into a set of components and to establish a specification for each of these components. Component specifications may be completely informal and expressed in natural language, semi-formal where a quasi-programming language is used for specification, or completely formal where a mathematically rigorous notation is used.

Formal component specifications use a notation in which syntax and semantics are completely defined. The development of these notations (generally based on mathematical logic) is still a research problem, and current specification techniques have not been demonstrated to be cost-effective for the specification of complex systems with many inputs and outputs. Because this book is concerned with software development techniques that are currently practical, we do not discuss formal system specification here, but concentrate on interface specifications. However, we predict that formal software specifications are likely to become widely used in the 1990s and we provide recommendations for further reading in Chapter 4.

At this stage, it is perhaps useful to distinguish between the terms 'subsystem' and 'component' as they are used here. A subsystem is a system unit which provides a set of related services, whereas a component is a system unit which provides a single, distinct service. For example, in an office automation system, all information transmission services might be gathered together into an electronic mail subsystem. Within this subsystem, there may be a 'file mail' component whose service is to save mail on a permanent storage device.

Because subsystems are multifunctional, it is very difficult to attempt to provide formal subsystem specifications before decomposing the subsystems into components. Rather, the subsystem specification is created after functional decomposition and is an aggregate of the component specifications. Unlike component specifications, therefore, it acts as a post-design documentation rather than as a guide to the designer.

The fourth substage in the design process is the activity of detailed design or algorithmic design. During this design stage, the software specification is realized as a number of algorithms. The most appropriate notation for this detailed design is some form of program design language such as PDL (Linger *et al.*, 1978). Program design languages usually have the same control constructs as high-level programming languages, but often have a more flexible syntax and higher-level data types such as queues, lists, sequences, etc. The use of PDLs is discussed in Chapter 5, where detailed software design is covered.

1.2.3   Implementation

The next stage in this detailed life cycle model is sometimes considered to be the final design stage and sometimes the initial stage in the implementation phase. This stage is code design, which involves deciding how the algorithmic description of the system may be realized in a programming language.

The work involved in this stage depends largely on the 'closeness-of-fit' of the implementation language and the program design language. If the design language is a form of Ada (say) and the implementation language is Ada, then code design is a relatively simple process. On the other hand, if the programming language is assembly code or FORTRAN and an Ada-based PDL is used, more work is involved in deciding how to map Ada constructs on to the low-level language features. After code design, the final implementation stage which converts the PDL to an implementation is relatively straightforward. In itself, the programming process, in whatever language, is not particularly difficult and simply requires attention to detail. It is software design rather than computer programming that is a creative and difficult task.

1.2.4   Validation and testing

During the coding process, it is usual to carry out some testing whilst the code is being developed. On completion of coding, however, a more formal test phase is entered whose aim is to check that the system to be

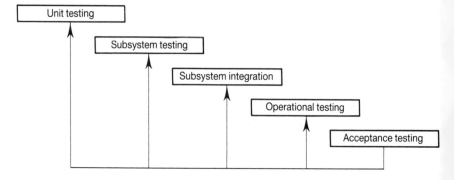

Figure 1.3 Phases of the testing process.

delivered matches that laid down in the requirements definition. This testing process is a multistage one which starts with the testing of relatively small software components and integrates the system in stages until the complete system has been built and tested. Each phase feeds back results, which may mean that previous phases have to be re-entered. This is illustrated in Figure 1.3.

The first substage of the testing process is called unit testing; program units (procedures, functions, etc.) are tested as they are written. In fact, the whole process of detailed design, implementation and testing is often incremental with detailed design, implementation and testing of different units all taking place in parallel. This entire process is usually the responsibility of individuals working in the program development group.

After unit testing, subsystem testing begins. This involves putting together entire subsystems and testing these with simulated input data. This substage might be undertaken by the program development group or might be the responsibility of an independent testing team. The principal aim is to test how the individual software components in a subsystem interact and work as a whole.

After each subsystem has been tested, the next substage in the software validation process is system integration. This involves taking all subsystems and exercising them together as a complete software system. Immense problems can arise if the detailed interface specifications were not available to subsystem designers or if programmers are undisciplined in their use of global data areas. It is during this stage that the majority of testing costs are incurred because of the complexity of subsystem interactions.This stage of testing and following stages are usually carried out by an independent software quality-assurance team rather than those responsible for the software development.

If a language such as Ada is used for system implementation, it is possible to devise software tools to process Ada subsystem definitions and check that interface specifications have been adhered to. On the other hand, if a lower-level implementation language is used, detailed interface testing procedures must be established as part of the operational testing process. After system integration, a final development testing phase called operational testing takes place. The system is presented with test inputs similar to those it is intended to process and operational testing is intended to check the conformance of the system with the software specifications.

Each stage of development testing discovers software errors and, after correction of these errors, all stages of system testing must be repeated. This means that the later an error is discovered by the testing process, the more expensive that error is to correct. It is therefore essential to devote sufficient resources to the early stages of system testing so that as many errors as possible are detected before system integration.

The final phase in the software development process before the system is brought into use is acceptance testing. Acceptance testing is a testing process carried out by the system user rather than the contractor responsible for software development. During acceptance testing, it is normal to exercise the system with 'real' data so that its operational performance may be ascertained.

1.2.5   Operation and maintenance

After the acceptance testing phase is complete, the system 'goes live' and is put into everyday use. Whilst the maintenance demands made after the system is in use vary dramatically from system to system, there are a number of maintenance phases, some of which may take place in parallel, which may be identified. These are:

- a honeymoon phase
- an error correction phase
- one or more evolutionary phases
- one or more perfective maintenance phases

During the honeymoon phase, users are learning about the new system and use it in a fairly unsophisticated way. They are not, therefore, driving the system hard and are not likely to detect many errors that are subtle and difficult to correct. The load on system maintenance staff is relatively light and may only involve correcting simple coding errors.

After some system experience, users begin to make heavier demands on the system and, typically, discover errors that were missed during system testing. These errors are often obscure and difficult to correct so that maintenance staff must spend a great deal of time on detailed debugging. Users also tend to discover, at this stage, errors or omissions in the software requirements and thus generate new requirements which define future system evolution.

After these initial phases (which may last months or even years!) large systems usually undergo a number of evolutionary phases. These evolutions are a result of changed system requirements and maintenance staff may be involved in redesigning and reimplementing entire subsystems.

For some large systems this process of evolution is continuous, but for others the system stabilizes with few changes to requirements. The maintenance load is relatively light, with most of the system maintenance being perfective.

1.2.6   Final comments on the life cycle model

For large software systems, the entire life cycle may last many years. For example, most large systems currently under development will still be in use at the beginning of the twenty-first century. It is therefore important to consider system costs over this time scale and not in the relatively short time devoted to software development. This is the topic of the following section.

The classical model of the software life cycle where separate development phases are identified seems to be appropriate for many classes of software system. It is probably most suitable for systems where it is possible to establish a fairly complete requirements definition. These include automated versions of existing systems where the requirements are defined by the existing system, and some types of embedded systems (such as small control systems) where the requirements are strictly defined by the other system components. However, various authors (McCracken and Jackson, 1982; Gladden, 1982) have suggested that this classical model is not appropriate for all types of software system. Broadly, they suggest that a model based on prototyping and the refinement of the system through a number of prototype versions is more appropriate.

For systems where the requirements are ill-defined and impossible (or very difficult) to define, the life cycle model we have described may not be appropriate. Examples are information systems where the facilities required may only be determined by experiment, and artificial intelligence systems where the actions of the system may be non-deterministic. Indeed, fitting the development of such systems to the classical life cycle model is probably impossible.

There is no doubt whatsoever that there are significant defects in the traditional model of the software life cycle, but we must be careful that attempts to correct these deficiencies do not introduce further, more serious problems. We have already suggested that good software management is essential to cost-effective software engineering and, realistically, good management is only possible when there are concrete deliverables (documents) produced at regular planned intervals during a project. The traditional model makes this possible and this is probably its principal strength. It is also a weakness as sometimes deliverables are produced because of management considerations and not because it is sensible to do so! Progress can be more difficult to assess using prototyping because the goals of the project are not clear, and thus such projects can be difficult to manage effectively. Because of the management difficulties of prototyping, it is likely that the traditional life cycle model or a variant will continue to be used for the development of large, embedded software systems.

1.3   Software costs

The so-called 'software crisis' originated in the 1960s when new computer hardware was introduced. These new computers were orders of magnitude more powerful than earlier machines as well as being much cheaper and more compact. Their power and cheapness meant that, in hardware terms, it was economic to use a computer for many new applications. However, these applications required large software systems to be constructed, and the failure of many of these large software projects brought the true costs of computer software to light.

If we consider computer systems built before 1965, the cost of the software for these machines was very much less than the hardware costs. Typically, the software costs for a large application system (including systems software) were about 30% of the total system costs.

By 1970, these figures had reversed so that, for a comparable system, software costs were about 70% of the total system cost. Hardware costs had fallen dramatically. During the 1970s, further developments in semiconductor technology resulted in even greater reductions in the cost of powerful hardware. Now, for large systems, the software cost may be over 90% of the total.

To give some impression of how much money is actually involved in software development, the annual cost of software in the United States in 1980 was of the order of $40 000 000 000. This was approximately 2% of the Gross National Product. The rate of growth of software costs is considerably faster than the general rate of economic growth so that, by 1990, it has been predicted that software costs will make up about 11% of the US Gross National Product.

The reason for the high cost of software is, of course, that software production is a labour-intensive activity. As yet, software tools that allow quantum increases in programming productivity are not available. Unlike the capital-intensive computer hardware industry, software production is still largely a manual process.

Essentially, therefore, increased programmer productivity is the key to cheaper software development. However, attaining such an increase is hindered by the fact that it is very difficult indeed to arrive at a generally applicable measure of programmer productivity. The most commonly used measure is the number of source instructions completed by a programmer in a day. This is simplistically computed using the following formula:

DSI /(NP TT)

DSI stands for the total number of delivered source instructions, NP is the number of programmers working on the project, and TT is the time taken in days to complete the work. There are obviously many problems with this definition. What is a delivered source instruction? What is the correspondence between programmer-days and calendar days given that programmers do not spend all their time programming? The answers to these questions are arbitrary, and global comparisons of productivity are very difficult because there are no standard definitions of the productivity parameters.

As discussed by various authors (Jones, 1978; Boehm, 1981), this is an imperfect measure of productivity. However, it is sufficient to illustrate here why software costs are so high. Measurements have shown that an approximate productivity figure is 20 DSI/programmer/day. This figure depends on a large number of factors and can vary dramatically from 2 DSI/programmer/day in complex embedded systems development to 100 DSI/programmer/day when systems are straightforward and well-understood.

Therefore, for a software system made up of 64 000 source instructions (a medium-sized system), the number of programmer-days required for system implementation is approximately 3200. Given an average of a 20-day working month and a 10-month working year (allowing for holidays, illness, training, etc.), this means that a total of 16 programmer-years are required to complete this project.

Converting this figure to an actual cost is quite difficult as the cost of employing a programmer does not simply include his or her salary. There are also many other overheads such as support staff costs, building costs, travel costs, etc., and these are computed in different ways by different organizations. An approximate figure, quoted to one of the authors, is that the average overhead costs for a software engineer in the UK are approximately £40 000. This means that the total cost of developing a 16 programmer-year system is about £640 000. Overhead costs and salaries are significantly higher in North America and in Japan.

1.3.1 Software life cycle costs

Although we have discussed programmer productivity in terms of delivered source instructions per day, this does not, of course, mean that a programmer can only write 20 lines of code each day. Rather, the low figure of 20 DSI/day reflects the fact that the programming phase is only one part of the overall systems development effort. Most of the time spent on software development is actually spent on activities apart from coding – such as software design, testing, documentation, etc.

In fact, a study by Boehm (1975) showed that somewhere between 17% and 28% of the effort devoted to software development was taken up by coding activities. The difference reflects the fact that the measurements were taken with different types of system. His actual figures showing the distribution of effort (and hence costs) over the phases of the software life cycle are shown in Figure 1.4. From this we see that the cost of coding real-time systems was about 20% of system costs whereas testing costs were around 50% of the total development costs. This reflects the high reliability requirements of real-time systems.

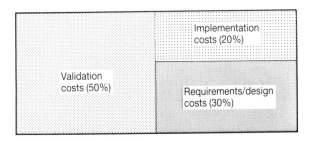

Figure 1.4   Cost distribution over the software life cycle.

So far, we have simply discussed the costs of software development and have not yet looked at the costs of the final stage of the software life cycle namely maintenance costs. Although up-to-date information on software maintenance costs is not available, a survey by Lientz and Swanson (1980) showed that software maintenance costs were typically 49% of data processing budgets, compared with 43% for software development costs.

By now, the figures are likely to show a greater imbalance as most software development is cumulative. As new programs are developed and put into use they must themselves be maintained, but their development does not necessarily mean that existing programs are scrapped. Therefore, there are more and more programs to be maintained and software costs necessarily increase, otherwise all resources, ultimately, must be devoted to software maintenance.

Furthermore, the ratio of development costs to maintenance costs does not reflect the fact that different types of program have vastly different maintenance requirements. In particular, some programs are 'one-offs', which means they are written to solve a particular problem on a particular hardware configuration. They may be configuration-specific with no requirement that they be moved to another system when the hardware becomes obsolete. Such programs, typically, need little maintenance. Another class of programs whose maintenance costs are low consists of those intended to solve very well-defined problems. For example, a program might be written to compute the eigenvalues and eigenvectors of a matrix: this uses a well-known algorithm and such a program will require virtually no maintenance except, perhaps, occasional error correction.

The software systems with the highest maintenance costs are the long-lived complex systems which must adapt to changing requirements and hardware. For such systems – typically command and control and avionic systems – maintenance costs generally exceed development costs by a significant factor. On average, this factor appears to be about 4, although Boehm (1975) quotes cases where the maintenance costs were more than 100 times the original software development costs.

1.3.2 Cost-effective software engineering

Cost-effective software engineering is the construction of software systems so that the overall software costs are minimized without compromising other system objectives, such as reliability and performance. This implies that the software engineer should concentrate on reducing the costs of the most expensive phases of software development, namely software maintenance and software testing. In fact, it may well be worth spending more on the early phases of the life cycle if this results in a comparable cost reduction during later life cycle stages.

For example, suppose the development costs for some embedded software system are estimated to be $y and the resulting maintenance costs are estimated to be $4y. The total life cycle costs are thus $5y. Presume now that an $x\%$ increase in development costs results in a comparable decrease $(x\%)$ in overall maintenance costs. Thus, if this development cost increase is accepted, the overall system costs are $(y + xy/100) + 4(y - xy/100)$ giving a reduced life cycle cost of $(5y - 3xy/100)$. If y has the value $1 000 000 and x has the value 5, the overall monetary saving is $150 000.

The high cost of software maintenance was the reason why the Ada project was initiated by the US Department of Defense. The principal design aim of Ada was that it should contain features that could contribute to a reduction in maintenance costs even if this meant an increase in development costs. As a result of this requirement, Ada programs are often longer than corresponding programs in other programming languages but, if the language is properly used, they should be easier to maintain.

Maintenance costs are governed by both technical and non-technical factors. Because of the way in which some software projects are funded, where maintenance is charged separately from development, there has been little managerial incentive to reduce maintenance costs at the expense of development costs. Indeed, to do so might reduce a software company's profits, so development practices which lead to high maintenance costs are tolerated by management. This is clearly a contractual rather than a technical problem which can only be resolved by the intervention of the purchasers of computer systems.

Of course, the maintainability of a software system is also governed by a number of technical factors:

1. *The completeness and consistency of the system documentation.* Maintaining a software system means more than simply changing a program. Changes made to a program might be reflected in requirements definition, specification and design documents and might require new test plans to be devised. If documents are not available or if document sets are inconsistent, software maintenance is more difficult and costly.

2. *The understandability of the program and its documentation.* The process of system maintenance means changing the program code and other associated documents. This change can only be made, without adversely affecting parts of the system that are not supposed to be changed, if the structure and details of the system are understood.

3. *The modifiability of the system.* This is related to, but distinct from the understandability of the system. A system can be thought of as being modifiable if a change made to one part of it affects that part and that part only. This implies that a modifiable system should be built up from stand-alone components (black-boxes) which do not interfere with other system components.

Ensuring the consistency and completeness of the system document-ation is a problem for software management and does not depend on the language used for system programming. However, the other major influences on maintainability – understandability and modifiability – are affected by the systems programming language.

As far as Ada is concerned, several features of the language that are explicitly geared towards producing readable programs may be identified. These include:

- the ability to define and to overload operators – this allows expressions on user-defined types to be written using familiar infix notation;

- the ability to use long identifier names and to separate constituent parts of these names so that meaningful descriptive phrases may be used to identify objects;

- the ability to assign names to formal parameters and to use these names in actual parameter association – this means that the reader need not know the ordering of the formal parameters in their original declaration.

Other language features such as user-defined types, structured control statements and the separation of interface specifications also contribute to program readability, but are not explicitly included in the language just for that purpose.

Program modifiability depends on separating functions and on concealing information from those parts of the program that do not need that information. Ada provides a number of constructs to assist in functional separation and information hiding. These include user-defined data-types, packages, functions and sub-programs. The importance of all of these constructs is discussed later in the book.

Apart from these technical factors, the widespread use of Ada will contribute further to a reduction in software maintenance costs because there will be a large number of software engineers trained in the use of the language. This means that training costs for staff moving to maintain a new software system will be reduced.

1.4   Ada, the life cycle and software costs

We have already seen how the use of Ada should reduce software costs over a project's lifetime by reducing the costs of software maintenance. In this section, we shall examine the effect that the use of Ada has on the other phases of the software life cycle and discuss the costs and problems of using Ada for software engineering.

The obvious life cycle phase where Ada will be used is the implementation phase, when a software design is translated to an executable program. For embedded systems, this is not the most costly phase – it typically takes up about 20% of the total development costs. Somewhat paradoxically, the introduction of Ada as an implementation language generally increases this cost. Although the language is too new for measurements to have been made, our guess is that implementation costs, when Ada is used, will be about 30–35% of the total system development costs. The reasons for the increase in implementation costs are as follows:

1. Because most embedded systems are, at the time of writing, implemented in low-level languages or in inadequate high-level languages, the software design must be developed to a high-level of detail. Using Ada, much of the detailed design is indistinguishable from implementation, so some present design costs will be shifted to the implementation phase.

1. Ada has been designed so that a great deal of compile time checking is possible and so that constructs that are error-prone in other languages, such as parallelism and exception handling, may be expressed directly. This means that the programmer may take longer to develop an Ada program, but that it ought to contain fewer errors than a comparable program in a lower-level language. Program testing and debugging costs should be reduced, so that there will be a cost-shift from the testing to the implementation phase.

2. Ada programmers have to be more highly skilled than programmers in FORTRAN or assembly code because they must understand the concepts underlying Ada to use the language properly. This means that they probably expect to be paid more for their services, thus increasing implementation costs. Later in this chapter, we discuss some of the problems of getting started with Ada as a language for software engineering, and we describe why higher skill levels are necessary to make effective use of the language.

Of course, it does not really matter if the cost distribution across the life cycle changes as long as the total software costs are reduced. Indeed, we have already seen that it is worth increasing software development costs if this produces a comparable reduction in software maintenance costs. However, various developments centred around Ada suggest that the use of Ada in software engineering projects will reduce overall development costs as well as maintenance costs. The influence of Ada and related notations on the phases of the life cycle is shown in Figure 1.5.

The most important of these Ada-based developments is the Ada Programming Support Environment (APSE) which we discuss in Chapter 2. The APSE is intended as a comprehensive, integrated software engineering environment to support the development of software systems in Ada. As well as implementation, testing and debugging tools, it is intended that the APSE should also support the earlier life cycle phases of requirements definition, software specification and software design.

The availability of a support environment like the APSE reduces

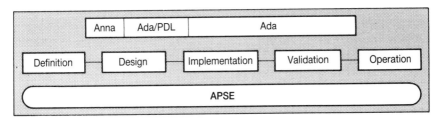

Figure 1.5   Ada influence on the software life cycle.

software development costs for two reasons:

1. It provides tools to speed up the production and validation of software designs, implementations, documentation, etc. Thus it increases the productivity of the individual software engineer.

2. It is a means by which the complexity of a software project may be kept under control. The major problems in a large software project include ensuring that all the documents associated with software components are consistent and complete, that accurate records and plans of progress are maintained and that costs are kept under control. The APSE is based around the notion that all project documents should be held in a database and tools should be provided to process documents in that database.

It is possible to view the APSE as the Ada programmer's toolkit and we subsume discussion of particular software tools under that heading. However, there are two Ada-related notations that affect life cycle costs and that are usable independently of the APSE. These notations are Ada-based specification languages such as Anna (Krieg-Bruckner *et al.*, 1980) and program design languages which are based on Ada (Ada/PDLs). Both specification languages and design languages are discussed in later chapters.

The advantages of using Ada-based notations for describing different phases of the software life cycle are twofold:

1. Training costs are reduced as Ada acts as a common base for all life cycle notations. Once Ada has been mastered, only a little extra work is necessary to learn Ada-based notations which are geared towards describing specification and design activities.

2. It is relatively simple to transform one notation to another if both have a common root. Indeed, it may be possible to devise automatic transformation processors which accept an Ada-based notation at one level as input and which generate an equivalent description in some related notation. Such transformation programs are beyond the current state of the art, but the use of notations with a common base will simplify their ultimate development.

The availability of the APSE and Ada-based specification and design languages in combination with Ada as an implementation language seems likely to reduce the costs of software development as well as the costs of maintenance. In effect, as Wegner (1984) suggests, software engineering may be changing from a labour-intensive to a capital-intensive activity. Capital-intensive activities are characterized by highly skilled workers supported by sophisticated tools who thus achieve high levels of productivity. The transition from our current way of working to this state is likely to be both expensive and traumatic.

There is no question whatsoever that the biggest problem in changing from Pascal, FORTRAN or assembly language programming to Ada is posed by the sheer size of the Ada language. Indeed, it has been argued by Hoare (1981) that Ada is so large and so complex a language that it will be impossible ever to have confidence in its implementation. Therefore, the use of Ada might actually reduce software reliability. Hoare's argument is flawed as, whatever its faults, Ada is better than assembly language which is often the only alternative. However, we accept that Ada is a large and complex language which could and should be trimmed in some areas.

Learning Ada is not like learning other, simpler programming languages. It is relatively easy for the FORTRAN programmer to learn Pascal (say) because Pascal is really quite similar to FORTRAN. Learning Pascal only involves the learning of one fundamentally new concept – that of data typing. Ada, on the other hand, introduces many new concepts – operator overloading, generics, packages, tasks, etc. with the result that learning Ada takes a considerable time.

Furthermore, the effective use of Ada constructs, such as packages to implement abstract data types, requires an understanding of the concepts that underlie these constructs. This implies that the effective use of Ada requires some formal training in computer science, and this will pose immense problems for those organizations whose software engineers do not have such a background. This is a fairly common situation and very large training costs must be budgeted for in the management of a transition to Ada as the principal programming language for systems development.

In conclusion, Ada and its derivatives have an important role to play in the specification, design and implementation phases of the software life cycle. It is likely that the use of Ada will reduce software development costs as well as software maintenance costs, particularly if the APSE is available to support system development. However, using Ada requires greater skill, and software technology seems likely to change from a labour-intensive to a capital-intensive technology as automated tools are developed to support highly-skilled craftspeople in the development of software systems.

1.5 Summary

Because the US Department of Defense made use of a great many different languages for embedded systems programming, software maintenance costs were higher than necessary and it was decided to develop a standard language (now Ada). After a competitive design exercise, a language designed by a consortium led by Honeywell-Bull in Paris was selected as the best for embedded systems programming.

We have discussed the notion of a software life cycle, namely the phases through which a software system passes whilst it is developed and used. We have described the fairly traditional life cycle model made up of requirements definition, design, implementation, validation and operation. Although there are defects in this model, we believe that it will dominate software development for many years and consider it unwise to rely on relatively untried approaches to sofware management.

Basically, software is expensive because software development remains a labour-intensive process and the skilled workers involved expect high rewards for their work. The costs are distributed across the life cycle in such a way that validation and design each take up about 40% of the total system costs, and programming only 20%. However, for large systems, the cost of maintenance far exceeds development costs by factors from 2 to 100.

We predict that using Ada for software development may increase overall development costs, but will lead to a reduction in the costs of software maintenance and is thus likely to lead to an overall decrease in costs over the whole software life cycle.

1.6   Further reading

Boehm, B.W. (1981). *Software Engineering Economics*. Englewood Cliffs, N.J.: Prentice-Hall.

A formidable piece of work which is not just concerned with the costs of software development. It contains many insights into software engineering in general.

Sommerville, I. (1985). *Software Engineering* (2nd Edn). Wokingham: Addison-Wesley.

A general introduction to software engineering. This is an advertisement!

Chapter 2 Software Development Environments

As we have seen, the original motivation for the development of Ada was the fact that, in 1975, over 400 different programming languages were used in the development of US DoD embedded systems. As well as actually maintaining the systems themselves, the Defense Department also had to maintain all the support software (compilers, assemblers, loaders, debuggers, etc.) associated with each programming language. This support software makes up the 'software development environment', that is, the context in which the software was developed. As the size of the support software often exceeded the size of the embedded system, support software maintenance accounted for a very significant part of the total maintenance cost.

As well as a common programming language, therefore, the US Department of Defense specified that there should also be a common set of software tools to support the development and maintenance of Ada programs. The term integrated support environment is sometimes used to describe a software toolkit where the individual software tools are integrated around some common core.

The notion of a software tool is not a new one. A software tool is simply any program that may be used to help create or maintain other programs. Thus, early software tools included compilers, editors, assemblers, loaders, etc. Such tools are provided as an integral part of most mainframe and minicomputer operating systems. In operating systems like the UNIX system (Ritchie and Thomson, 1978), these basic tools are supplemented by a variety of others for source-level debugging, formatting, file checking, etc. In essence, the user of UNIX is provided with a powerful software toolkit for program development.

However, there is an important distinction between software toolkits and integrated support environments. In a software toolkit, each tool works in isolation and it is the responsibility of the user to combine the software tools in an effective way. Tools are not aware of the existence of other tools. UNIX is particularly successful as a software development environment because it provides mechanisms such as a command language and pipes, which allow tools to work in unison and to interchange information.

In an integrated environment, tools may be aware of the existence of other tools and the system is set up so that output from any one tool may act as input to some other tool. This implies the existence of some central information store and integrated environments are always built around some form of database system.

Software development environments (integrated or otherwise) are needed to support software development because writing software is inherently labour-intensive. When hardware costs were high, software costs were a significant, but not a major part of total system costs. Now, in a large system, the costs of the software development are likely to be three or four times the costs of the system hardware. Therefore, to reduce costs in general requires much more effective use of human resources in systems development.

In large system development, there is an immense amount of 'housekeeping work' to be carried out. There may be many programmers working at geographically dispersed sites and there are likely to be hundreds if not thousands of distinct documents associated with the project. With many programmers working on a project, a large amount of time is spent not actually in software development, but in reading and abstracting information from the work of others, finding and retrieving documents and checking that tasks undertaken by different team members may be successfully integrated.

Most of the costs of software development are not a result of the development process itself, but of this housekeeping and other routine tasks undertaken by software engineers. It is this work that may be automated by an effective set of software tools. Whilst tools to support the implementation of software are essential, it is important to realize that they support only a small part of the work involved in system development.

Historical evidence suggests that the most dramatic increases in individual productivity in any job come about when automated tools are provided to supplement individual skills. For example, the productivity of construction workers increased by several hundred per cent with the introduction of earthmoving equipment, and Wegner (1982) argues that software engineering, too, should become a capital-intensive technology. Very sophisticated tools are required to take over virtually all of the non-creative tasks of the software engineer. The software engineer of the future will not spend a great deal of time in routine tasks, but will be a highly skilled professional supported by a powerful development environment. His or her productivity should be very much greater than that of the programmer of the 1980s.

Building an effective environment for software development is an ambitious project. Many of the tasks involved in software development are unquantifiable. Tools to support these tasks must therefore be developed on a trial and error basis. However, the rewards (in terms of increased productivity) of producing a successful integrated environment are great and this whole area is currently a major software engineering research topic.

The aim of this chapter is to look at different types of environment that are intended to support different tasks and activities. We examine and compare current environments used for software engineering support and then go on to consider the Ada Programming Support Environment. This proposed environment is intended to be a portable, standard environment to support the development of software projects implemented in Ada. We look at the components making up that environment and critically examine its suggested structure and facilities.

2.1   Environment classification

It is possible, in theory, to use any programming language for any programming task. However, it is obvious that particular problems are best solved by using a language whose facilities are geared to solving that class of problem. For example, artificial intelligence programs are easier to encode in Lisp or Prolog rather than Ada, which is designed for building embedded computer systems. COBOL is designed for the development of business systems and Pascal for teaching computer science.

The same principle holds for programming environments. Just as the development of a 'general-purpose' programming language which is equally suited to every possible task is an unrealistic objective, so too is a universal software development environment. Different kinds of programmers solving different problems require different sets of software tools, so we need many different kinds of environment with each geared towards a different class of user.

In this section, we identify six classes of development environment where each is best suited towards supporting different kinds of software production. We also discuss how some of these environments might be integrated into a general-purpose environment to support all of the phases of the software life cycle. Finally, we describe current research programmes to develop integrated project support environments (IPSEs) which are intended to support all of the phases of the software life cycle.

The types of programming environment we describe here may be classified as follows:

1. **Teaching and learning environments**. These environments are equipped with tools which help the novice programmer in his or her learning activity. Such examples are typified by the Cornell Program Synthesiser (Teitelbaum and Reps, 1981) whereby the learner interacts with an integrated system that provides assistance with programming language syntax and program debugging. Thus, the novice is free to concentrate on problem solving and program

development and his or her involvement with arbitrary syntactic detail is minimized.

2. **Programming environments for non-professional programmers**. This class of environment is provided on most current microcomputer systems and is intended to support the development of small programs by workers who are not professional programmers and who need to develop applications software as quickly as possible. They are typified by systems such as UCSD-Pascal.

3. **General-purpose language-independent environments**. These are intended for professional programmers, but are not oriented towards any specific programming language. Typically, they provide a wide range of tools to support implementation and testing and, perhaps, documentation tools, but few tools to support other life cycle phases. Perhaps the best known example of such an environment is the UNIX Programmer's Work Bench (PWB) environment described by Kernighan and Mashey (1979) and by Ivie (1977).

4. **Language-oriented environments**. This class of environment provides a set of tools tailored to support the development of programs, by professionals, in a specific programming language. Such environments integrate the computer operating system, language processing, support tools and program execution. The programmer using the supported language L sees, in effect, an L-machine rather than a Brand X computer running some operating system which includes a compiler for L. Well-known in this class are the InterLisp environment (Teitleman and Masinter, 1981) and the Smalltalk environment (Goldberg, 1984).

5. **Software design environments**. Here, toolkits are geared towards the development of software designs rather than implementations. Many of these environments have been developed as proprietary tools to support particular design methods. Examples are the AIDES environment (Willis, 1981), PRISM (Rosenberg, 1985) and the Analyst (Stephens and Whitehead, 1985).

6. **Integrated project support environments**. This class of environment is geared towards supporting the entire software life cycle from initial requirements through to operation and maintenance. Thus, as well as development tools, they also provide tools for control such as configuration management, documentation, planning, etc. Such environments are not yet widely available, but several research projects in this area (Standish, 1981; Stucki and Walker, 1981; Alderson *et al.*, 1985; Hall *et al.*, 1985) are under way.

Figure 2.1 shows the sizes of projects for which each of these types of environment is appropriate. Notice that it is not always sensible

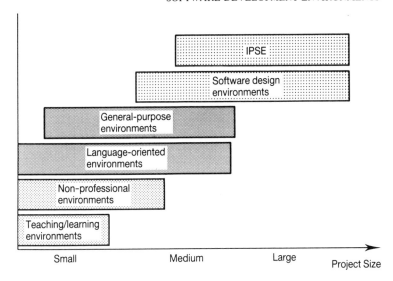

Figure 2.1   Project sizes and classes of environment.

to make use of the most powerful environment for software development. For small projects, the overhead involved in learning about the facilities may actually exceed the benefits gained from that environment. As this book is concerned with the development of large rather than small software systems, we shall say no more about environments for novices and non-professionals. Rather, we now discuss, in more detail, environments in the classes 3–6 above.

2.1.1   General-purpose language-independent environments

This type of programming environment is, at present, the most commonly used for large systems development. Indeed, any system that provides program development facilities (compilers, editors, etc.) might be considered as falling into this class, although we prefer to exclude systems that do not provide explicit mechanisms for tool integration.

Probably the best example is the UNIX system. This system was originally developed by an individual who became frustrated by the development facilities available on the computers in his organization. He thus built his own development system. From these small beginnings, the UNIX system has evolved through a number of versions, and it is now an important software product which is available on more than 100 different types of computer from small microcomputers to large mainframes.

The facilities of UNIX are not geared towards any specific programming language and the system is used for program

UNIX	
Unstructured file organization	Pipes for process connection
Command language (shell)	Software tools

Figure 2.2   UNIX environment facilities.

development using many different programming languages. However, there are probably most tools available to support programming in C (Kernighan and Ritchie, 1979), which is the language used to write the UNIX system itself. In addition to language support tools, UNIX also provides tools for documentation (tbl, spell, troff, eqn, etc.), file searching and checking (grep, diff, awk, etc.) and configuration management (make and SCCS).

The facilities of UNIX which contribute most to its effectiveness as a programming environment are shown in Figure 2.2. These exemplify, in an elegant way, essential characteristics of a software development environment that is an extension of an existing operating system and they have had significant influence on our thinking about environments. It is therefore worth looking at them in more detail here.

UNIX file organization

Files in UNIX have no structure imposed upon them by the operating system. They are considered as variable-length streams of characters which may be structured according to the needs of user programs. Thus these programs are not constrained by inbuilt system file structuring mechanisms.

This seemingly simple feature, which might appear to give the user additional work, actually ensures that the system is language and application independent. Any file structure which is imposed by an operating system is inevitably more suited to some applications than others. Therefore some applications (often program development) are less well-supported by the system.

Furthermore, because there is no file structure, there is no distinction made between files which reside on different devices. The details of each device are hidden by the system and, indeed, devices themselves are simply viewed as files. A terminal keyboard, for instance, is seen as an input file producing a stream of characters and a printer is viewed as an output file. This general-purpose view means that executing programs may receive input from a keyboard, a file or some other device without change and without having to be aware of the source of the input.

UNIX was designed as an interactive system and the default input and output files for most processes are the user's keyboard and screen respectively. However, an I/O redirection mechanism is provided and this facility alone allows software tools to be interconnected. For example, the following command line calls a tool named spell to find words that do not appear in a dictionary. Input is taken from a file called doc and output is placed on another file called doc.badwords. This file is input to a word counting program named wc. Thus, the user can find out how many distinct misspelled words there are in his or her document:

```
spell <doc >doc.badwords; wc <doc.badwords
```

Both spell and wc are set up so that they accept input from the so-called 'standard input' (the user's keyboard) and send output to the 'standard output' (the user's terminal screen). The symbols < and > specify redirection of the standard input and output respectively so that spell above takes its input from the file doc and sends its output to the file doc.badwords. Similarly wc takes its input from this file, but outputs to the user's terminal.

Input/output redirection using < and > is one possible way of connecting UNIX tools. However, there is a more elegant tool connection mechanism called 'piping', which we shall describe shortly.

UNIX command language

The UNIX command language (called the shell) is more than a command interpreter which identifies commands and initiates processes to execute these commands. The shell has extensive control facilities which allow command sequences to be combined, parameterized and executed conditionally or repeatedly. It also has a limited variable declaration facility, so it may be regarded as a programming language whose operations are the executable system commands and whose variables are of type 'file' and 'string'.

The shell is simply a program executing under UNIX and the command language is not 'hard wired' into the operating system. Thus, alternative shells can be provided and many UNIX systems support at least two variants. These are the Bourne shell (Bourne, 1978) which uses some of the conventions of Algol68 and the C-shell whose syntax resembles that of the programming language C. Example 2.1 is defined using the C-shell which offers more facilities than the relatively simple Bourne shell.

Example 2.1 uses a parameter ($1) to control whether a file ($2) should be printed on the user's terminal or on one of a variety of

```
#   Set up some abbreviations for configuration files used by prt. This is
#   accomplished using the setenv command which defines a variable name
#   and initializes it to the character string which follows.
#   Thus, the variable T has the value "/usr/rsch/is/consts/tform",
#   P is "/usr/rsch/is/consts/prelude" etc.
#
    setenv T /usr/rsch/is/consts/tform
    setenv P /usr/rsch/is/consts/prelude
    setenv H /usr/rsch/is/consts/any.h
#   if a filename prefixed by .h has been input as a parameter use it.
#   Otherwise use default .h file
    if (-e $2.h) setenv H $2.h
#   if there is a file called prelude in the working directory use it,
#   otherwise use default prelude file
    if (-e prelude) setenv P prelude
#   The switch statement is like a case statement - it matches parameter
#   1 with possible strings
    switch ( $1 )
#   If match "-t" print onto terminal
    case "-t":
        nroff -ms -Tcrt $3 $4 $5 $6 $P $H $2 | more;
        breaksw ;
#   If match "-p" print onto line printer
    case "-p":
        nroff -ms $3 $4 $5 $6 $P $H $2 | lpr;
        breaksw ;
#   if match "-d" print onto daisy wheel printer
    case "-d":
        nroff -ms -e -Txerox12 $3 $4 $5 $6 $P $H $2 | lpr -Pdaisy -h;
        breaksw ;
#   if match "-l" print onto laser printer
    case "-l":
        nroff -ms -e -Tlaser $3 $4 $5 $6 $P $H $2 | lpr -Plaser-h;
        breaksw ;
#   if match "-c" print onto matrix printer
    case "-c":
        nroff -ms -e -Tcanon $3 $4 $5 $6 $P $H $2 | lpr -Pcanon -h;
        breaksw ;
endsw
```

Example 2.1   A C-shell procedure.

printers. The command nroff calls a formatting program and its output is sent to the appropriate driver for the required printing device. Actions are explained by embedded comments introduced by a # symbol.

Given that this command is called prt (for print), it may be executed as follows:

```
prt -t myfile – – formats and prints myfile on terminal
prt -d myfile – – formats and prints myfile on daisy wheel printer
prt -p myfile – – formats and prints myfile on line printer
```

Pipes

The foregoing shell programming example uses a symbol '|' as a separator of executable commands. This symbol means that the output from one command should be connected to the input of another command. By analogy with plumbing, a pipe is said to connect the two processes.

The notion of a pipe is feasible on UNIX because of the general-purpose view of files as character files. A pipe is simply a communication channel with its input connected to the output of one process and its output connected to the input of some other process. Using pipes the word counting example may be written:

```
spell <doc | wc
```

There is no need for an explicit intermediate file to be set up by the user – this is handled automatically by the piping mechanism. Pipelines may be arbitrarily long and may include several processes. For example, the pipeline below may be used to build an index from the file BOOK. This pipeline consists of a mixture of standard UNIX commands and specially written programs.

```
split <BOOK | killjunktoks | formterms | putpagenos | sort -u | catentries |
       lookup index.terms
```

UNIX tools

One of the immense strengths of UNIX as a programming environment and probably the main reason for the system's success is the large number of useful software tools included with the system. These include tools for supporting program development in a number of languages (C, Pascal and Lisp, for example), tools for file manipulation and tools for text processing. The importance of text processing tools cannot be over-estimated as most of a software engineer's time is probably spent in writing documents and it is extremely useful to have these documents accessible along with the programs being developed.

The philosophy underlying UNIX tools is that each tool should be built to do a single job and that tools should be combined using pipes and the shell to create more complex tools. This has meant that UNIX is one of the few examples where non-mathematical software is genuinely reused, as a matter of course, during systems development.

General-purpose programming environments like UNIX are well-suited to building small and medium-sized software systems. However, although UNIX has been used to build large systems, and configuration management tools such as the Source Code Control System (Rochkind, 1975) are provided to help in this task, it is not really geared to software engineering support. The reason for this is that UNIX tools are not tightly integrated. It is serendipitous if they work well together. The tools provided with UNIX were not designed as an integrated toolkit, and while simple tool communication mechanisms are one of the strengths of UNIX, they are also a weakness when the system is used for large system construction.

Large system building requires more complex tool interactions than can readily be implemented using UNIX pipes and shell operations. As a result, it is now recognized that for large software system support, tools must communicate through a database. The other classes of programming environment described below all make use of some kind of central database for tool communication. However, because of the general usefulness of UNIX and the fact that it is a widely available operating system, many current environments use it as a starting point and build extra features on top of the UNIX system for software engineering support.

2.1.2 Language-oriented programming environments

In a language-oriented programming environment all programs are written in a single programming language. This means that there is no need for a general-purpose program editor, say, to create and edit program text. Rather, a special-purpose editor may be provided with built-in knowledge of the programming language in use. This editor incorporates primitives to support the creation and maintenance of programs in that language.

A characteristic of such environments is that the operating system and the language processing are integrated. Rather than calling the compiler from the operating system, the user of an environment oriented towards language L, say, is presented with an L-processor which includes constructs often considered to be operating system commands.

Many systems provided with home computers may be considered as language-oriented environments as they are geared towards the creation of BASIC programs. However, they provide only a minimal toolset (editor and BASIC interpreter) so will not be discussed here. Instead, we are interested in environments that provide a comprehensive set of software tools to assist in the development of medium to large programs.

InterLisp	
File package	Information retrieval
Error correction	Programmer's assistant

Figure 2.3   InterLisp environment facilities.

In such environments, all tools have knowledge of the programming language constructs that may be used. They are also aware of the existence of other tools and of the output produced by these tools. The environment provides a mechanism for any one tool to make use of information produced by another. For example, a debugging tool may use the symbol table generated by the language compiler, the editor operates on a tree representation of the program generated by a parser, and so on.

The best examples of language-oriented programming environments are the InterLisp environment (Teitleman and Masinter, 1984) and the Smalltalk environment (Goldberg, 1984). We shall describe the InterLisp environment here as an excellent example of a tightly integrated environment. However, the reader should be aware that this was built to support the development of programs, in the general application area of artificial intelligence, which are usually refined through a series of prototypes. It does not include facilities to support the software life cycle model activities discussed in Chapter 1.

As the name implies, the InterLisp environment is designed to support the development of programs in InterLisp, a dialect of the widely-used AI programming language Lisp. The tools provided by the environment to support InterLisp program development include a structure editor, a compiler, a filing system and an automatic error corrector. Whilst these may be viewed as separate tools, they are, in fact, tightly integrated so that the user sees a single powerful system rather than a set of discrete tools.

The facilities of the InterLisp environment that make it an extremely effective program development system are shown in Figure 2.3.

The file package

InterLisp users may choose to view their collection of programs in two ways. They may work in a mode where the programs are seen to reside on an external filing system and make use of editing and retrieval tools to manipulate these programs. Alternatively, they may operate in 'residential mode', where the program they are working on is in the random-access memory of the computer and the file package is used to move the program data structure to and from a backing store.

However, this movement need not be explicitly initiated by the user, but can take place automatically. Users, therefore, do not have to think about backing store organization, but can view their working environment as a very large memory. The file package handles, in a way that is transparent to the user, transitions from one level to another in the system's memory.

As a result, users are freed from the burden of saving copies of modified programs in the filing system and need not keep track of exactly what is contained in each file. Furthermore, they may define their own file package operations or may redefine built-in system operations, thus tailoring the file package to their own needs.

The information retrieval system

As the size of systems built using InterLisp grew larger, it became harder for users to predict the effects of a proposed change to their programs. The need for a program information system was perceived and thus a tool called Masterscope evolved.

Masterscope is an interactive program for analysing and cross-referencing InterLisp programs. It can answer questions such as 'which functions make use of object X?', 'where is object Y bound?', etc. In addition, Masterscope is integrated with the system editor so that the user can retrieve information and then, on the basis of that information, can make program changes.

The error corrector

One of the principal tenets underlying the InterLisp system was that computer time is cheap whereas human time is expensive. As a result, the system incorporates a sophisticated error correction facility called DWIM (Do What I Mean). Given incorrect input, DWIM uses contextual information to try to identify what was intended by the user. It then initiates this action.

Examples of modifications that might be carried out by DWIM are spelling corrections and parameter passing corrections. For example, say a user program incorporates a function called GetInp, but the user actually refers to a name GetIn. When an unidentified name is encountered, DWIM tries to find the closest match to that name, so that GetIn would probably be understood as GetInp.

Another example of a correction that might be made by DWIM occurs when a user calls a function with an invalid argument. If there is a sensible way to convert this invalid argument to the correct argument, this will be invoked by DWIM. Thus, if a function expects a list as a parameter, but the user provides a single atom as an argument, DWIM will turn that into a list for the user. Similarly, the user may sometimes omit parameters and DWIM will automatically substitute 'sensible' values for these.

The use of an error corrector can be dangerous as the corrections made automatically may not correspond to the intent of the user. To avoid unintended corrections causing damage, the InterLisp system incorporates an **undo** command which reverses the previous action. Thus the state which prevailed before the automatic error correction was invoked can always be restored.

The programmer's assistant

The reasoning behind the programmer's assistant is that a computer should not simply be a passive device responding to and then forgetting the user's commands. Rather, it should actively try to help users, particularly in repetitive tasks, so that it actually appears to help with their work.

As the programmer interacts with the system, the assistant constructs a 'history list' of the user's input, results and the side effects of their operations. Commands are provided to manipulate this history list. A user can repeat a sequence of operations with a single command, can edit previous command sequences and then re-execute them, and can undo the effects of previous operations.

The InterLisp environment has been characterized as friendly, cooperative and forgiving and has probably taken the integration of programming support tools and programming language to its logical extremity. The InterLisp system user need not know whether a facility is an inbuilt language facility or a system facility, so that there is no explicit context switch when moving from one tool to another.

There are two reasons why this highly integrated approach to programming support is successful:

- The programming language Lisp is one that lends itself to user extensions. Thus, facilities may be added at will without affecting the basic operations of the language.

- The users of the InterLisp system are sophisticated and are willing to expend considerable time and effort in learning about the system. Many facilities of the InterLisp system were provided by system users in response to personal needs. They were not anticipated by the system designers.

The InterLisp system is an excellent example of a tightly integrated programming environment, but it is unlikely that environments to support the development of programs in other languages, such as Ada, can be integrated in the same way. Not only is language extension forbidden in Ada, but the Ada programming community will exhibit a wider range of abilities than the InterLisp community who are all highly skilled programmers. Less skilled and motivated workers are not likely to be willing to expend the time required to learn about a complex, extensible programming environment. Nor are they able to produce powerful tools to extend that environment. So, although Ada-oriented programming environments may be built, they are unlikely to be as tightly integrated as InterLisp.

2.1.3   Software design environments

Recall from Chapter 1 that, in large software engineering projects, the costs of program specification and design are approximately twice the costs of programming itself. Therefore, it may be more cost-effective to provide tools to support these phases of the software life cycle rather than expend the effort required to develop tools for programming support. This does not imply criticism of an environment like InterLisp which is intended to support research in artificial intelligence and not as a development environment for software products. In research work, specifications and design are more fluid and need not be so well developed before programming begins.

Software design is a creative activity. It is unlikely that, in the near future at least, we shall be able to automate the software design process. Original design will remain the province of the human designer. The role of a software design environment is to take over the repetitive aspects of the designer's work. Broadly, these can be identified as follows:

- the construction and maintenance of design representations such as data flow diagrams, structure charts, PDL descriptions, etc.
- the checking of designs for consistency and completeness
- the establishment of measures of the quality of a software design.

The motivation for the development of the design environment called AIDES (Willis, 1981) was the problem of maintaining very large and complex design structure charts. The implementors of AIDES make use of a modified version of the Structured Design methodology (Constantine et al., 1974; Constantine and Yourdon, 1979). This involves producing graphical representations of the design hierarchy called structure charts, and AIDES provides a graphics system which allows these charts to be produced and edited.

However, AIDES is more than just a graphics system. The generated structure charts are held in a database, which means that other software tools may operate on these charts. For example, there are tools that enforce company software design standards and report generation tools that use the structure charts and other information to generate progress reports for management.

The philosophy adopted by the designers of AIDES was that the

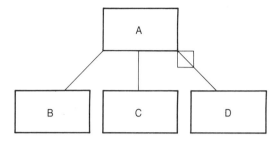

Figure 2.4   AIDES output.

system should not simply be a draughting system which automated the generation of diagrams. Rather, the designer interacts with AIDES to create a software design (not a diagram) and this is expressed in a design specification language. Diagrams are generated from this language.

Therefore, rather than specifying that Box A is connected to Boxes B and C, the designer specifies that procedure A calls procedures B and C and conditionally calls procedure D. From this input, AIDES would generate a structure chart as shown in Figure 2.4.

The designers of AIDES emphasize the necessity of such a design-oriented interface, and given that AIDES was based on slow-speed graphics devices, a textual design language undoubtedly speeds up diagram production. However, it does mean that design diagram layout must be handled entirely by the system. Whilst layout automation is straightforward for simple diagrams, it is very difficult to lay out a complex design in an elegant way without manual intervention.

With modern personal computer workstations which provide high-resolution bit-mapped graphics and two-dimensional input via a puck, or a mouse, there is less need for a design description language such as that provided in AIDES. Using a menu of graphics symbols and placing symbols using the puck, a design diagram can be produced quickly, with the layout left to the user rather than to the system. Such a system is described by Sommerville et al.(1985).

AIDES does not provide tools to check design consistency and completeness, but does provide other quality-control tools. Prominent amongst these are tools to assess the 'quality' of a software design. Although it may appear that design quality is an intangible, there are various measures that appear to correlate with manual assessments of the 'goodness' of a design. AIDES includes tools which process the design and which provide measures of the following characteristics.

- complexity of the software module interconnections
- the modifiability of a substructure design
- the testability of a design.

These quality-control features mark AIDES as an important development in software engineering. As well as simply supporting the designer, the AIDES system also attempts to force the production of 'good' designs and thus reduce overall software costs.

Unlike InterLisp, say, where the programmer's tools are integrated through the internal program representation, AIDES tools communicate via a shared database. This means that these tools cannot be as tightly integrated, but are initiated explicitly by the user rather than automatically by other software tools.

2.1.4   Integrated project support environments

So far, the classes of environment we have described are geared towards the support of one or two phases of the software life cycle. Although they may contain tools which partly support other life cycle phases, UNIX and InterLisp are primarily intended to support program development whereas AIDES provides tools to support software design. Indeed, the designers of AIDES have proposed that a marriage between AIDES and the UNIX/PWB system might be an effective way to provide tools for both the software designer and the programmer.

In this section, we describe a more ambitious software development environment. This has been termed an 'integrated project support environment' (IPSE) which should provide an integrated toolkit to support all life cycle phases from initial requirements definition to software maintenance. In the UK, the Alvey directorate (which was set up to support research in information technology) has based its software engineering strategy on IPSEs and has funded two major IPSE projects for completion in 1987 (Hall et al., 1985; Alderson et al., 1985). Other IPSE projects are described by Stenning (1986) and Campbell (1986).

IPSEs are designed so that they provide support for all phases of the life cycle from initial requirements definition through to software maintenance. In addition, they should support software management activities, configuration control and provide office automation facilities such as word processors, diagramming systems and electronic mail. Whilst these activities are supported using individual software tools, IPSEs differ from software toolkits like UNIX/PWB in that they are integrated around a database rather than a collection of files. The APSE, discussed in the following section, is an Ada-oriented IPSE, and the tools that might be provided in an IPSE are described in that section.

A typical IPSE architecture is layered as shown in Figure 2.5. IPSEs are usually built around a general-purpose operating system such as UNIX (used because it is portable), but the filing system is effectively concealed from users by a database system that is used to store all IPSE objects. The next layer is an object management system which allows

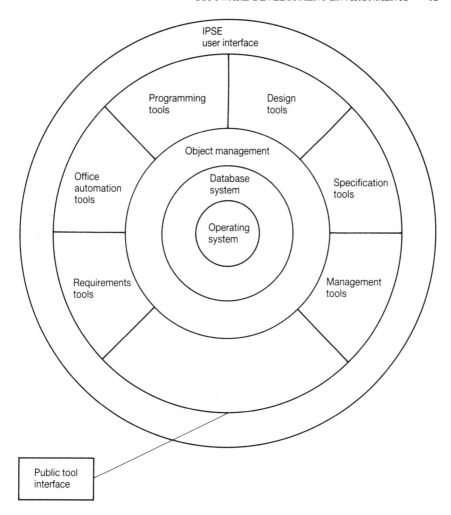

Figure 2.5 Typical IPSE architecture.

relationships between objects to be specified and which provides version management facilities for use by configuration management tools. Support for systems that exist in multiple versions is an essential characteristic of an IPSE, and an integrated object management system is one of the distinguishing features of this class of environment.

The software tools provided with the IPSE should support all of the activities involved in software design, including document preparation and project management. Many of the tools will be integrated, which means that they interface directly with the configuration control system in the IPSE. However, it is also important to provide support for imported tools and these normally interact with the IPSE via the public tool interface. Imported tools are less tightly integrated with the IPSE as, obviously, they have been designed to operate in stand-alone mode, and it is the responsibility of system management to ensure that they are compatible with other IPSE tools.

The outermost IPSE layer is the user interface system. This may have to support a variety of devices from slow dial-up terminals to powerful personal workstations equipped with high-resolution bit-mapped graphics displays and pointing devices (such as mice). One of the most important integrating factors of an IPSE is that it provides a consistent interface to all of the IPSE tools so that the user does not have to learn a variety of arbitrary interfaces to different tools.

The design of an IPSE is an extremely difficult task because we do not have effective notations for describing the products of all of the life cycle phases and sub-phases. Furthermore, software maintenance is essentially an *ad hoc* activity, with the consequence that deriving effective tools to support maintenance is very difficult indeed. By contrast, the programming and design phases are better understood, and hence it is much easier to build tools to support these activities. However, current R & D projects are likely to lead to production-quality IPSEs by the late 1980s with IPSEs in widespread use to support software development from then onward.

2.2   The Ada programming support environment

It is likely that Ada will become the principal programming language for the development of large embedded software systems. As a result, the most widely used software development environments, apart from personal computer environments, will be those intended to support the production of systems written in Ada.

It was recognized at an early stage in the planning of Ada that, as well as a common programming language, there must also be a common support environment providing tools for the development of Ada programs. Without such an environment, many of the portability advantages gained by using Ada are lost. The reason for this is that it is impossible for the programming language to be isolated from the underlying machine and operating system so that programs produced using different machines and operating systems are often difficult to port to some other system configuration.

If a common environment is used for developing and executing Ada programs, the machine and operating system dependencies are concealed from the programs by that environment. Thus, in principle at least, programs developed under any one standard Ada environment should run under any other such environment. Furthermore, a large part of the costs of large system maintenance are incurred in the maintenance of that software's supporting environment. A common environment should mean that this maintainance cost will be significantly reduced. Environment support costs should be minimized as the support tools are generally shared.

In the same way as the requirements for Ada evolved through a number of different stages (STRAWMAN to STEELMAN) so too did the requirements for an Ada programming support environment (APSE). In 1978, three years after the issue of the requirements document for the language which became Ada, a document called SANDMAN was issued by the US Department of Defense. This document contained preliminary thoughts on programming environments and, later the same year, a revised version of this document called PEBBLEMAN was issued. After further work, a final version of the requirements for an Ada support environment was issued in February 1980. This document, called STONEMAN, forms the basis of the requirements for APSEs which are currently being developed. For convenience, we subsequently refer to this document, which defines the APSE requirements, as the STONEMAN document.

Although it is to the credit of the planners of Ada that the need for a support environment was recognized, less time and effort was expended in establishing the requirements for that environment than was spent in the formulation of the language requirements. This was probably a mistake as software engineering tools are as important a part of the software development process as the programming language used. In fact, had the APSE and Ada been designed as an integrated system, some of the complexity inherent in Ada might have been factored out into the APSE.

However, in spite of the limited time spent on the APSE proposals, the final STONEMAN document is a specification for an integrated project support environment that is more complex and more comprehensive than any other currently available support system. It takes state-of-the-art techniques and integrates them so that an APSE is more than a language-oriented programming environment. Although lacking in some respects (notably support for system specification and design) the APSE proposals are, in essence, a definition of a language-oriented software engineering environment. It is important to realize that the author of the STONEMAN document envisaged that there would be a number of different APSEs and that the proposals are generic rather than specific.

Each APSE is a very large system and it is unlikely that APSEs will

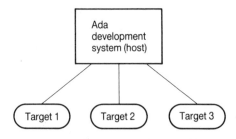

Figure 2.6   Host-target development.

be available on all computers for which software is to be developed using Ada. Therefore, the normal mode of development of Ada programs will be based on the notion of host and target systems. Host machines will be equipped with an APSE and contain comprehensive facilities for Ada program development. Target machines, the machines on which the developed software will execute, will usually have much simpler support software or, occasionally, no software whatsoever. Thus an APSE must provide target machine cross-compilers, simulators and loaders to allow this mode of software development to be effective. Host-target working is illustrated in Figure 2.6.

It is the aim of this section to give readers an overall view of what to expect from an APSE. In the remainder of the section, we describe the proposed APSE architecture as this is a good starting point for a description of the system facilities. The APSE architecture is layered into a Kernel-APSE, a Minimal-APSE and the full APSE and the facilities provided by each of these layers are described in turn. In the final section of this chapter we discuss limitations in the APSE requirements definition.

2.2.1   APSE architecture

One of the principal reasons for introducing Ada was the fact that the use of a common programming language reduces the problems of transferring software from one machine to another. However, as well as language portability, it is equally important that the environment which supports system implementation and maintenance is also portable. Without environment portability, many of the advantages of a common language are lost as the work involved in rehosting a development environment is at least comparable with the work required to reimplement a very large applications program.

This portability requirement was a major factor in the design of the

APSE architecture. It is intended to achieve portability by placing the following constraints on APSE implementations:

- All software tools used in the development of Ada programs must themselves be written in Ada.

- The APSE must be structured in layers with each layer being built using the facilities of its subsidiary layer. This approach has the advantage that rehosting a system may be accomplished by reimplementing the innermost machine-dependent layers.

- One of the layers, the Kernel-APSE, must provide a complete set of facilities to permit access to a system database and to facilitate tool communications. This layer is that which presents a machine-independent portability interface to the user.

The layered structure of the APSE is illustrated in Figure 2.7. The role of each layer is as follows:

1. **System hardware**. The computer on which the APSE is provided.

2. **System software**. The host operating system. This may be an existing operating system such as UNIX or may be a system that is specifically designed for APSE support. In all cases, it must be possible for this system to support an APSE database. The APSE requirements do not specify the class of database system that should be used.

3. **A Kernel-APSE (KAPSE)**. The APSE is centred around a system database and the KAPSE is intended to provide database access primitives, tool communications and run-time support. According to the STONEMAN proposals, the KAPSE is the outermost machine-dependent layer, so rehosting an APSE should be possible by reimplementing the KAPSE on the new host system.

4. **A Minimal-APSE (MAPSE)**. The MAPSE is intended to be made up of a basic toolkit for the development of Ada systems. It comprises tools for program development such as editors, debuggers, configuration management systems, etc. In general, MAPSEs are expected to evolve into full APSEs.

5. **An APSE**. The APSE is seen as an extension of the MAPSE to provide more complete support for Ada system development. The STONEMAN document envisages that there will be no single standard APSE, but that a range of APSEs will evolve to support different applications of Ada.

It is explicitly specified that the tools provided by the APSE should be able to communicate through a commonly accessible system database. This implies that a standard internal representation of Ada programs should be available and, at the time of writing, a representation

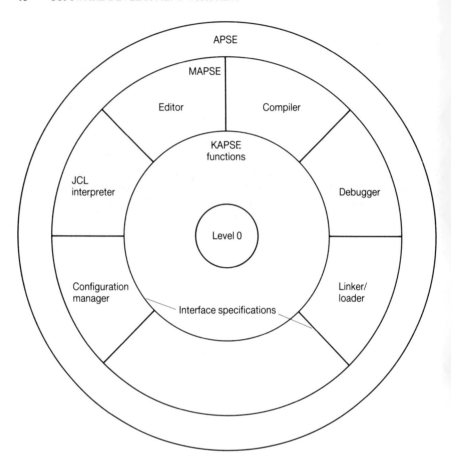

Figure 2.7   The architecture of the APSE.

termed Diana (Wulf *et al.*, 1983) seems to be favoured by most (but not all) implementors of APSE compilers and language support tools.

2.2.2   The APSE database

It is an explicit requirement that APSEs should be built around a database holding all relevant information about the Ada system under development or being maintained. Access to this database is via KAPSE-provided primitives which ensure that the user-view of the database is machine-independent. In some ways, the database may be considered to be part of the KAPSE, but we consider it to be important in its own right so it is discussed separately here.

The database is the central component of the program support system. The APSE system itself is stored in the database along with details of all other systems developed using that APSE. Tool communication is coordinated using the database. Recall that the STONEMAN document places no limitations on the type of database to be provided. Given that the KAPSE database access primitives are supported, they may be mapped on to any underlying special-purpose or general-purpose database management system.

As far as the APSE user is concerned, the database is composed of an aggregation of objects, where an object is any identifiable collection of information that may be treated as a unit in its own right. Examples of objects, therefore, are source programs, Ada compilation units, editor scripts, executable object programs, reference manuals, system specification documents, etc.

All objects may be separately identified using a unique name and may have associated attributes which provide meta-information about the object. There may be any number of attributes associated with an object, but the STONEMAN document defines three attributes that *must* be provided. These are:

1. **An access rights attribute**. This defines who may make use of the object and, to some extent, what use they may make of it. For example, User X may be allowed to read the object, User Y may be allowed to execute the object and User Z may be allowed to modify the object.

2. **A history attribute**. This records the manner in which the object was produced and all subsequent changes to the object.

3. **A categorization attribute**. This classifies the object in a manner which may be used by other APSE tools. Examples of possible classifications are Ada source code, text, executable binary, etc.

All objects in the database have a unique name, but some objects may have a common or very similar specification. In such cases, these objects may be regarded as different versions of the same abstract object. In fact, different versions of a system may be defined by grouping different objects together into configurations.

Software configurations are a particular type of object and hence have a name, attributes, etc. Configurations may be loosely structured or tightly structured collections of objects and may overlap completely or partially. It is a requirement of the APSE that a grouping of objects into configurations be supported and that configuration management tools should be provided for the APSE user.

Because of this configuration management requirement, it is essential that a user should be able to determine how any object evolved and should be able to access previous versions of the object. This means that every object in the APSE database must have a history attribute recording all the changes that have been made to it. Given such a history attribute, it is possible to reconstruct particular versions of an object as they are used in different configurations.

The categorization attribute indicates the type of information held in the object. For example, Ada source code might be classified as 'source' and compiled and linked code might be classed as 'executable'. This categorization attribute may be used by APSE tools to protect an object from invalid use. Therefore, knowledge that only compiled code may be linked might be built into the linker so that attempts to link source code, say, would be immediately aborted. Similarly, configuration management tools might use this attribute to determine which dependent source objects must be recompiled after changes to a compilation unit have been made.

The access attribute associated with each object specifies who has the right to read, write and use that object. Effective and secure provision of this attribute is particularly important as one of the principal uses of Ada is in building military systems. Such systems may require the use of classified data so it is very important that object access is carefully controlled.

A general problem that must be faced by builders of an APSE is whether the chosen database should support a fine-grain or a coarse-grain view of the objects being managed. A fine-grain view means that objects may be very small (typically less than 1000 characters) and that very precise relationships between objects may be recorded. For example, an object may be a single Ada-type definition, and a recorded relationship might be 'used by' which is represented by a link to all other objects that use that type definition. By contrast, a coarse-grain database uses much larger objects and has the disadvantage that only more general relationships may be recorded.

It seems that the obvious choice of database management system is therefore one that supports a fine-grained view of data but, unfortunately, current DBMS technology is such that these systems usually offer a very poor response to users. Thus, APSE developers must trade-off the precision offered by a fine-grain system and the better performance offered by a coarse-grain DBMS. The argument that performance is not important in this area does not hold, as a system with poor performance will simply not be acceptable to professionals used to fast interactive systems.

2.2.3 The Kernel-APSE

The aim of the KAPSE is to conceal all details of the underlying operating system and hardware from the tools supporting the development of Ada programs. This means that these tools may be viewed as executing on a KAPSE virtual machine. They may thus be transferred to some other host computer by porting the KAPSE to that machine. Given that the KAPSE is very much smaller than the APSE, this activity ought to be less expensive than reimplementing each Ada support tool.

The STONEMAN document does not define the KAPSE virtual machine in detail, but merely indicates which facilities must be provided by the KAPSE. It was envisaged that several different prototype KAPSEs would be developed and that, after experimentation, one of these would become a *de facto* standard system. In fact, some time after the publication of STONEMAN, it was realized that the emergence of a *de facto* standard would take several years and that there was an urgent need for some interim standard interface. A joint industry/university working group was set up called KIT/KITIA and they were charged with the responsibility of defining a Common APSE Interface Set (CAIS). The first report on this was published in 1983 and, by the time this book is available, agreement should have been reached on an APSE interface set. The most recent version of this report is available from the US Department of Defense.

The functions to be provided by the KAPSE may be classified under a number of different headings:

1. **Database access**. The KAPSE provides a database for use by the user and by MAPSE and APSE tools. It must therefore provide facilities to allow objects in the database to be created, accessed and destroyed. Furthermore, the KAPSE is responsible for maintaining some database object relationships such as the 'SOURCE CODE – OBJECT CODE' relationship. It should also provide some means for user-defined relationships to be established – for example, the user should be permitted to say that 'A.spec *is a specification of* A.source'.

2. **Ada program run-time support**. Some components of an executing Ada program require run-time support to be provided by the virtual machine on which that program is executing. For example, if use is made of dynamic data structures (such as linked lists) there may be a need for run-time garbage collection. This should be provided in the KAPSE, as should facilities to support Ada's parallel processing constructs.

3. **Ada program input/output support**. The Ada standard package INPUT–OUTPUT is made up of a collection of I/O functions that may be invoked by an Ada program. These functions allow the programmer to open and close files, to read information from and to write information to these files, and to detect conditions such as 'file not open for reading', 'end of file', etc. Clearly, the implementation of these operations requires access to the

underlying input/output primitives provided by the host operating system. It is the task of the KAPSE to map Ada's I/O operations into these more fundamental constructs.

4. **Software tool invocation and communication**. The APSE database is used to store software tool outputs and these outputs may act as inputs to other tools. However, other means of tool communication, such as UNIX pipes, may be provided by the KAPSE. Furthermore, the KAPSE must provide a mechanism for one tool to invoke other tools and, if appropriate, to pass parameters to the invoked tool.

5. **Interactive terminal control**. During program execution, a user may wish to interrupt the program. For example, the program may be producing incorrect output and the user may wish to terminate execution. Alternatively, the user may wish to suspend his or her current work, execute some other program and then recommence the suspended task. Generally, such facilities can be provided by associating particular meanings with terminal control keys, and it is a requirement of the KAPSE that it provides such facilities and maps control keys to their associated actions.

In general, these KAPSE facilities are presented to the user as a set of Ada package definitions or abstract data types as discussed in later chapters. For example, the KAPSE may provide an abstract data type SYMBOL_TABLE which may be used by the Ada compiler and other tools and which acts as part of the interface between the Ada compiler and the system database.

An examination of the KAPSE requirements shows that it defines a kernel system which is heavily biased towards the hardware technology of the 1970s. Its terminal support, in particular, assumes that only simple character terminals will be used for Ada system development. However, by the time a full APSE is implemented, high-resolution bit-mapped graphics workstations incorporating a powerful processor will be in common use. There is a need for a revised KAPSE requirements document which includes requirements concerning the support of such devices, although, because of the lack of standards in this area, this is not a straightforward task.

2.2.4   The Minimal-APSE

The APSE database and the KAPSE are the bases on which the higher levels of the support environment are built. The STONEMAN document defines a minimal APSE which is made up of a software toolkit consisting of those tools necessary to create, compile and debug Ada programs. The facilities provided by the MAPSE are broadly comparable to those offered to programmers by many modern operating systems used for program development.

It is expected that MAPSEs will be provided initially as Ada development environments. These would gradually evolve through a series of releases until full APSE facilities were available. Although MAPSE tools are comparable to those provided by systems such as UNIX, the use of a MAPSE for program development should offer the programmer much better tool communication facilities. As the MAPSE is an APSE, it must be possible to store all tool outputs in the APSE database and use these outputs as inputs to other tools.

The MAPSE toolkit specified in the STONEMAN document is made up of twelve components:

1. **An Ada translator**. Obviously, a fundamental requirement of a MAPSE is an Ada translation system which converts Ada source text to a form that may be executed on some target machine. As Ada is principally intended for developing embedded systems, the translator should be able to produce executable code for at least one target machine, apart from the host machine.

2. **A text editor**. As all objects must ultimately be represented as characters, this tool allows objects to be created and modified. The editor is not simply a program editor, but may be used for manipulating any textual object including source programs, program data and documentation.

3. **One or more prettyprinting systems**. It is often convenient to store database objects in some compressed form which is not readily readable by people. The role of a prettyprinter is to take this form and to display the object's structure in a legible way. Given that many different categories of object may exist in the database, there may actually be a need for several tools of this type to handle the printing of these different object types. For example, a text processor might be used to format free text, a program formatter might print Ada programs neatly, and a file dumper might be used to convert binary files to their octal or ASCII representation.

4. **Program linkers**. Linkers are programs that take a number of independently compiled units as input, resolve external references, adjust program addresses if necessary and output an executable object. Linkers must be provided for the MAPSE host and for all target machines supported by the MAPSE.

5. **One or more program loaders**. Program loaders are programs that take an executable object as produced by a linker and load this into the logical or physical address space of the host or target machine. So-called 'down-line loading' may be used to load and

execute a program on a target machine connected to the host system via some communications channel.

6. **A set-use static analyser**. This is a tool that can scan an Ada program and provide information about the types associated with names, where names are declared and where names are referenced within the program. It may also indicate statements which might change the value of a named object.

7. **A control flow static analyser**. This tool processes Ada source text and provides information about possible program control flows. It indicates which procedures are called from where in the program and may provide information about exceptions and inter-task communication.

8. **A dynamic analyser**. This tool allows analysis of a program's execution. It should provide details of how often each program statement has been executed as well as trace and symbolic dump facilities. It may provide an interface simulator so that dummy program units may be used and their actions simulated by the user at their interactive terminal.

9. **Terminal interface routines**. Typically, different systems use different types of interactive terminal so there is a need for device drivers for each terminal class to be provided by the MAPSE. These drivers interface the terminal to the relevant structures and functions in the KAPSE.

10. **A file administrator**. This is a tool that allows file transfer and comparison. Facilities that should be provided include file comparison, error control and file/attribute transmission.

11. **A command interpreter**. It is envisaged that all APSE tools may be invoked using a command interpreter. This tool accepts user commands and parameters, stores them in the database then initiates the specified tool. An example of such a system is the UNIX shell .

12. **A configuration manager**. This tool is required as an aid to system developers and managers in configuring a system from a large number of objects. In addition, the system must be able to recompile objects if necessary and handle the general problems associated with change control. Of all proposed MAPSE tools, this is perhaps the least understood and is likely to cause most problems for MAPSE implementors.

In addition to this toolset, the MAPSE should also provide better I/O support for Ada programs than the relatively simple INPUT–OUTPUT standard package supported by the KAPSE. These I/O facilities should be implemented as Ada packages and corresponding facilities for both host and target machines should be available.

At the time of writing, a number of MAPSEs are under construction and, by the time this book is published, some of these should be in use. However, it is unlikely that the final layer in the APSE-onion will be available until the late 1980s as this represents a significant development in the state of the art of programming environments.

2.2.5   Ada programming support environments

It is not intended that there should be a single Ada programming support environment. Rather, the author of the STONEMAN document suggests that many APSEs should be developed with each APSE tailored towards a particular application of Ada, towards a particular software development methodology or towards a particular set of software management practices. However, the requirements for an APSE emphasize that an APSE is also an IPSE, that is, it is intended to provide support for all of the activities involved in software development and not just those activities associated with programming. In this respect, the title of the STONEMAN document is misleading as it emphasizes programming rather than project support.

Because it is not intended that there should be a single APSE, the STONEMAN requirements are very vague indeed about which tools must be provided in the APSE. Broadly, a number of specific tools are suggested which supplement MAPSE tools. In addition, he also suggests directions in which the APSE might develop so that tools to support all phases of the software life cycle are provided for the software engineer.

Some specific tools which will probably be provided in most APSEs are:

1. **An Ada program editor**. This is a syntax directed editor which has built-in knowledge of Ada syntax and which only permits syntactically correct Ada programs to be created. Such editors have already been created for other programming languages like PL/C and Pascal (Teitelbaum and Reps, 1981).

2. **A documentation system**. This is a system to assist with the production and control of software project documentation. It should be made up of tools for document preparation, filing and checking. Such a system might be modelled on the Writer's Workbench (Cherry and MacDonald, 1983) which is a set of programs available under UNIX to assist authors of software documentation.

3. **A configuration management and control system**. A fundamental requirement of the KAPSE is that sufficient information about system objects should be maintained so that automated configuration management and control is possible. However, only minimal configuration management tools are envisaged at the

MAPSE level, and it is intended that the full APSE should provide more extensive tools in this area. Notice that there is a distinction between configuration management and configuration control. Configuration management is concerned with the activities involved in maintaining system configurations. Configuration control is concerned with ensuring these activities are carried out on the right objects, by the right people and at the right time.

4. **A fault report system.** The process of software maintenance in a large software project involves handling a large number of requests for system changes, evaluating the impact of these changes, changing the system and then revalidating the system to ensure that modifications have not had adverse effects on unmodified parts of the system. This process is both time-consuming and error-prone. The STONEMAN proposals include a requirement that a fault reporting system should be an inherent part of an APSE.

5. **A project control system.** This is a management tool that makes use of information in the APSE database to keep track of the progress of a software project. Such a tool will compare actual progress against estimates, measure programmer productivity and produce reports for management about the status and progress of the software development project.

In addition to these support systems (which are suggestions rather than requirements), a number of other classes of software tool are suggested. The author of the STONEMAN report goes into very little detail of what specific facilities might be provided in the tool systems suggested below:

1. **System measurement.** There is a pressing need for methods that will allow the quantification of the software development process. It is suggested that software tools be provided in the APSE to support this quantification.

2. **Requirements specification.** Requirements specification tools are those tools which help analyse system requirements and which relate requirements to functional specifications, designs and implementations. Examples of such notations are PSA/PSL (Teichrow and Hershey, 1977) and RSL (Bell *et al.*, 1977).

3. **Software design.** It is suggested that an APSE might provide tools to support both system design and program design. Examples of such tools might be design diagram editors, design verifiers, etc. Examples of systems which incorporate such tools are AIDES (Willis, 1981) and ECLIPSE (Alderson *et al.*, 1985).

4. **Verification.** The formal verification (proof) of programs is emerging as an important software validation technique. However, the

work involved in formally verifying a large software system is immense and can only be cost-effective if automatic verifiers can be developed to assist in this process. Prototypes of such tools have been built (London and Robinson, 1979) and it is suggested that, as production quality versions of such tools become available, they might be incorporated into an APSE.

5. **Command interpreters.** In addition to a fairly simple command interpreter which will be included as part of the MAPSE, the APSE may include more sophisticated command language processors where the command language might be based on Ada itself.

Although some of the suggestions for APSE tools are very general, the overall picture to emerge is of a very powerful and useful environment which should support all of the stages in the software life cycle. However, some of the proposed tools are beyond the existing state of the art or exist only in simple prototype versions. It is therefore unlikely that complete APSE implementations, providing life cycle support, will be available until the 1990s.

2.3   A critique of the APSE requirements

STONEMAN is a seminal document because it legitimizes the view that software development support environments are at least as important as the programming language used for software implementation. However, much less time and money was devoted to the specification of the APSE requirements than was spent in deriving the requirements for Ada itself. This has meant that the document, inevitably, is couched in very high-level, general terms and this is likely to hinder the development of cost-effective, portable, Ada programming environments.

Another, potentially more serious, problem is that the STONEMAN document seems to have made little attempt to anticipate hardware developments and how they might affect the APSE. This is particularly important as the requirements for the APSE were written in the 1970s, but the system will not be built until the late 1980s. Furthermore, APSEs will probably be in existence for at least 20 years – well into the twenty-first century. Given the rate of hardware development, it is inconceivable that we shall still be using the same equipment as in the late 1970s.

The main area to be affected will be in the user's interface with the APSE. STONEMAN is oriented largely towards simple character terminals, but it is likely that most software engineers in the 1990s will make use of personal workstations with bit-mapped high-resolution graphics displays. These open up opportunities for providing a much more powerful and productive APSE interface, yet some of the APSE requirements (such as the need for all communication being via the Ada character set) may preclude taking full advantage of the power of these systems.

The major criticisms that can be made of the document fall under a number of distinct headings:

- It omits any mention of how particular software development methodologies (Structured Design, JSD, etc.) might be supported.

- It fails to suggest a basis for a KAPSE interface or a MAPSE command language.

- It fails to suggest, except in terms that are so general as to be of little use, how the initial phases of the software life cycle, namely requirements definition, software specification and software design, might be supported by an APSE.

Since the early 1970s, a number of different methodologies of software development have evolved. Almost all of these have their roots in 'structured programming' as described by Dahl *et al.*, (1972). They propose that a software system should be viewed as a hierarchical structure. Although alternative methodologies such as object-oriented design (Booch, 1983) have been proposed and are discussed later in this book, some form of hierarchical functional decomposition or top-down design is likely to be the most widely used software development methodology until at least the mid-1990s. The use of this methodology results in systems that are both understandable and maintainable and it is now extensively used for production software development. In spite of the fact that top-down methodologies are extensively used, and in spite of the fact that Ada is well-suited to such techniques, there is no mention whatsoever of top-down design in the STONEMAN requirements. This we believe to be a significant omission.

Our second criticism is related to the omission of methodology support. The document devotes a total of two sentences to the software tools that might be used to support software requirements definition and design. This is in spite of the fact that the process of specification and design has been estimated to consume about 40% of total software development costs.

Whilst it is true that tools for requirements and design are neither well-developed nor widely used, there is a significant body of work in this area which might serve as a basis for a minimal toolset. Furthermore, the underlying database/KAPSE model is probably adequate to support such tools so that they could be readily integrated into an Ada development environment.

Whilst these criticisms of STONEMAN document are essentially philosophical – they criticize the view of software development environments described in that document – our final criticism is much more practical. It is quite contrary to the initial aims of the APSE project to omit a detailed requirements definition for a KAPSE interface and a MAPSE command language. Without such a specification, it is inevitable that different implementations of APSEs will use completely different interfaces and command languages. The STONEMAN proposals expect a *de facto* standard to emerge, but we believe that this is unlikely, at least in the short-term. Whilst work on this is now under way (CAIS), this has come too late and, whilst it might ·not have been appropriate to include such a detailed description with the document, its publication should have followed soon after.

Without a standard interface and command language, tool portability will be reduced very significantly indeed. Training costs will be increased as each time a software engineer moves to a new environment he or she must learn the particular interface and command language used in that environment.

In conclusion, then, we believe that the APSE proposals were, at the time of writing, critically important in promoting the importance of software development languages. As an early attempt at a specification for an Ada support environment they are very good indeed, but it must be recognized that it is now time for a radical revision of the proposals to take into account criticisms and changes since they were initially written.

2.4   Summary

Software development environments assist the software engineer in developing software systems. We have introduced a number of different types of environment that are currently in use and described in some detail a toolkit environment built around UNIX, a language-oriented, tightly integrated environment (InterLisp) and an environment intended to support the software design process. We have also described the facilities that an integrated project support environment should include.

A support environment specifically designed for Ada (the APSE) has been described. The architecture of such an environment consists of three layers namely a Kernel-APSE, a Minimal-APSE and the APSE itself. However, it was never intended that there should be a single APSE, but that a number of different application-oriented APSEs would be developed to support different classes of Ada system development.

The APSE is an interesting and ambitious development, but the original APSE requirements suffer from a number of problems.

Perhaps the most serious of these problems are the lack of methodology-orientation of the APSE requirements and the fact that it is assumed that character terminals rather than bit-mapped graphics workstations will be the major user interface devices connected to an APSE.

2.5   Further reading

Hunke, H. Ed.; (1981). *Software Engineering Environments*. Amsterdam: North-Holland.

> A collection of papers on environments used to produce large-scale software systems. Progress has been quite rapid in this field so some of the papers are a little out of date. Nevertheless, the book is still well worth reading.

Barstow, D.R., Shrobe, H.E. and Sandewall, E.; Eds. (1984).*Interactive Programming Environments*. New York: McGraw-Hill.

> A collection of papers on environments which places emphasis on language-oriented environments like InterLisp and environments to support exploratory programming rather than software engineering, although an interesting rationale for STONEMAN is included here.

McDermid J.; Ed. (1985). Integrated Project Support Environments. London: Peter Peregrinus.

> A recent collection of papers on IPSEs presented at a conference on integrated project support environments.

Sommerville, I.; Ed. (1986). *Software Engineering Environments*. London: Peter Perigrinus.

> The proceedings of a conference on software engineering environments which includes most UK developments in this area.

Chapter 3 Designing Software Architecture

Software design is a creative process and so cannot be completely formalized. It is impossible to present the user with a recipe that will always result in a 'good' software design, and personal creativity, wisdom and experience are of paramount importance.

The most general definition of a 'good design' is one that meets the system requirements and costs as little as possible; but this is so general that it is practically useless to the software engineer.

However, given the fact that most software costs in large systems development are incurred in changing the system to accommodate new requirements, we consider a 'good software design' to be one that meets the following criteria:

- *The design should be readily understandable* by other software designers and programmers. To achieve this, the designer should exclude low-level implementation details which tend to confuse the software design.

- *The design should be readily modifiable.* This suggests that components of the design should be as independent of other components as is practically possible. Therefore, only the minimal number of components are affected when changes to the system become necessary.

- *The design should be checkable*, where the term 'checkable' encompasses testing, formal verification, design reviewing, etc.

In this book we describe design techniques which we believe will lead to a software design satisfying the above criteria. A number of different views may be taken of the design phase of the software life cycle but, in general, it may be seen as a sequence of specification/realization steps whereby the realization implements the specification set out in the previous phase. The view we have adopted in this text is to consider that the design stages are:

1. **High-level or architectural design**. Using the system requirements definition as a guide, the software system is decomposed into a set of interacting subsystems. These subsystems may be multifunctional, that is, they may do more than one thing. If so, all of the functions

provided by a subsystem should be related in some way. Depending on the subsystem size, this high-level design process may be repeated for each subsystem until subsystems amenable to decomposition using steps 3 and 4 below are produced. Subsystems often operate concurrently in the overall system, particularly if this is a real-time embedded system.

2. **Interface design**. The data flows to and from subsystems are defined and specified in a precise way, as is the procedural interface published by each subsystem. This design process is closely associated with high-level design and is normally carried out in parallel with that activity.

3. **Component specification**. During this stage of the design process, each subsystem is decomposed into its components and the task of each of these functions is specified. It is at this stage that mathematically formal specification techniques, such as those summarized by Liskov and Berzins (1979), may be useful in defining all or part of the design. If formal techniques are not used some other precise specification technique should be adopted.

4. **Algorithmic or low-level design**. During this phase of systems development, the function specifications are used to derive algorithm designs describing how the specifications are to be implemented. It is at this stage of the design that decisions concerning control flow, data type representation, etc. should be made.

Of course, for many systems the splitting of the design into these sub-phases is artificial. Depending on the system size, the number of project staff and the project organization, other ways of partitioning the design phase may be more appropriate. In particular, if the system is not large, the detailed design definition may be derived directly from the requirements definition. However, for large systems made up of several distinct subsystems, each of which may be implemented by a separate project group, it is useful to adopt the above view of software system design.

Naturally, the design sub-phases overlap. Whilst the structure of this book suggests that there are clear distinctions between the sub-phases, in practice the activity of design is an iterative one. As design progresses from one stage to another, errors and omissions in previous stages are discovered and must be corrected. Unfortunately, this cannot be illustrated (without excessive repetition) by examples that are presented in sequence.

As the activity of design is not amenable to formalization, we have followed the practice, used in other creative disciplines, of illustration by example. We have chosen a system which processes electronic mail as our base example and we use this as a linking theme throughout the remainder of the book. This system includes facilities for classifying, redirecting, filtering and automatically acknowledging mail. These facilities are described, in outline, later in this chapter.

Of course, such an electronic mail system is not a particularly large system, but neither is it a trivial example. Attempting to use a truly large system as an example would make this book far too long! However, large systems are normally split into smaller systems – about the size of this example – for implementation, and the technical problems encountered are comparable to those described here. The fundamental problems encountered in developing very large systems are managerial rather than technical, and these are outside the scope of this text.

The aim of this chapter is to describe an approach to the high-level design of software systems and to show how Ada can be used to specify that design. A technique of subsystem decomposition based on subsystem types is described, and this is demonstrated using the example of an electronic mail system decomposed into several subsystems. We then go on to show how the interfaces between these subsystems may be defined using Ada. We pay particular attention to the definition of abstract data types as the means of defining the objects that are shared between subsystems.

3.1   Decomposing a system into subsystems

The first stage in the design process involves analysing the system requirements definition to identify logically related services which may be grouped together and provided by distinct subsystems. As far as we are aware, there is no 'ideal' way of doing this. Indeed, we do not have system evaluation techniques that allow us to compare different decompositions, so we cannot really say if one decomposition is 'better' than another. However, it is possible to provide some guidance for the designer.

The material here is not based on any single design methodology. We believe that large systems are so complex that no single design methodology is appropriate and that different approaches might be used for different parts of the system. As a result, the techniques described here are loosely derived from the work of Wirth (1971, 1976), Constantine and Yourdon (1979), Linger et al. (1979) and others who describe a design methodology based on top-down functional decomposition. We also make use of object-oriented design techniques described by Robson (1981) and by Booch (1983) who showed how Ada may be used for object-oriented design. Object-oriented design is an evolution of a design methodology based on information hiding first described by Parnas (1972). Finally, we have borrowed from the work of Jackson

(1975, 1982) whose design methodology is based on the notion that the structure of the system should reflect the structure of the data being processed by that system.

In order to derive a technique that allows us to identify subsystems, we first define those attributes which we believe subsystems in a 'good' design should exhibit. Obviously, the attributes of a subsystem are partially dependent on its purpose, but we consider that a subsystem design should exhibit at least the following three characteristics:

1. **Logical coherence**. The services provided by a subsystem should be logically related to each other. This means that services identified from the system requirements definition should not just be arbitrarily packaged for the purpose of implementation by different groups.

2. **Independence**. It is not uncommon for subsystems to be implemented as stand-alone programs rather than as a sub-program of some larger system. It is therefore necessary to ensure that subsystems are as independent as possible and that their operations are not highly dependent on other subsystem implementations.

3. **Simple interfaces**. It is essential for subsystems to communicate with other subsystems, and the interfaces through which this communication takes place should be as conceptually simple as possible. This does not necessarily mean that interfaces should be limited to one or two data items. Rather, it means that as well as the subsystem operations exhibiting logical coherence, so too should the data on which the subsystem operates.

Our aim, then, is to decompose the system into subsystems having these characteristics. This process is simplified if we make use of the fact that subsystems themselves frequently fall into one of three classes:

- user utilities
- resource management utilities
- service utilities

User utilities are subsystems that are directly responsible for providing user services as set out in the software requirements definition. For example, in a hospital patient monitoring system there may be several requirements describing which reports on a patient's condition are to be produced. In this case, these services may be collected together into a reporting subsystem whose functions are connected with the provision of reports for the system users.

Resource management utilities are those subsystems responsible for looking after a system resource or class of resource. For example, a resource management subsystem might be responsible for all I/O traffic to a particular device or all operations on a shared table. A resource management utility may also be associated with a particular file or set of files and be responsible for all operations on these files. An example of a resource management utility taken from a patient monitoring system might be a console subsystem which handles all operations associated with a nurse's console.

Service utilities are subsystems that exist to provide a service required by several other subsystems. Naturally, they may call upon resource management subsystems as part of the provision of that service and an aspect of the service may involve user subsystems. For example, in a patient monitoring system there may be several information displays, such as a display on the nurse's console, a display at each patient's bedside and a remote display in a doctor's office. A display management subsystem might be responsible for managing all of these displays and would be called by other subsystems that required information to be displayed. Service subsystems often act as the 'layer' above resource management subsystems concealing their existence from user utilities.

The distinction between service utilities and resource management utilities is in the logical coherence of the subsystem functions. In service utilities, the subsystem encapsulates operations whose relationship is based on functionality. For example,the display subsystem collects together all display functions in the monitoring system and calls on resource management systems associated with each display device. Both the data on which the subsystem operates and the particular operation required are passed to service subsystems through their interfaces.

The functions provided in resource management utilities need not have any similarities. Rather, their coherence is based on the fact that all the functions are necessary to support the resource being managed by the subsystem. Given that there may be multiple instances of a resource in a system, an effective way of managing these resources is to define a single resource management subsystem whose operations are applicable to a specific class of resource. This subsystem then takes a parameter to identify the particular resource instance that is to be manipulated.

This classification of subsystems should not be taken as completely rigid as it is quite possible for subsystems to fall into more than one of the above classes. For example, a requirements definition might specify that a facility is to be provided for the user to list files on a printer. The subsystem for this function might be considered as a user utility since it provides a user service, or as a resource management utility since it is responsible for managing the printer resource.

For real-time systems, a fourth type of subsystem – namely a control subsystem – may be identified. This is dedicated to some control function such as temperature control. The system accepts input from sensors and, on the basis of these inputs, produces control outputs. This is actually very similiar to a user utility which accepts user inputs and produces outputs for the user, so a control subsystem might be considered as a special form of user utility where the 'user' is a hardware or software subsystem rather than a person.

When decomposing a system into subsystems, the first step should be to identify the user utilities that provide services defined in the software requirements document. The difficulty of this task depends on the completeness of the requirements definition. If this is complete and detailed, the subsystems can be identified by listing the services that the system must provide, partitioning them into logically related groups and dedicating a subsystem to each group of services.

On the other hand, if the software requirements document is not sufficiently detailed, the designer must take each generalized requirement and, using some kind of system decomposition, identify more details of what might be provided. By doing this for each requirement, logically related functions can be identified and grouped into subsystems. Problems often arise at this stage which are sometimes left unresolved until the system is put into use. Such problems are due to differing assumptions made by the author of the requirements document and the software designer, with the result that subsystem facilities are not as envisaged by the user. It is really the responsibility of the designer to ensure that the system meets the actual requirements, although this is sometimes very difficult as the requirements may not have been considered in detail by the user and may be subject to change as system development proceeds.

This stage of software design is probably the one that is most dependent on the creativity of the designer. Because systems differ so much, there are really no general guidelines that can be established to define how this stage should be tackled. However, after the identification of user subsystems is complete, subsequent stages in subsystem decomposition can be tackled in a methodical way.

The first stage in this methodical approach is to take each subsystem and describe, at a very high level, how the services provided by that subsystem might be implemented. This top-level decomposition having been made, each subsystem should be examined and common elements factored out as resource management or service subsystems.

To illustrate this process, consider a foetal monitoring system used to monitor a baby's heartbeat and the mother's contractions during childbirth. Such a system monitors heart rate and intra-uterine pressure and displays them on a bedside console. The user services provided by this system are heart-rate monitoring, and pressure monitoring so user utility subsystems can be associated with each of these. They may be decomposed as shown in Example 3.1. In each of these subsystems, there is a display requirement, so it is appropriate to factor this out and implement it as a service subsystem.

A first-level decomposition is often sufficient to identify service subsystems, although, in some cases, another decomposition level

```
procedure Heart_monitor is
begin
  loop
    Get_heart_rate ;
    Display_heart_rate ;
    exit when Power_off ;
  end loop ;
end Heart_monitor ;

procedure Pressure_monitor is
begin
  loop
    Get_pressure ;
    Display_pressure ;
    exit when Power_off ;
  end loop ;
end Pressure_monitor ;
```

Example 3.1   Outline design of a foetal monitoring system.

may be necessary. To identify resource management subsystems, however, the functional decomposition should not be continued. Rather, a strategy based on identifying system resources and associating a subsystem with each of these resources or resource classes should be adopted.

The advantage of this approach is that all the operations associated with a resource are gathered together in one place. Should the representation of this resource change, system changes are confined to a single subsystem. In most cases, other subsystems using the resource need have no knowledge of its representation. Any changes to that representation are transparent to users of the resource management subsystems.

For example, say the foetal monitoring system introduced above has two output devices. These are a plotter where the heart rate and intra-uterine pressure are recorded on a continuous roll of paper, and a digital display where the current heart rate and pressure are output as numbers. In accordance with the strategy above, subsystems PLOTTER and DISPLAY would be constructed to handle all operations on these output devices. If, subsequently, the type of display was changed from a display which used vector graphics to a bit-map display, the system changes necessary because of the changed hardware are isolated in a single subsystem. Only the DISPLAY subsystem need be modified.

This technique of system design which starts with the notion of an object (the resource) and then identifies the operations on that object is sometimes called object-oriented design. It is quite distinct from top-down functional decomposition which is based on the notion that functions are central to the design. Objects that are manipulated by these operations are seen as secondary and are defined at a later stage of the decomposition process.

Object-oriented design has the advantage that it is straightforward to change the representation of low-level objects in the system without affecting the rest of the system. For this reason, we consider it to be well-suited to resource management as it allows decisions on the concrete realization of a resource to be deferred. We return to the advantages and disadvantages of object-oriented design in Chapter 5.

The general principles of decomposing a system into subsystems is best illustrated by a non-trivial example. We therefore describe an electronic mail system in the following section and go on to show how that system may be broken down into interacting subsystems.

3.2   An electronic mail system

The electronic mail system described in this section is used as a source of examples throughout the remainder of the book so we cover it in some detail here. However, our intention is simply to provide an overview of the system such as might be found in the introduction to a software requirements document. Space does not allow a full requirements definition of the electronic mail system. However, we assume that the concepts of electronic mail systems will be familiar to many readers and hope that a system overview is enough to give an appreciation of the system and its design.

The electronic mail system (subsequently referred to as the EM system) provides the usual electronic mail facilities. Users may send mail to other users and may read mail that other users have sent to them. Each system user has his or her own unique identifier, and the sending of mail simply involves the receiver despatching the text of the mail to that identifier.

As well as being able to send and receive mail, the EM system also includes facilities that allow users to get help on how to use the system, to find out which mail has been sent, but not read, to cancel mail sent by mistake and to set up a personal 'mail profile' which specifies mail filtering actions to be carried out on incoming mail.

This notion of mail filtering is a powerful one which is intended to support automatic mail redirection and classification according to the receiver's preferences. The user may define in his or her mail profile that mail from particular users or mail containing particular phrases should be redirected to some other user. For example, say a user, whose identifier is JohnDoe, is a member of some committee and all mail concerning that committee is mailed to him electronically by the committee secretary whose identifier is ComSec. When John Doe is away, his place on the committee may be taken by user Joe Soap, so in his absence all committee mail should go to JoeSoap rather than JohnDoe. If John Doe includes the line ComSec -> JoeSoap in his mail profile, this redirection will be automatically set up. Incoming mail from ComSec will be intercepted and redirected to JoeSoap without ComSec having to be aware that a change in committee membership has taken place.

Similarly, if John Doe is also responsible for collating equipment fault reports mailed to him electronically on a form headed EQUIPMENT FAULT REPORT, the line EQUIPMENT FAULT REPORT –> SueBell in John Doe's mail profile causes all such fault reports to go to user Sue Bell. The mail system scans all mail as it is sent to JohnDoe, and when mail containing the string EQUIPMENT FAULT REPORT is detected it is immediately rerouted to SueBell.

The mail profile may also contain instructions on how the mail should be ordered for presentation. This facility is based on the notion that any item of mail may be classified by the sender to have an importance rating ranging from 1 to 8, with 8 taken to be the most important mail. The sender classifies the mail as it is sent, but the receiver may modify the assigned importance rating by including instructions in the mail profile to redirect the mail to his or herself with a modified importance rating.

For example, the line DerekSmith -> SELF;4 in the mail profile ensures that all mail from user Derek Smith is given an importance rating of 4 irrespective of the rating placed on that mail by the sender Derek Smith. Similarly, a profile entry SYSTEM UPDATE -> SELF;8 ensures that all mail containing the string SYSTEM UPDATE is given the highest importance.

Normally, mail is presented to the sender by the receive mail function and the default presentation order is in descending order of importance. However, the receiver can modify this presentation order so that the mail is sorted alphabetically by title, by expiry date, a date specified by the sender after which the mail is valueless, or alphabetically by sender. After an item of mail is presented, an acknowledgement is automatically generated by the electronic mail system and sent to the mail sender. Acknowledgements, naturally, are not themselves acknowledged.

After reading the mail, the system user may redirect the mail to another user or put it back into the mailbox for later reading. Alternatively, the mail may be filed in the user's personal directory or may be discarded. If none of these options are chosen, the mail is retained by the EM system for later retrieval by the user.

One of the problems with computer systems is that the activity of deletion is a final one. Once a file has been deleted from the filing system it is usually impossible to recover the contents of that file if it is subsequently discovered that the deletion was a mistake. Manual systems of deletion are much more flexible. We delete mail by throwing it into a waste paper bin and we have some time to recover it before it is irretrievably lost when the bin is emptied.

An electronic analogue of a waste paper bin is provided by the EM system to implement the discarding of mail. There is no delete operation built into the system. Rather, deletion of mail is accomplished by redirecting it to the special user whose identifier is wpb. This is the user's own waste bin and items remain there for some time before being permanently deleted. Thus, if mail is discarded by mistake, it can be recovered from the waste bin.

This summary of the facilities offered by the EM system has simplified the system and has glossed over many aspects of it. However, it should be adequate to give the reader an indication of the facilities offered and thus understand the design and implementation of the system covered in the following chapters. A fuller description of this system and outline details of a prototype implementation is given by Sommerville and Smith (1984).

3.3   A design for the EM system

In this section, we show how the guidelines for decomposing a system into subsystems may be applied to our electronic mail system example. Recall from the system description that the EM user sees the system as a set of facilities as follows:

- send mail (Send_mail),
- receive mail (Receive_mail),
- get help (Help_me),
- cancel mail sent by mistake (Cancel_mail),
- find out what mail has been sent, but not read (Find_unread_mail),
- set up or edit the mail profile (Profile_editor).

The guidelines set out in Section 3.1 imply that the EM system might be built from six user subsystems whose names are those in parenthesis in the list.

A particular action is selected by the user to invoke one of these subsystems. There are various ways to implement this selection, but perhaps the simplest is via a command menu. Therefore, a top-level system design, expressed in a notation based on Ada, is shown in Example 3.2. Notice that no attempt has been made at this stage to specify subsystem interfaces – this comes later in the design process.

```
procedure EM_system is
begin
  loop
    case Get_user_choice_from (Command_menu) is
      when Send => Send_mail ;
      when Receive => Receive_mail ;
      when Help => Help_me ;
      when Cancel => Cancel_mail ;
      when Edit => Profile_editor ;
      when What_mail => Find_unread_mail ;
      when Quit => exit ;
    end case ;
  end loop ;
  Shutdown ;
end EM_system ;
```

Example 3.2   Outline design of the EM system.

At this stage in the design process, whilst the design is developed, it is far too early to think about design details and the notation used to express the design has to be flexible yet adequate for the designer to express the detail that he or she considers necessary. A programming language (such as Ada) is far too inflexible a notation for design expression, although many programming language features may be included in a design description language.

The notation used here to describe the top level of the system design uses the same control constructs as Ada, but has a flexible syntax and no requirement that names and types must be declared before use. In addition, an informal approach is taken to parameterization so that parameters to procedures etc. are only introduced when the detail they provide becomes important to comprehensibility.

A particular problem with using Ada as a design description language is that all dependencies (with clauses) must be specified before a program can be compiled. This conflicts with top-down design where high-level decisions are made and dependencies sorted out at a later stage. We use an Ada-based design description language throughout this chapter to illustrate top-down design, but the examples here are not directly compilable as dependencies are not specified.

The next stage in identifying subsystems is to take each of the user subsystems and formulate its top-level design. A process of top-down decomposition where high-level abstractions are expressed in terms of lower-level abstractions is used during this stage. Operations required by

```
procedure Send_mail ( Mail_sender: User.ID ;
                      Mail_form: in out Mail_item.INSTANCE) is
   Blank_form: Mail_item.INSTANCE ;
begin
   Display_the (Mail_form) ;
   -- Get the displayed form. We assume some kind of screen editing
   -- process to fill in the form
   Mail_form := Get_form_filled_in_by (Mail_sender, Mail_form) ;
   Put_into_receivers_mailbox (Mail_form) ;
   case Get_user_choice_from (Send_menu) is
      when Edit_mail =>
         -- The same mail or a variant of it is to be sent to another
         -- user. Display the same form for the user to edit it
         Send_mail (Mail_sender, Mail_form) ;
      when New_mail =>
         -- Call send mail again with a blank form for new mail
         Send_mail (Mail_sender, Blank_form) ;
      when Quit => return ;
   end case ;
end Send_mail ;
```

Example 3.3   The send subsystem design.

more than one subsystem may then be provided as service utilities. We show this decomposition for the two subsystems Send_mail and Receive_mail in Examples 3.3 and 3.4 respectively.

The implementation adopted here is to present the user with a mail form which he or she fills in with the sender's identity, the mail title, the expiry date, the mail text and, perhaps, other information. This filled-in form is collected by the EM system and entered into the receiver's mailbox for subsequent presentation. An example of a possible form design is shown in Figure 3.1. Notice the naming convention used here for names such as User.ID and Mail_item.INSTANCE. This identifies externally defined type names and suggests that these should be provided in a package whose name is the component of the type name before the dot (e.g. User) and whose name within the package is that part of the name in upper-case letters. When implemented, the subsystem here is dependent on these packages, but no design decisions concerning them are made at this stage.

This form-based approach means that it is simple to send the same mail to different users. Rather than present the sender with a blank form, the previously filled in form is presented to the sender. The receiver field and, indeed, any other part of the form may then be edited

Mail Message		
To: RCW	From: IS	Date: 8/5/86
Subject: Reuse project meeting		Expires: 11/5/86
Cancellation Key: 23251		Priority: 8

I can't go to the next reuse project meeting as I have a
dental appointment. The meeting is at 10am in 12.13
on Wednesday 12th. Can you please take my place? I
will ask Tony to mail an agenda to you.

Ian

Figure 3.1   A mail form design.

before entering it into the system again. The Send_mail subsystem is then
called recursively to send the mail to the new recipient. Readers who are
not familiar with the notion of recursion will find a short explanation in
Chapter 4. The Receive_mail subsystem is rather more complex than the
Send_mail system as it must provide facilities for the user to reorder his
or her mail, to summarize it (print titles and senders), to file it and to
redirect it to other users. A design for this subsystem is shown as
Example 3.4.

This routine empties the user's mailbox and holds the contents in a
list called Unread_mail. As mail is read, it is transferred to another
list called Examined_mail. The user is presented with a menu of choices
and he or she can carry out operations on the mail in Unread_mail or on
mail which has already been read (all operational functions take both
lists as parameters and ask the user which list to manipulate). On
completion of the receive mail operation, any unread mail is returned to
the mailbox and mail that has been read and not filed is placed in a
'pending tray' for future filing.

Notice how, in Examples 3.3 and 3.4, we continue the design in a
top-down way and introduce a number of procedures without
worrying about the details of the procedure definition. This is normal
practice in top-down design. However, one step we have taken is to try
to identify which of these undefined operations should be implemented
by calls on other subsystems and which should be implemented by local
routines.

In the examples above, subsystem calls are distinguished using the
Ada naming convention where the routine name (or type name if

```
procedure Receive_mail (Mail_receiver: User.ID) is
    Unread_mail: Mail_list.INSTANCE := Mail_list.Create ;
    Examined_mail: Mail_list.INSTANCE := Mail_list.Create ;
begin
    Unread_mail := Mailbox_manager.Empty (Mail_receiver) ;
    Unread_mail := Discard_expired_mail_from (Unread_mail) ;
    Unread_mail := Sort_on_priority (Unread_mail) ;
    loop
      case Get_user_choice_from (Receive_menu) is
        when Read =>
          Present_mail (Unread_mail, Examined_mail) ;
        when Summary =>
          Present_summary (Unread_mail, Examined_mail) ;
        when Redirect =>
          - - Redirect also handles mail discarded to wpb
          Redirect_mail (Mail_receiver, Unread_mail, Examined_mail) ;
        when File =>
          File_mail (Unread_mail, Examined_mail) ;
        when Reorder =>
          Reorder_mail (Unread_mail, Examined_mail) ;
        when Quit => exit ;
      end case ;
      exit when Is_empty (Unread_mail)
    end loop ;
    Return_to_mailbox (Unread_mail) ;
    Place_in_pending_tray (Examined_mail) ;
end Receive_mail ;
```

Example 3.4 The receive subsystem design.

that is published in the subsystem interface) is preceded by the subsystem name and separated from that name by a dot. Therefore, Mail_list.Create refers to the function Create in subsystem Mail_list and Mailbox_manager.Empty refers to the function Empty in subsystem Mailbox_manager. When these subsystems are implemented it is, of course, necessary to bring these names into scope by including the appropriate **with** clauses at the head of each subsystem implementation.

By contrast, names such as Return_to_mailbox, Redirect_mail and Sort_on_priority are assumed to be routines that are part of the Receive_mail subsystem. In some cases it is not really obvious whether a function should be provided as part of a subsystem or should be provided by calling some external subsystem. An example of this is the

Get_user_choice_from operation whose task is to return the user's chosen option from a menu of possibilities. As all menus are different, it can be argued that each subsystem might do some of its own menu management through Get_user_choice_from and that only the display of menus and the return of user inputs should be handled by a shared service subsystem.

There is no need to make a definite decision at this stage as the design at this level is not affected one way or another. We do, in fact, decide that there should be a generalized menu management system (discussed in Section 3.5.1) and when it comes to design refinement Get_users_choice_from is replaced by a call to a function that is part of the menu management system. The actual refinement that includes this change is shown in Chapter 5 (Examples 5.6 and 5.9) where further refinement of these routines is discussed.

Given the system description, it is clear that, for each user, one possible data organization might include the electronic equivalent of a waste paper basket for discarded mail, a pending tray for mail which has been put aside, but not discarded, and a mail box containing mail which has not yet been dealt with. There are various ways of realizing these objects but, at this stage, it is best to delay making a decision on concrete representations as this inevitably places constraints on the freedom of the software designer.

Rather, we identify three resource management subsystems. These are a mailbox subsystem, a pending tray subsystem and a waste-bin subsystem. As each user also has an individual profile which is used to control mail filtering (with no non-electronic analogue), a profile manager subsystem controlling this resource might also be introduced. It is also clear that there is a need for a menu management subsystem (at some level) as the processing of menus is a common shared activity.

Therefore, the following subsystems might be identified as components of the electronic mail system:

- Send_mail,
- Receive_mail,
- Help_me,
- Cancel_mail,
- Find_unread_mail,
- Profile_editor,
- Menu_manager,
- Mailbox,
- Wastebin_manager,
- Pending_tray_manager,
- Profile_manager.

As the system design evolves, the need for other subsystems may become apparent or this original decomposition might be changed. In particular, we have made no mention of how the system actually communicates with the user at his or her terminal. Whilst it is sometimes sufficient to distribute this communication throughout the system, it is good design practice to isolate I/O operations as these are often the most machine dependent aspects of the system.

3.4 Subsystem communications

Once the subsystems in a system have been identified and named, the next step is to work out how they should communicate with each other. It is then essential to define, in a precise way, the subsystem interfaces and only then commence detailed subsystem design.

However, before any formal definition is possible, a more general picture of subsystem communications should be established. This should give an overall picture of the system architecture, showing the subsystems making up the system and their relationships. One of the most useful notations for expressing this general picture is the data-flow diagram whose purpose is to show the flow of data between subsystems.

There are different conventions used in the construction of data-flow diagrams, but they are all broadly equivalent and can be expressed using the following symbols:

- a rounded rectangle representing a subsystem or process, annotated with the name of the subsystem;
- an arrow indicating a data flow between subsystems, marked with a mnemonic data name;
- a rectangle representing a data source or a data sink, annotated with the name of the data store/sink;
- a lozenge representing an interaction with the user, annotated with information about the data displayed;
- an unannotated arrow between a process and a data store/sink or a user interaction (this may be a two-way arrow indicating bidirectional information transfer);
- the keywords **and** and **or**.

The keywords are used when two or more data flows enter or leave a bubble. The word **and** between two data arrows means that both data flows are input or output, whereas **or** means 'exclusive or' meaning that one of the possible data flows is input or output.

Given this notation and the subsystems included in the EM system, a data-flow diagram describing the most abstract level of the system may be constructed. For readability we have split the system into a

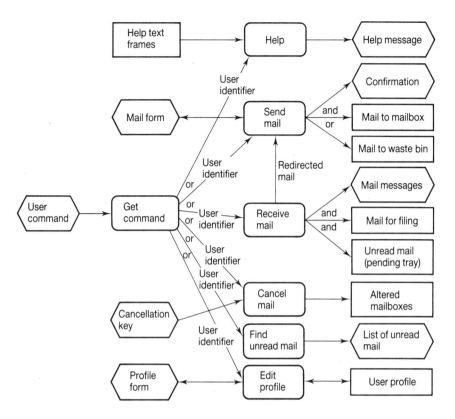

Figure 3.2   Electronic mail system – user utilities.

number of parts. In Figure 3.2, the user subsystems, their inputs and outputs and their interactions are displayed. In fact, only the send and receive subsystems interact directly when mail is redirected during a 'mail receive' operation. This involves calling the send subsystem to send the mail to the new recipient.

As the user subsystems in the EM system are independent, data-flow diagrams for each of these subsystems can be produced showing how they make use of the service and resource management subsystems. This is illustrated for the send subsystem in Figure 3.3. Notice that the subsystem interacts with the user in two ways. It interacts directly to get the user mail and through the menu manager to present a list of options to the user.

In a similiar way, the data-flow diagram for the receive subsystem can be derived as shown in Figure 3.4. The decompositions of the other user utility subsystems to data-flow diagrams may be carried out in a comparable way. We leave this as an exercise for the reader.

One of the important advantages offered by graphical notations is

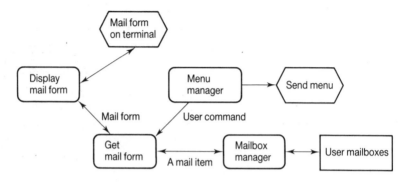

Figure 3.3   The send subsystem.

that the visibility and understandability of the design is enhanced. This seems to be because these notations use a richer symbol vocabulary than textual notations and our understanding processes have less work to do in identifying the design abstractions. However, it is very important to realize that graphical notations usually have imprecise semantics and must be supplemented by more precise specifications if the design is to be fully documented.

After constructing the data-flow diagrams for the user utilities, the next stage in the design process should be to examine these and check if the initial subsystem partitioning is still the most appropriate. In particular, if some service or resource management subsystem is not used by more than one user utility subsystem, then it should not be incorporated at this level in the design. Rather, it should be a part of the utility subsystem that makes use of that facility. Similarly, if we find that several user utility subsystems appear to have very similar inputs or outputs, it might be appropriate to handle these through a shared subsystem.

In the case of the EM system, we find that the pending tray manager is only used by the receive subsystem and not by any others, so it should be factored out of the design at this level. We cannot, however, identify any other shared subsystems at this stage.

A data-flow model of a system does not include control information and, in particular, makes no assumptions about the sequence of activation of the identified subsystems. In most real-time systems, at least some of the subsystems execute concurrently and will be implemented as Ada tasks. However, it must be emphasized that decisions on parallelism are often arbitrary and dependent on the need to meet timing constraints. It is important to defer them until as late as possible in the design process and simply to consider the system as a logically interacting set of subsystems without regard to whether these are executing in parallel or in sequence.

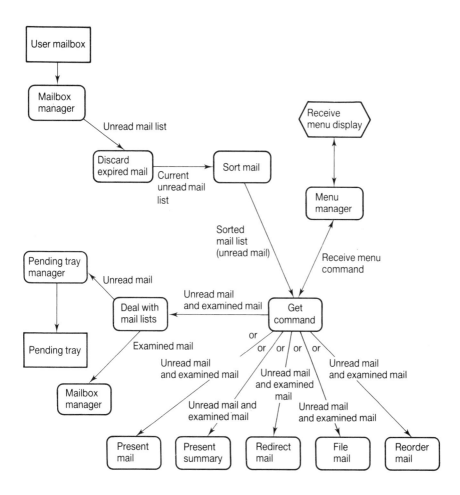

Figure 3.4   The receive subsystem.

Whilst it may be argued that parallelism is fundamental and should be taken into account at a very early stage in the design, the need for parallel computation is partly a consequence of the fact that infinitely fast sequential hardware cannot be built. For any particular application, available hardware may be adequately fast to support a sequential computational model. Whilst a parallel implementation of some algorithms may be appropriate, we reject the notion that parallelism is somehow more natural than sequential computation and consider the degree of parallelism in any system to be a design decision that should be postponed until the stage of detailed system design. Of course, the designer should not preclude parallel implementations when setting out the high-level design description. Parallelism is discussed in some detail in Chapter 9.

In Figures 3.2–3.4, information that flows to and from a system user is shown as data flows which enter or leave the diagram. These might be implemented directly as I/O statements in each of the processes but, in general, this is poor design practice. Rather, there should be a single resource management subsystem which is responsible for handling all user input/output, and all I/O traffic should go through this subsystem. This means that user interaction is localized, so subsequent changes only require a single subsystem to be modified. For example, different types of terminal may be supported by modifying the I/O package, and changes to other parts of the system are unnecessary. In the EM system, the I/O handling subsystem is called User_info and examples of its use can be seen in Chapter 5. At this stage of the design where we are basically concerned with the system architecture, the details of I/O can often be treated as a later design decision.

Given the data-flow diagrams for the system, the next task is to design the interfaces between subsystems. This is particularly critical for shared subsystems as the design decisions made at this stage affect all other subsystems that make use of the shared system. Interface design is the topic of the following section.

3.5   Interface design

It has been estimated that the majority of the validation costs for a large system arise when the subsystems making up that system are integrated and incompatible interfaces are discovered. These incompatibilities arise partly because subsystem interfaces are not specified in a formal way, and partly because most programming languages do not support facilities for safe interface construction. In particular, many languages force subsystem communication via global or common variables that are unprotected from misuse by other subsystems.

The designers of Ada have gone some way towards solving both of these problems. The formal specification of interfaces is supported by the Ada typing model and Ada's type checking mechanisms, whereby checking is carried out at compile-time and run-time and typing errors are reported. It is also possible to program in Ada without using globally accessible objects as the package construct allows objects to be shared in a controlled way.

In designing the subsystem interfaces, two principles should be borne in mind:

- The interfaces should be conceptually simple.
- The actual concrete representation of data is irrelevant to the subsystem user and is a later design decision. This should be reflected in the interface design, and abstract data types (see later) should be used whenever possible.

Interface design involves more than just designing the structure of the data that is passed from one subsystem to another. It also means defining those service or resource management operations that are available for use by other subsystems. These operations are largely dependent on the type of resource managed by the subsystem or the service provided by that subsystem. For example, the menu management subsystem may have a visible operation Get_choice_from, whereas the mailbox subsystem may provide Put and Empty operations.

The fact that large software systems are often made up of independently developed subsystems and the importance of formally specified subsystem interfaces was recognized by the designers of Ada. It is probably the first widely used programming language to make provision for specifying subsystem interfaces without forcing the designer to make decisions about implementation.

The features of Ada that make it particularly suitable for interface specifications are:

- the ability to separate a program unit header definition from the body of the associated program unit

- the ability to define structured types, which means that objects passed through subsystem interfaces may be conceptually simple

- the ability to conceal the structure of types in a package and to limit the allowed operations on these concealed types. The package is also the way in which the accessability of variables may be controlled.

The type definition mechanism in Ada can be used to impose constraints on the values of objects passed across interfaces. For example, if an object passed to a subsystem must have the value 1, 2 or 3, it might be declared to be of type TINY_INTEGER as follows:

type TINY_INTEGER **is range** 1..3 ;

If an attempt is made to pass a value outside this range, this will be trapped by the system at either compile-time or run-time. The Ada compiler attempts to evaluate all variables, and if it detects that they inevitably fall outside the range, an error is indicated. If evaluation is impossible, a call to a run-time range checking routine is planted in the code and raises a constraint exception if the value is outside the range.

However, the type definition mechanism is inadequate for expressing some kinds of constraint. For example, say an array object is to be passed between subsystems. The constraints that are to be imposed are that all values in this array lie in the range 1 to 10 and that there is at least one array element whose value is 10.

Ada's typing mechanism can be used to express the first of these constraints:

type ELEM **is range** 1..10 ;
– – ARRAYINDEX is declared elsewhere
type SOMEARRAY **is array** (ARRAYINDEX) of ELEM ;

The type system is inadequate for expressing the second constraint. To do so, constructs based on predicate calculus may be used. For example, the constraint that at least one of the array elements must be 10 may be expressed in a comment as follows:

$--|$ **exists** I: ARRAYINDEX $=>$ SOMEARRAY (I) $= 10$;

This constraint is expressed in a form of predicate calculus. It specifies that for all arrays of type SOMEARRAY there must exist some member of that array whose value is 10. Such constraints may be expressed in comments associated with type definitions, as we discuss in Chapter 4.

Let us now look at some of the shared subsystems in the EM system and consider the interface that they offer to other subsystems. We show the design of three resource management subsystems – namely the menu manager, the mailbox manager and the waste bin manager. These have a broadly comparable structure, as do the other resource management subsystems which are not described here.

3.5.1   Menu manager design

In the design of the send and receive subsystems, we identified the need for an operation that returned a user's choice from a menu. However, we did not commit ourselves as to whether this should be provided by a local function or by a call to an external subsystem. Clearly, at some level, it makes sense to have an external subsystem handling menu management, as activities such as 'display a menu at a particular position on a screen', 'return the response made by the user', etc., are common to all menus. The question really is whether or not the menu management system should have higher level concerns, such as checking the validity of a user's response, setting up menus, converting the user's keyed response (a keyboard character or, perhaps, a mouse button selection) to the type expected by the calling subsystem, etc.

At the lowest level, the menu management system is only really concerned with very simple types (characters) input by the user and output to the screen. There is a correspondence between these characters and the logical types (lists of choices) identified by the user which make up the menu. It is a straightforward matter to implement a low-level menu manager which deals with low-level types and then leave it to the calling routine to sort out the correspondence between the input and output and the logical types.

However, this is not really satisfactory as it necessarily involves a great deal of duplicated code, so we prefer to carry out type conversions (characters to menu types) within the menu management subsystem. Of course, Ada's philosophy is to forbid explicit type conversions but, fortunately, it provides a facility (generics) that makes the construction of a generalized menu management system straightforward.

We describe generics in detail in Chapter 8. In essence, a generic subsystem is a template for a subsystem and instances of subsystems corresponding to that template, but operating on different types may be created. Assuming that decisions on exactly where a menu is to be displayed, how it is to be displayed, etc., are low-level ones made within the menu management system, we can identify three operations common to all menus:

1. Bring a menu into existence. This means initializing the menu with a title and the names of user options. We assume this is done from some file, so the file name should be a parameter to this function.
2. Identify a user's choice from a menu. This operation must obviously be preceded by a display of the menu on the user's terminal.
3. Inform the calling subsystem that the user has input an invalid choice.

These can be considered as Ada subprograms as follows:

procedure Get_choice_from (Menu : A_MENU ;
                                    Choice: **in out** A_MENU_SELECTION ;
                                    Error: **in out** STATUS) ;

procedure Setup_menu (Menu : **in out** A_MENU ;
                             Setup_filename: STRING ;
                             Error: **in out** STATUS) ;

function Explain_error (Menu: A_MENU ;
                           Choice: A_MENU_SELECTION ;
                           Error: STATUS) **return** STRING ;

For the moment, we ignore the definition of the types of object manipulated by these procedures. The first of these operations, Get_choice_from, takes an object of type A_MENU as its parameter and returns objects of type A_MENU_SELECTION and STATUS as its results. Choice is the menu item picked by the user, and Error returns a value which is set if some error has occurred. More information about this may be obtained by calling the procedure Explain_error. The Setup_menu procedure initializes a menu by taking information from the file called Setup_filename. It is implemented in this way so that dynamic menus which may change during system execution may be provided. Procedures rather than functions are used to allow two results (the result required and an error indicator) to be returned by the menu manager.

In order to build a generic menu manager package, the above procedures are transformed by removing the parameter representing the menu from their parameter list. Rather than access the menu information through the parameter, the menu representation is hidden in the body of the menu manager package and its type is passed as a generic parameter (A_MENU). The procedure Setup initializes this, and it is used by Get_choice (notice the name change) when offering a menu of possibilities to the mail system users.

The types A_MENU, A_MENU_SELECTION and STATUS are generic types and these must be instantiated to actual user-defined types before the menu manager may be used. Thus, the user may instantiate A_MENU to SEND_MENU_TYPE, RECEIVE_MENU_TYPE, etc. to create an instance of the menu manager for each type of menu. In addition, the package takes another generic parameter of type STRING, which is the name of the file whose contents are used to initialize the menu displayed on the user's terminal. Thus, the final form of the menu manager interface is as shown in Example 3.5.

```
- - MENU MANAGER SUBSYSTEM

generic
    Entry_length: NATURAL := 16 ;
    type INDEX is range <> ;
    type A_MENU_SELECTION is private ;
    type STATUS is range <> ;
    type A_MENU is array (INDEX) of STRING (1..Entry_length) ;
    Setup_filename: STRING ;
package Menu_manager is
    type ERROR_MESSAGE is new STRING (1..256) ;
    procedure Get_choice ( Choice: in out A_MENU_SELECTION ;
                           Error: in out STATUS) ;
    procedure Setup ( Error: in out STATUS) ;
    function Explain_error ( Choice: A_MENU_SELECTION ;
                             Error: STATUS) return ERROR_MESSAGE ;
    end Menu_manager ;
```

Example 3.5   The menu manager subsystem interface.

In general, resource management and service subsystems should always be defined as Ada packages where the subsystem operations and types are specified. Because Ada allows the package specification to be separated from the package body, it is a particularly suitable construct for expressing an interface design.

Now, the interface specification for the menu manager has been specified and some semantic constraints associated with the interface by means of the typing mechanism. No further decomposition of the design is necessary at this stage.

3.5.2   Mailbox manager design

In this design of the EM system, it has been decided to provide each user with a single electronic mailbox. There are various strategies that could be adopted here to cope with mail of different priorities, such as multiple mailboxes with different types of mail in each. However, a fairly arbitrary decision has been made to simulate a manual mail system. Incoming mail is placed in this mailbox and mail to be read by the user is taken from it. As all users have the same form of mailbox, identified by the user's identifier, the subsystem used for mailbox management is considered as a resource management subsystem manipulating a class of resource.

The interface for the mailbox manager is derived and specified using Ada packages. First, mailbox operations are identified and defined as procedures or functions. These are as follows:

> **procedure** Put (Item : Mail_item.INSTANCE ; The_user: User.ID) ;
> **function** Empty (The_user: User.ID) **return** Mail_list.INSTANCE ;
> **procedure** List (The_user: User.ID) ;

Notice that single mail items are entered into a mailbox by the Put operation, but all mailbox items are retrieved at once by the Empty operation. This is analogous to what happens in a manual system where mail may arrive in a mailbox item by item, but may be removed all at once by the mail receiver. Again we use a naming convention which suggests that the types Mail_item.INSTANCE and User.ID are declared in the packages Mail_item and User which we have still to design. These will be defined later. Using such a naming convention, it is possible to devise a design tool which abstracts the scope information and automatically adds **with** clauses to the package specification.

Notice that the representation of mailboxes and the operations that manipulate the mailbox are completely concealed from other parts of the program which make use of the mailbox manager. Good design practice suggests that the types Mail_item.INSTANCE and Mail_list.INSTANCE should be

---

```
-- MAILBOX MANAGER SUBSYSTEM

package Mailbox_manager is
    procedure Put (Item : Mail_item.INSTANCE ; The_user: User.ID) ;
    function Empty (The_user: User.ID) return Mail_list.INSTANCE ;
    procedure List (The_user: User.ID) ;
end Mailbox_manager ;
```

Example 3.6   The mailbox manager subsystem interface.

types which are private to the package Mailbox and which are really under the control of the mailbox manager. However, good design practice also suggests that these types should be implemented as abstract data types (packages) and, unfortunately, one of the deficiencies of Ada is that the package construct is not precise enough to control the visibility of information. Whilst, logically, these abstract types should be part of Mailbox_manager, it is not possible to make part and not all of the specification of Mailbox_manager visible where only these types are required.

In fact, these types are fundamental to the system and are used in other subsystems (such as Wastebin_manager) which have no need to have access to the operations defined in Mailbox_manager. Whilst we could explicitly export the types Mail_list.INSTANCE and Mail_item.INSTANCE (we would have to use other names, of course) we have chosen to implement these shared types as separate packages, as this gives more control over which operations are accessible to users of these packages.

3.5.3 Waste bin manager design

Let us now look at another subsystem which also has a very simple interface – the waste bin manager. This is a resource management subsystem as all users have a waste bin of the same form identified by their own user identifier, and this subsystem is responsible for looking after all of these waste bins. The operations that are available to other subsystems which use the waste bin manager are as follows:

1. Put an item of mail into the waste bin.
2. List the contents of the waste bin.
3. Retrieve a particular item from the waste bin. (Each item is referenced by some identifier).
4. Discard all items in the waste bin.

The list and retrieve operations are used when the user wishes to retrieve an item which was discarded by mistake. The user may also clear his or her own waste bin, although this function would normally be carried out automatically by the system at regular intervals. A definition of this subsystem interface is given in Chapter 5 and a formal specification of the type Wastebin.INSTANCE is provided in Chapter 4.

3.5.4 User utility interfaces

Having defined the interface specifications of the shared subsystems, the next step in the interface design and specification process is to define the interfaces of the user utility subsystems. In this example of an electronic mail system this is a straightforward task, although this will not always be the case. All of the user utilities may be considered as Ada procedures which are completely self-contained. Except for the Send_mail subsystem which interfaces with the Receive_mail subsystem, these operations do not require explicit inputs and outputs. Inputs are collected from and output is generated by other subsystems called from within each user subsystem.

However, it is useful for all of these procedures to have access to some identification of the system user, and the most convenient way to provide this is to pass it as a parameter to each procedure. Thus, all user utilities have a parameter of type User.ID and thus make use of the User package where that abstract type is defined. Furthermore, the Send_mail subsystem is also used in the implementation of mail redirection, so a mail form containing information about mail sender, receiver as well as the mail text (if any) is passed to the send subsystem as a parameter. This mail form is of type Mail_item.INSTANCE as defined in the package Mail_item.

The specifications for the user utility subsystems can therefore be written in Ada as follows:

```
procedure Help_me (The_user : User.ID) ;
procedure Profile_editor (The_user: User.ID) ;
procedure Cancel_mail (The_user: User.ID) ;
procedure Find_unread_mail (The_user: User.ID) ;
procedure Receive_mail (The_user: User.ID) ;
procedure Send_mail (Form : in out Mail_item.INSTANCE; User : User.ID) ;
```

3.5.5   Global variables

In this example of an electronic mail system, global variables are not used. It is good practice to avoid the use of global variables when developing large systems as this reduces the complexity of subsystem interfaces. When all subsystem communication is through parameters, the interface is explicit, more readable and safer than interfaces implemented using shared variables. When global variables are used, the entire interface specification is not defined in the same place as the subsystem. Not only does this make the subsystem interface harder to understand, it also means that accidental use of the global variables may cause unforeseen effects in that subsystem.

3.5.6   System configuration

Although we do not make use of global variables in the EM system, it is necessary to share some constant information that defines a particular system configuration. In general, any system that is intended to run on more than one computer may exist in a number of different configurations, with these configurations defined using constant values. These must be shared so that parts of the system may take configuration dependent actions.

One way of providing this configuration information is via a package of shared constants, but this approach lacks flexibility. If, for some reason, the configuration changes, this package and all dependent packages must be modified and recompiled. A better alternative is to access configuration information via function calls. This means that the system can be dynamically configured by reading the configuration information from a file as it is required.

Part of the specification for the EM system configuration package is shown as Example 3.7.

```
package Configuration is
    function Get_wastebin_size return INTEGER ;
    function Get_profile_size return INTEGER ;
    function Get_uid_size return INTEGER ;
    - - Other configuration information here.
    - - This is not included for the sake of brevity
end Configuration ;
```

Example 3.7   System configuration package.

3.5.7   Shared types

When the interface definitions for the subsystems are studied, it is clear that there are a number of types that are shared by several subsystems. These are:

1. User.ID. A user identifier
2. Mail_item.INSTANCE. A descriptor for an item of mail in a mailbox
3. Mail_list.INSTANCE. A list of mail item descriptors.

There will also be other types (such as Date) which are shared between subsystems but, for brevity, there are not discussed here.

In a language like Pascal, it is necessary to establish a representation for these types and to declare them as global types. In languages such as FORTRAN which do not have facilities for user type definition, the designer must map the logical type representation on to an underlying physical representation which makes use of the built-in language data types.

It is actually premature to make decisions on type representation at this stage in the design process. To specify the system interfaces, it is necessary to establish the names of the shared types and the names of the operations that may be used to access objects of these types. In doing so, we are effectively defining what are termed abstract data types whose representation is a decision made at a later stage in the design process.

We have already come across the use of these abstract data types in the previous examples in this chapter. The notion of an abstract data type is a very important one for the software designer and we discuss abstract types in detail in Chapter 6. At this stage, all we have to know about these abstract types is that the Ada package specification may be used to set out the type name (usually specified as a **private** type) and the operations on the type.

When designing abstract data types, the first stage is to decide what logical information is represented by that type. The next step is to decide what operations should manipulate that logical information and, finally, the abstract type specification should be defined as an Ada package specification. Unfortunately, Ada is not ideal for abstract data type definition: it forces a premature decision on to the designer in that a type representation must be set out as part of the private part of the package specification. This is logically unnecessary for type definition, but is included so that the compiler may make space allocation decisions for these type representations.

We concentrate in this chapter on defining those abstract data types that are used in subsystem interface definition. The first of these is the type User.ID which is a specification of the form of some user identifier. Given that the EM system is running under an operating system, the representation of this will be operating system dependent, so it is important to hide that representation in an abstract type. There are few operations on this type – the only one which is of interest here is the operation Get_uid which returns an object of type User.ID. Notice how this type is actually named ID in the Ada package specification so that its full reference is the meaningful User.ID.

To design the structure of a mail item, the system facilities must be examined and analysed to find out what logical information should be held in items of this type. This analysis can be summarized as follows:

1. **Mail delivery**. This requires the receiver's user identifier, the sender's user identifier and the mail to be delivered.

2. **Mail classification**. This requires information about the priority of the mail.

3. **Automatic mail expiry**. This requires a user-provided mail expiry date.

4. **Presentation in order of posting**. This requires the date and time at which the mail was entered into the system.
5. **Mail cancellation**. This requires a user-provided cancellation key.
6. **Mail summarization**. A summary consists of a list of mail titles and senders so this requires a user-assigned mail title and the sender's user identifier.
7. **Mail input from file**. It is possible to create a mail file and then give that file name rather than the text of the mail. Thus provision must be made for this in the design of Mail_item.INSTANCE.

From this analysis, it is clear that procedures to interrogate and access the following components of Mail_item.INSTANCE may be necessary:

- mail sender,
- mail receiver,
- the date the mail was sent,
- the expiry date of the mail,
- the mail cancellation key,
- the mail priority,
- the mail message text.

Apart from the operations that are concerned with the text of the mail message, the other operations may be provided by simply reading and assigning to objects of the appropriate type. It may therefore seem to be redundant to provide many similiar 'get' and 'put' operations when the same could be accomplished by making a simple record declaration visible. However, the advantages of hiding record structures

```
-- User abstract data type
with Configuration ;
package User is
    type ID is private ;
    -- Assume this is implemented by picking up some system variable
    function Get_uid return ID ;
private
    Id_length: constant := Configuration.Get_uid_size ;
    type ID is array (1..Id_length) of CHARACTER ;
end User ;
```

Example 3.8   The User abstract data type.

are that they can be completely changed at some later date without change to other parts of the program, and their representation can be optimized for a particular implementation without the user being concerned with these details. For example, objects of type Mail_item.INSTANCE are likely to be sent over communication lines so it is desirable to minimize the number of bits in their representation. However, this is of no interest to the user of the package who requires a more abstract view of such objects.

```
- - Mail item abstract data type specification
with Date, User ;
package Mail_item is
  type INSTANCE is private ;
  type MAIL_MESSAGE is record
    Title: STRING (1..50) ;
    Filename: STRING (1..256) ;
  end record ;
  type PRIORITY_TYPE is range 0..9 ;
  type CANCEL_KEY_TYPE is new NATURAL ;
  - - This is an incomplete list of function
  - - and procedure definitions. All procedures have the same form
  function Get_sender (Item_is: INSTANCE) return User.ID ;
  procedure Put_sender (User_is: User.ID ; Item_is: in out INSTANCE ) ;
  function Get_expiry_date (Item_is: INSTANCE) return Date.STAMP ;
  procedure Put_expiry_date (Date_is: Date.STAMP ;
                             Item_is: in out INSTANCE ) ;
  - - more access procedures of the same form here
private
  type INSTANCE is record
    Sender: User.ID ;
    Receiver: User.ID ;
    Date_sent: Date.STAMP ;
    Expiry_date: Date.STAMP ;
    Message: MAIL_MESSAGE ;
    Cancellation_key: CANCEL_KEY_TYPE ;
    Priority: PRIORITY_TYPE ;
  end record ;
end Mail_item ;
```

Example 3.9   The Mail_item abstract data type.

```
– – Mail list abstract data type specification
with Mail_item ;
package Mail_list is
    type INSTANCE is private ;
    function Create return INSTANCE ;
    function Add (List: INSTANCE; Item: Mail_item.INSTANCE)
            return INSTANCE ;
    function Head (List: INSTANCE) return Mail_item.INSTANCE ;
    function Tail (List: INSTANCE) return INSTANCE ;
    function Is_empty (List: INSTANCE) return BOOLEAN ;
private
    type MAIL_ELEMENT ;
    type INSTANCE is access MAIL_ELEMENT;
end Mail_list ;
```

Example 3.10   Mail list abstract data type.

A shortened version of the package specification for Mail_item is shown as Example 3.9. Note that the sizes of Title and Filename in MAIL_MESSAGE are arbitrary and could actually be passed as generic parameters.

Notice that, as well as the abstract type name Mail_item.INSTANCE, this package also defines some other types, namely MAIL_MESSAGE, CANCEL_KEY_TYPE and PRIORITY_TYPE. These are used in the access functions to Mail_item.INSTANCE, but are not defined as abstract types as their operations are fundamental operations provided in Ada. We also make use of the type Date.STAMP which is assumed to be defined in the package Date. For brevity, we have excluded the definition of this package from this section.

The final abstract data type we consider is the type called Mail_list.INSTANCE. Objects of this type are an unbounded list of mail items and operations are provided to add and remove items from the mail list, check if any items are on the list, create the list and so on. A specification is shown in Example 3.10.

3.6   Overall system design

It is now possible to go ahead with the separate development of the designs for each of the subsystems. Before doing so, however, it is useful to specify the highest level in the system. This was introduced at the beginning of Section 3.3 and may now be expressed in more detail and

```
– – Appropriate with declarations should appear here
procedure EM_system is
   type TM_INDEX is range 1..7 ;
   type TOP_MENU is array (TM_INDEX) of STRING (1..16 ) ;
   type OPTIONS is (Help, Send, Receive, Cancel, Edit, What_mail, Quit) ;
   type MENU_ERROR is range 1..4 ;
   Command_menu_file: constant STRING := "Command_file" ;
   – – Instantiate the generic menu manager package to create a menu
   – – manager for the top level menus used by EM_system
   package Command_menu is new Menu_manager (
                    INDEX => TM_INDEX ,
                    A_MENU => TOP_MENU ,
                    A_MENU_SELECTION => OPTIONS ,
                    STATUS => MENU_ERROR ,
                    Setup_filename => Command_menu_file) ;
   Action : OPTIONS ;
   Error: MENU_ERROR ;
   The_user : User.ID :=User.Get_uid ;
   Blank_form : Mail_item.INSTANCE ;
begin
   Command_menu.Setup (Error) ;
   loop
      Command_menu.Get_choice ( Action, Error) ;
      case Action is
         when Send => Send_mail (Blank_form, The_user) ;
         when Receive => Receive_mail (The_user) ;
         when Help => Help_me (The_user) ;
         when Edit => Profile_editor (The_user) ;
         when Cancel => Cancel_mail (The_user) ;
         when What_mail => Find_unread_mail (The_user) ;
         when Quit => exit ;
      end case ;
   end loop ;
   Close_down_the_EM_system ;
end EM_system ;
```

Example 3.11   The top-level design of the EM system.

with interface details included. This is shown as Example 3.11.

We have now reached the stage in the design of the EM system where the highest level abstractions have been identified and their interfaces defined. The next step is to refine each of these abstractions, to remove ambiguities in the design and to develop precise, perhaps formal, specifications of the operations of each subsystem. The development of such precise specifications is the topic of the following chapter.

3.7   Summary

This chapter has been concerned with the early stages of the software design process – namely the establishment of an overall system architecture and the design of the interfaces between subsystems. We believe that decomposing a system into subsystems should be done on the basis of subsystem type, and we have identified three typical types of subsystem – namely user utilities, resource management subsystems and service subsystems – which seem to be part of many types of system.

An electronic mail system is used as a linking theme throughout the book. Although this is not, in itself, a large system, we believe that it is sufficiently complex to reveal the design principles.

The process of top-down design has been illustrated by decomposing the electronic mail system into subsystems, and we described some of these in a design language based on Ada. We then discussed subsystem communications and suggested that data flow diagrams are a good first step in describing how subsystems communicate.

In the final sections of the chapter, we looked at the interface design of a number of service and resource management subsystems making up the EM system and showed how Ada could be used to specify their interfaces without including any information about the subsystem implementation. We also introduced the important topic of abstract data types as a means of concealing interface representation, and defined some of the abstract data types used in the mail system.

3.8   Further reading

The specific approach to software design we have advocated here is derived from a number of different design methodologies, and the further reading we recommend looks at these design methodologies in more detail.

Booch, G. (1983). *Software Engineering with Ada*. Reading, Mass.: Addison-Wesley.

This is one of the most interesting introductory texts for Ada as Booch advocates, very strongly, the use of an object oriented approach to software construction. It contains many examples on object-oriented design using Ada.

Jackson, M. A. (1982). *System Development*. London: Prentice-Hall.

An exposition of Jackson's ideas on how a software design should be viewed as a set of cooperating sequential processes. This is an excellent book covering a sound design methodology.

Constantine, L.L. and Yourdon, E. (1979). *Structured Design*. Englewood Cliffs, N.J.: Prentice-Hall.

This is the definitive text on structured design and the methods are explained very clearly. Unfortunately, all of the examples are from commercial data processing and the use of this technique in designing embedded systems is not discussed.

Chapter 4 Software Specification

The word 'specification' is one of the most overloaded terms currently used in computing. Unfortunately, there is no agreed, precise definition of what is meant by that expression, so each user tends to have their own idea of when the term should be used. This leads to frequent misunderstandings and mutual disagreement. It is not our intention to attempt to establish a definitive meaning of specification in this book; but before discussing software specification, it is very important that we say what we mean by that term and how we view the role of specification in the software life cycle.

We are interested in *precise* rather than *formal* specification because we believe that the precision of a specification is more important than the notation in which it is expressed. Whilst imprecise specifications are generally expressed in natural language and the most precise in a rigorous formal way, there are many states in between. We believe that the pragmatic software designer should attempt to achieve as precise a specification as is practicable within whatever constraints of staff, time, expertise, etc. he or she is presented with. Normally, this will involve using multiple notations, with some parts of the system specified more formally than others.

We consider software specification to be the part of the design process where the actions of the system's software components are described. This activity is distinct from what is sometimes called requirements specification. In fact, we have tried to avoid the term 'requirements specification' in this book and prefer to use the expression requirements definition. Unfortunately, in the terminology used by many systems analysts, the expression 'functional specification' is also used to describe this activity, so it is not surprising that confusion is common.

In short, we view the requirements definition phase of the software life cycle as an expression of the services provided to the system user, the constraints under which the system must operate and, perhaps, a statement of the goals of the system. The software specification of the system, on the other hand, is intended to describe the operations of the software system (not just user services) to software designers and programmers. It need not be couched in terms that are understandable to users.

94

Of course, there is no reason why parts of the requirements definition of the system may not be expressed in the same notation as is used for system specification. However, it is important to emphasize that the requirements definition is intended to communicate the needs of the system's users to the system designers. It must therefore be expressed in a language that is understandable to the user even if this is not an ideal notation from the designer's point of view.

The documents produced during the software specification stage of the life cycle, however, are intended for designer–designer communication. Therefore, precise technical terminology and notations may be used as it may be assumed that the designers involved share a common vocabulary. That vocabulary may be a restricted form of natural language, a programming language, or a formal notation that is specifically intended for expressing software specifications.

Our own position on a formal approach to specification is that of a software engineer rather than that of a computer scientist. However, unlike some software engineers who suggest that formal specification will be of future value, but is not yet well enough developed for practical use, we believe that, in some areas, such techniques may be used *here and now* in the design of practical software systems. In particular, we believe that a formal approach to the specification of interfaces is of immense value and is now cost-effective. By contrast, overall system specifications are much harder to develop and, whilst they are very valuable indeed, it is arguable if existing tools, techniques and staff allow them to be developed in a cost-effective way.

Of necessity, the approach here is opinionated because no consensus on specification techniques has yet emerged. We differ from some computer scientists in that we do not currently favour the use of mathematical symbolisms for expressing specifications. The reasons for this are twofold. Firstly, it is our experience that, rightly or wrongly, many readers are 'turned off' by apparently complex notations, although the underlying concepts may not be at all difficult. Secondly, notations that use mathematical symbols force a separation between specification and program, and we believe that, in many cases, including specifications as program comments is very valuable indeed. Thus, we use a mnemonic notation here which can always be typed on a normal keyboard.

As this is a chapter rather than a book about specification we have been forced to be very selective in the material presented and have made an arbitrary decision to cover only techniques for specifying interfaces between software components. The principal reason for this decision is that this is perhaps the most critical part of the software engineering process when software is being developed by a team. Furthermore, the techniques are now usable and are understandable by most software engineers, whether or not they have experience of working with formal specification techniques. We have successfully used the techniques described here in developing a real software system (a graphics editor for a workstation) and are convinced that these simple specifications improve communication between designers and lead to more reliable software systems.

The techniques described here are useful, but are not really adequate for completely specifying all of the actions of a software system. Although there are different approaches to this problem, specification techniques that are based on mathematical set theory (such as Z (Abrial, 1980) and VDM (Jones, 1980)) have been successfully used in specifying non-trivial software systems. Lack of space prevents us from discussing these approaches to specification. Currently, it is unclear if the use of notations such as VDM is cost-effective, as there are few staff trained in their use and few software tools exist to assist with their use. However, we believe that, in future, these techniques will become more widely used and will play a very important part in the software process.

The aims of this chapter are to convince the reader of the value of a formal approach to software specification, and to show how interface definition may be made complete by the use of additional specification information. We do not attempt to describe available specification techniques, but concentrate on demonstrating how interface definition can be made more precise by associating predicates with the interface types and by showing how algebraic specification may be applied to abstract data type definition.

4.1   Why formal specification?

The activity of software specification is sometimes described as defining 'what' the software system should do. By contrast, the software design process is seen as a description of 'how' the specification may be executed on a computer. It seems to us, however, that this distinction between specification and design is a spurious one. It has arisen because it is sometimes convenient to use notations for software specification which, given the current state of hardware and software technology, cannot be translated directly into an efficient form.

In fact, these hardware and software technologies change very rapidly indeed and what is today's specification language is tomorrow's implementation or design language. Let us illustrate this by considering a situation which might have arisen before any kind of high-level programming language was devised.

Before high-level languages, programs were written in assembly code or even in binary machine code and all kinds of tricks were used to optimize the use of store and to increase processor speed. Now imagine that a specification language called FORTRAN was proposed which ignored machine details and allowed design solutions to be expressed in a machine independent way. A statement such as 'DIFF = DIFF * VAL/32' would certainly not have been considered, in the early 1950s, to be an executable statement. It could be hand translated into assembly code, but it is unlikely that the actual code would contain either multiplication or division operations.

Nowadays, FORTRAN is seen as a fairly low-level implementation language allowing very efficient programs to be generated. No one would consider using it for software specification. Given developments in technology, 'what' can very quickly become 'how', and we believe that the development of computers that will execute today's specification languages is very probable indeed.

It seems to us, therefore, that a system specification is simply another way of describing a design. However, it is generally true that the design is expressed in such a way that low-level details are eliminated. It is thus either impossible or very inefficient to execute the specification and, for efficient execution, the specification must be transformed into some other, more readily executable form.

As an example of this, consider the specification for a factorial function shown as Example 4.1. This is not expressed in Ada, but in a simple specification language whose meaning is, we hope, obvious.

```
factorial (N : integer)
    if N = 0 then return 1
    if N < 0 then return UNDEFINED
    if N > 0 then return N * factorial (N–1)
```

Example 4.1   The specification of a factorial function.

This specification states that if a function's input is 0, the value of the factorial is 1, if the input is less than 0, the factorial is undefined. If the input is greater than zero the factorial may be computed by multiplying the input value N by the factorial of the predecessor of N, namely N − 1.

The use of recursion, where the actions of a function are described in terms of that function itself, is very common in software specifications. Recursion should be a familiar concept to those readers experienced in the use of Pascal or a similiar block-structured high-level language. However, it may be somewhat alien to readers whose past experience has been confined to FORTRAN, assembly code or some other low-level language.

A recursive procedure or function is simply one which calls itself.

Naturally, the procedure or function parameter must be modified in some way within the procedure before the next procedure call. Typically, the parameter might be reduced or increased and the recursion terminates when the parameter attains some value. The procedure must contain a 'recursion termination' statement where the self-calling process is not activated. In Example 4.1, the recursion terminates when the input parameter N has a value of zero. Notice that for values greater than zero, factorials are defined using other factorials, but for zero we know that 0! is 1.

Recursion is best viewed as a description of a process, although, in most cases, it is executable. It is actually possible to express the foregoing specification directly in a functional language such as Lisp but, for efficient execution, it may be translated to Ada as shown in Example 4.2.

```
type FACTORIAL_TYPE is record
    Input_defined : BOOLEAN ;
    Value : INTEGER ;
end record ;

function Factorial (M : INTEGER) return FACTORIAL_TYPE is
    Temp : FACTORIAL_TYPE :=
        (Input_defined => TRUE, Value => 1) ;
    N: INTEGER := M ;
begin
    if N < 0 then
        Temp.Input_defined := FALSE ;
    else
        while N > 1 loop
            Temp.Value := Temp.Value * N ;
            N := N - 1 ;
        end loop ;
    end if ;
    return Temp ;
end Factorial ;
```

Example 4.2   A factorial function in Ada.

There are, of course, many possible Ada implementations of the given specification, including implementations which make use of recursion. However, we have chosen not to use a recursive approach here, to emphasize the distinction between specification and implementation. Notice how a record is returned by the function with a field of the record indicating whether the input value is valid or not. This permits the effective return of an undefined value if the function input is negative. An alternative strategy would have been to raise an exception if the input value was less than 0 or to define the input parameter to be of type NATURAL and let the Ada type checker catch any type errors.

The example exhibits those characteristics we consider to be most important, namely:

- It provides a clear description of the function for the designer and the programmer.

- It provides information that allows the implementation of the function to be validated.

This latter point is particularly important. Not only do formal specifications provide a framework for program verification, they may also be used by the software tester to guide his or her choice of test data. The factorial specification clearly suggests that the test data set for the factorial function should contain, at least, values less than zero, zero, and values greater than zero.

The development of mathematically formal notations for the expression of software specifications is currently the subject of much computer science research. A mathematically formal notation is one where the syntax and the semantics of the notation are rigorously and completely defined so that the meaning of a specification in that notation is unambiguous. It is likely that, in future, all or part of a software system will be formally specified, although the state of the art is such that formal software specification is not yet widely used.

The advantage of using formal specifications is that they are amenable to mathematical analysis and can be processed using computer-based tools. For example, it may be possible to analyse the specification and detect inconsistency or incompleteness, specifications may be shown to be equivalent and, of course, proving that a program is correct depends on the existence of a formal specification.

Furthermore, some researchers now believe that it will be possible to transform program specifications into efficient implementations on current hardware. Effectively, this means writing a compiler for the specification language and, should this come about, the work involved in low-level system design could be eliminated or drastically reduced.

Even when automated manipulation is impractical, formal specifications are an unambiguous way of communicating a software design. In addition, Liskov and Berzins (1979) suggest that the use of a formal specification language makes the construction of incomplete specifications less likely because the incompleteness cannot be hidden behind vague, informal terminology.

This does not mean that formal specifications, however unambiguous, cannot be misunderstood. Parnas (1979) reports that, in his experiments, formal specifications were more often misunderstood than informal specifications. He attributes this to the background of the users but, whatever the reason, it seems to be unwise to rely entirely on formal specifications for any software system.

Perhaps the best approach is to construct informal specifications which act as comments in the formal specification language. The reader may then get an intuitive feel for the concepts being described by reading the informal description, yet still be able to find out details from the formal representation. Given that, at the time of writing, the construction of complete formal specifications for a large system is unlikely to be cost-effective in most organizations, this approach means that formal specifications can be developed for critical parts of the system with less critical functions specified in an informal way.

4.2 Ada-based specification languages

There have been a number of research projects aimed at inventing a specification language based on Ada. Probably the furthest advanced of these efforts is the Anna project (Krieg-Bruckner *et al.*, 1984) whose aim has been to develop a specification language for axiomatic and algebraic specifications. By contrast, the work of Hill (1983) has been devoted to the development of a specification language (Asphodel) to support the denotational approach to software specification.

Both Asphodel and Anna are annotation languages in which Ada text is annotated with formal comments defining the specification. Anna, in particular, is intended for use with automatic verification tools so the user is forced to provide considerable specification detail.

The notion of using an Ada-based language to annotate and specify Ada programs has obvious advantages:

1. The notation (or parts of it at least) is familiar to Ada programmers.

2. The program plus specification may be processed without change by Ada compilers, with the specification acting as program document-ation.

3. Specification compilers may be developed which translate the specification into self-checking executable code. This would be an important extension to the run-time checking facilities of Ada.

4. Programs may be developed by expanding specifications and programs, and specifications may be kept in step as one or the other is updated.

However, the annotation language approach does have some dis-advantages:

1. Specifications are not as concise as they might be. Ada is a verbose language and this is reflected in the specification notation.

2. The use of an Ada-based language tends to make users think in terms of Ada constructs. This constraint may not always be a beneficial one. For example, it is often useful to think of a problem specification as a conditional expression. This is not encouraged by Ada-like languages.

3. Ada-like languages preclude the use of mathematical symbolism. Although we believe that for novices to formal specification, mnemonic notations are best, more experienced developers of specifications usually prefer mathematical symbols to mnemonics.

We subscribe to the general notion that Ada-based specification languages are a 'good thing'. Much work remains to be done in this area, however, particularly in the development of specifications for parallel programs.

The examples below are presented in a notation that follows the style of Anna and which borrows much of its syntax. The notational constructs are introduced as they are used and we rely on the intuition and experience of the reader to understand their semantics. Space precludes any kind of formal definition of the notation. We have deliberately avoided using either Anna or Asphodel as this would involve dedicating too much space to notational descriptions.

4.3   Type constraints

We have already discussed, in Chapter 3, the importance of well-defined subsystem interfaces. Without a formal interface specification, there is a high probability that subsystem interfaces will be incompatible, thus increasing the costs of integrating these subsystems into a compatible software system.

These problems were recognized by the designers of Ada and the package construct was included in Ada to facilitate the definition of subsystem interfaces. However, the mechanisms provided in Ada are only sufficient to define the syntax of interfaces and the types of the objects passed through interfaces. The only constraints associated with an interface are those inherent in the interface types, and there is no way to define the semantics of the operations which are visible through the interface. Furthermore, it is not possible to associate stricter constraints with data passed across interfaces than those constraints implied by the type system.

In this section and in the following section, we describe how more complete subsystem interfaces may be defined. This section concentrates on type constraints, and the following section is devoted to the important topic of abstract data type specification.

The type definition features of Ada offer advantages over other commonly used programming languages in that they allow a fairly precise definition of the range of values associated with a particular type. For example, if a type MONTH is defined, its value may be restricted to an integer between 1 and 12, if a type DAY is defined, its value may be restricted to values from 1 to 31, and so on. It is also possible to define a type as a list of values. The type facilities of Ada are discussed in Chapter 6.

The ability to define types and associate objects with these types is a useful safety mechanism, but the Ada facilities are not adequate for describing all type constraints that might be desired by the user. For example, it is not possible to describe relationships between components of composite types using the type definition mechanism, nor is it possible to associate what might be called 'nonlinear' constraints with types.

For example, say it is intended to store prime numbers less than 1000 in an array. The type definitions for this might be as follows:

type PRIME **is range** 2..1000 ;
type PRIME_ARRAY **is array (range** <>**) of** PRIME ;

Whilst limitations on PRIME might be established if only a few prime numbers are to be stored, this is not feasible if the specification was changed so that primes up to 1 000 000 (say) were to be held in the array. Rather, an explicit type constraint might be associated with the type PRIME:

type PRIME **is range** 2..1000 ;
– –: P: PRIME ;
– –: Top: INTEGER := INTEGER (Math.Square_root (P)) ;
– –| **for_all** x, 2..Top => P mod x /= 0 ;

This constraint states that for all values in the range 2 to Math.Square_root (P) (converted to integer type) it is the case that there is no value that divides exactly into P. We assume that some package of mathematical functions called Math is available and this contains a function Square_root which computes the square root of its input. The symbol => can be read as 'it is true that'.

The specification makes use of the **for_all** construct which is derived from the universal quantifier as used in predicate calculus. As used here, it means that for every value in the specified range, the following predicate must hold. A completely formal specification would probably make use of set theory to model the array, and this would be essential if any automated specification checkers or program proving tools were to process the specification. However, if the annotations are intended to provide information for human readers, this relatively informal approach is more precise than natural language specification yet is easily read and understandable by readers who are unfamiliar with mathematical notations or set theory.

The type constraint is specified using formal comments as introduced in Anna. The specification is made up of valid Ada annotations which are introduced using the formal comment symbol '– –:' and statements in the specification language which are introduced using the symbol '– –|'. For simply reading specifications, there is no real advantage in using two types of formal comment symbol, but if the specifications are to be processed automatically, distinguishing Ada text from specification language statements is very valuable indeed. In this book, the advantage is that we may assume that the reader will understand the Ada text and can confine additional explanations to the specification language statements.

As an example of how constraints on composite type components may be established, consider the abstract type Date defined in Example 4.3 and used in our mail system example. This is a fairly trivial example, but it illustrates how additional Ada functions may be added to an interface specification to provide greater precision.

The range constraints set out in the type definition of HOUR and

```
package Date is
    type MONTH is (January, February, March, April, May, June, July,
                August, September, October, November, December) ;
    type DAY is range 1..31 ;
    type HOUR is range 0..23 ;
    type MINUTE is range 0..59 ;
    type YEAR is range 1985..2050 ;
    type STAMP is private ;
    – – Setdate uses the system clock to find out the date
    function Setdate return STAMP ;
    function Get_minutes (D: STAMP) return MINUTE ;
    function Get_month (D: STAMP) return MONTH ;
    function Get_day (D: STAMP) return DAY ;
    function Get_hour (D: STAMP) return HOUR ;
    function Get_year (D: STAMP) return YEAR;
    function "<" ( D1, D2: STAMP ) return BOOLEAN ;
    function ">" ( D1, D2: STAMP ) return BOOLEAN ;
private
    type STAMP is record
        Elapsed_mins: NATURAL ;
        This_Year: YEAR ;
    end record ;
end Date ;
```

Example 4.3   The definition of the abstract type Date.

MINUTE are sufficient to ensure that objects of this type always have a valid value. However, the range constraints associated with MONTH and YEAR do not ensure that the date is always valid. Clearly, the month of June does not have 31 days with our current calendar, so extra constraints are required. These constraints (shown in Example 4.4) provide information to the designers of the functions provided by the Date package.

In this example, we identify the months which do not have 31 days, and then place a constraint on the value returned by Get_day for each of these. The specification annotations would normally be included in the package specification and they apply to every entity which is of type Date.STAMP. In principle, the checks specified could be compiled with the program and a run-time exception raised if the conditions were violated. This is one of the aims of the Anna specification and annotation language.

We assume that readers are sufficiently familiar with the calendar to deduce the meaning of the above specification. Notice that we introduce a function called Leap_year as part of this specification and, if the specification is to be complete, this must be defined. Its definition is shown as Example 4.5 – notice that it is a valid Ada function, so each line is introduced by the comment symbol '− −:'.

In order to create specifications that are easily read, it is very important to develop these specifications in a top-down manner and to introduce functions such as Leap_year which are defined later as the

---

```
− −:   D : Date.STAMP ;
− −|   if Get_month ( D ) = February then
− −|     if Leap_year (Get_year (D) ) then
− −|        Get_day (D) <= 29 ;
− −|     else
− −|        Get_day (D) <= 28 ;
− −|     end if ;
− −|   elsif   Get_month (D) = April or
− −|           Get_month (D) = June or
− −|           Get_month (D) = September or
− −|           Get_month (D) = November then
− −|     Get_day (D) <= 30 ;
− −|   else
− −|     Get_day (D) <= 31 ;
− −|   end if ;
```

Example 4.4   Additional constraints added to type Date.

```
− −: function Leap_year (Y : YEAR) return BOOLEAN ;
− −: begin
− −       A year is a leap year if it is divisible by 4 and not by 400
− −:      if Y rem 4 /= 0 then
− −:          return false ;
− −:      elsif Y rem 400 = 0 then
− −:          return false ;
− −:      else
− −:          return true ;
− −:      end if ;
− −: end Leap_year ;
```

Example 4.5   The Leap_year function.

specification is developed. We take the pragmatic view that the easiest way to specify this function is to provide its implementation and we do not attempt to express this function in some specification language.

Now let as look at one of the types used in the electronic mail system and see how it may be constrained by predicates. A type that is used in the electronic mail system represents the information which must be recorded for each item of mail. In Chapter 3, we specified this as an abstract data type called Mail_item which exported a type called INSTANCE and a number of functions allowing the state of objects of that type to be interrogated. However, in addition to these functions, there may be various checks which should be applied to objects of type Mail_item.INSTANCE, and it is often convenient to specify these checks as constraints on the type definition. Recall that the type Mail_item.INSTANCE was defined in the **private** part of Mail_item as follows:

```
type INSTANCE is record
    Sender: User.ID ;
    Receiver: User.ID ;
    Date_sent: Date.STAMP ;
    Expiry_date: Date.STAMP ;
    Message: MAIL_MESSAGE ;
    Cancellation_key: CANCEL_KEY_TYPE ;
    Priority: PRIORITY_TYPE ;
end record ;
```

Now let us introduce some arbitrary constraints and illustrate how these can be specified as predicates restricting the actions on the type. Possible constraints might be:

1. The expiry date associated with the mail must be after the date when the mail was posted.

2. If a mail message is of the highest priority, its length must be less than 801 characters.

The following annotations might be added to the private part of the Mail_item package to specify these constraints. The constraints thus apply to all instances of that type.

```
-- expiry date must be after date sent. This implies that, in all
-- cases, the mail must have an associated expiry date.

--:   with Date ; use Date ;
--:   M : INSTANCE ;
--|   M.Expiry_date > M.Date_sent ;

-- The maximum length of mail messages of the highest priority
-- should be restricted to 800 characters. The predicate thus states
-- that either the priority of the mail is less than 8 or, if it is 8,
-- the message length must be less than or equal to 800 characters.

--|   M.Priority < 8 or
--|   M.Priority = 8 and Length (M.Message <= 800 )
```

Here, we make use of a function called Length which operates on objects of type MAIL_MESSAGE and which returns the number of characters in the message. This is a relatively simple function, and to avoid excessive detail we do not define it here.

So far, we have written predicates that allow the statement of constraints which cannot be expressed using Ada's type system. The information provided there helps the designer of the package bodies implementing these types to include the appropriate checks in type access and update routines, and gives the test case designer hints on how test cases should be formulated to test the abstract data type package. What this specification technique does not do is to state what the access functions mean – this topic is discussed in the following section.

As well as being able to associate general constraints with every instance of a type, this technique of specifying predicates can also be used to constrain specific objects in a system. For example, say a program made use of two arrays of integers called *A* and *B*. These lists contain the same values, but array *A* is unordered whilst array *B* is ordered so that its values are in ascending order. This might be specified as follows:

```
type INDEX is range 1..Some_maximum ;
type AN_ARRAY is array (INDEX) of INTEGER ;
A, B: AN_ARRAY ;
--| for_all x: INDEX, exists y: INDEX =>
--|    A (x) = B (y)
--| and
--|    for_all j: INDEX ' FIRST..INDEX ' LAST-1 => B (j) <= B (j + 1) ;
```

The first part of this specification states that if a value exists in array A, a corresponding value must also exist in array B. The **exists** clause is similiar to the existential qualifier as used in predicate calculus, but here we are applying it to array values rather than set values. It means that there should be at least one value in the range 1.. Some_maximum that allows the following predicate to be true. Thus the constraint may be read as 'for every value x which is a valid index of array A there must be an index value y of array B such that the value of A (x) is the same as the value of the B (y)'. The second part of the specification states that it is always true that the ith + 1 value of B is greater than or equal to the ith value.

This appears to be a correct specification, but it is, in fact, incomplete. For example, the following arrays meet the conditions specified, but B is most definitely not an ordered version of A:

$A = 1, 2, 1, 1, 3$
$B = 1, 1, 2, 2, 3$

For every value in A (1, 2, 3) there does exist a corresponding value in B, and B is ordered as specified. What the specification has not taken into account is the possibility that arrays may have duplicate values. In some ways, using notation derived from set theory when operating with arrays can be misleading as sets do not have duplicate values, and the above specification would indeed be correct if A and B were ordered sets. A complete specification which takes the possibility of duplicate values into account is as follows:

```
type INDEX is range 1..Some_maximum ;
type AN_ARRAY is array (INDEX) of INTEGER ;
A, B: AN_ARRAY ;
--| for_all x: INDEX, exists y: INDEX => A (x) = B (y)
--| and
--| for_all j: INDEX ' FIRST..INDEX ' LAST-1 => B (j) <= B (j + 1) ;
--| and
--| for_all x: INDEX => Count (A, A (x)) = Count (B, A (x)) ;
```

To get round the problem of duplicate elements, we introduce a function which counts the number of occurrences of each element and specify that this should return the same value when applied to A and B for any particular element of A. The function itself is simple and is shown in Example 4.6.

Again, pragmatically, we do not hesitate to use an implementation as part of a specification as this is the simplest and most precise way to define what we mean. A general rule of thumb that may be followed is that, if the specification in a specification notation is comparable in length with its implementation, it may simply be sensible to provide the

```
--:   function Count (A: AN_ARRAY ; X: INTEGER) return NATURAL is
--:      Counter: NATURAL := 0 ;
--:   begin
--:      for i in INDEX loop
--:         if A (i) = X then
--:            Counter := Counter + 1 ;
--:         end if ;
--:      end loop ;
--:      return Counter ;
--:   end Count ;
```

Example 4.6   The Count function.

implementation and to forget about the specification altogether. After all, if the specification is being used without automatic tools that can help to check it, the number of errors in a specification of length N is probably comparable to the number of errors in a program of the same length. We believe that specifications are only really valuable when they are much shorter than their corresponding implementations.

The technique of associating predicates with declarations is a valuable one, but it has the limitation that it is not really suitable for the specification of actions, nor does it allow the meaning of access and update functions operating on an abstract data type to be defined. In the following section, we look at a specification technique for this problem – namely defining the effect of functions associated with a type.

4.4   The specification of abstract data types

The notion of an abstract data type is one of the most important ideas that has emerged from computer science research. Rather than define a type by its representation (record, scalar, array, etc.), an abstract data type is defined by the operations allowed on objects of that type. There is no need for the representation of that type to be visible to its users.

This is an important concept for two reasons:

1. It allows users to view a system at a more abstract level. They need not be concerned with representational details and with the direct manipulation of representations.

2. It allows systems programmers to change the representation of abstract data types without affecting their use in any way. Thus, representations may be changed from arrays to lists, extra fields may

be added to records, etc. This is clearly of great benefit when the system has to be tuned or enhanced during system maintenance.

It can be argued that it is possible to build complete systems as hierarchies of abstract data types. This somewhat extreme view is undoubtedly true, although it is the authors' opinion that this is not necessarily the most natural view of most systems. After all, the user sees a system as a set of functions, and it is often more natural to map these directly on to software components than to conceal them as data type operations.

There have been a number of different techniques used to specify abstract data types, and a good summary of these is given by Liskov and Zilles (1977). We concentrate here on what is called the algebraic approach as we believe that this is both straightforward to understand and directly applicable to interface specification. This algebraic specification technique was first put forward by Zilles (1974) and since then has been developed by Guttag (1977) and rigorously formalized by Goguen *et al.*, (1977).

In essence, the algebraic approach involves listing the functions that are used to update and access an abstract data type, defining the signatures of these functions, and setting out a set of algebraic equations which relate the access operations and the update operations on the type. Basically, these equations provide a precise definition of what the functions operating on the type actually mean. These equations are usually referred to as axioms as they are deemed to be always true for all instances of the type.

The starting point for creating an algebraic specification of an abstract data type is to write down an informal definition of the functions that operate on the type. For example, the functions operating on an abstract type STACK might be as follows:

STACK

Create	Brings a stack into existence and initializes its state.
Push	Adds an element to the top of the stack.
Top	Returns the value of the top stack element.
Retract	Returns the stack minus its top element.
IsEmpty	Returns true if there are no elements on the stack.

Notice that the conventional stack pop operation is missing from this list. When choosing functions that operate on a data type, it is good practice to define functions that have no side effects and which return a single value. As often implemented, the pop operation returns the value on the top of the stack and, as a side effect, modifies the stack by removing its top element. Actually, the pop operation is not primitive as it is a catenation of the top and retract operations set out above.

The next stage of algebraic specification is to define the signatures of the functions that operate on the type. This means that the formal names and the types of parameters of each function must be set out. For example:

STACK of V

Operations

Create	Brings a stack into existence and initializes its state.
Push	Adds an element to the top of the stack.
Top	Returns the value of the top stack element.
Retract	Returns the stack minus its top element.
IsEmpty	Returns true if there are no elements on the stack.

Signatures
Create **return** STACK of V
Push (STACK of V, V) **return** STACK of V
Top (STACK of V) **return** V
Retract (STACK of V) **return** STACK of V
IsEmpty (STACK of V) **return** BOOLEAN

The stack operations have now been described and their syntax has been defined. The operations fall into two classes, namely **constructor** operations which build a stack and **access** operations which provide information about the stack. Essentially, algebraic specification involves specifying what state information is returned by the access operations for each different constructor. In the stack example here, the constructor operations are Create which brings a stack into existence and Push which adds an element ot the stack.

The final stage in the definition is to write down the axioms that define what each operation means. What we are really trying to do here is to express what the access functions mean with respect to the constructor functions. We thus identify the constructor operations and define the other operations in terms of these. Thus, the complete definition of STACK is as shown in Example 4.7.

From this example, we can see that the Top operation and the Retract operation can result in errors if they are applied to empty stacks. Strictly, therefore, in these cases the signature of the function is different unless we have an explicit UNDEFINED value for each type. Of course this is possible; but an alternative approach is to change the signature of the functions which may result in errors so that a tuple rather than a single value is returned by the function. One of the values returned specifies whether or not the operation was successful. Say a type was defined as follows:

type ERROR_STATUS **is** (Ok, Error) ;

The stack example might be rewritten as shown in Example 4.8.

When the result of a function is specified as a tuple, it is an implementation decision as to whether the function should return a record with a field holding the result of the operation, or whether the function should be transformed into a procedure which outputs an error message (functions cannot have **out** parameters). Which of these approaches is adopted depends on circumstances and local standards. Particular error message texts may be specified informally in the descriptive part of the specification.

We have deliberately avoided using an Ada-like notation in the first part of this section as much of the detail of Ada tends to clutter the specification. Of course, the same approach as was taken with type constraints may be adopted here and annotations added to the package

---

STACK of V

Operations

Create	Brings a stack into existence and initializes its state.
Push	Adds an element to the top of the stack.
Top	Returns the value of the top stack element.
Retract	Returns the stack minus its top element.
IsEmpty	Returns true if there are no elements on the stack.

Signatures

Create **return** STACK of V
Push (STACK of V, V) **return** STACK of V
Top (STACK of V) **return** V
Retract (STACK of V) **return** STACK of V
IsEmpty (STACK of V) **return** BOOLEAN

Axioms

— — If Top is applied to Create, the result is undefined
Top (Create) = UNDEFINED (V)
— — Top returns the last item pushed on to the stack
Top (Push (S, X)) = X
— — If Retract is applied to a newly created stack, the result is undefined
Retract (Create) = UNDEFINED (STACK of V)
— — Retract applied to push operation leaves the stack as if the Push had
— — not occurred
Retract (Push (S, X)) = S
— — A newly created stack is empty
IsEmpty (Create) = **true**
— — After a push operation, the stack is not empty
IsEmpty (Push (S, V)) = **false**

end STACK of V

Example 4.7 Algebraic specification of a stack.

STACK of V
Operations

Create	Brings a stack into existence and initializes its state.
Push	Adds an element to the top of the stack.
Top	Returns the value of the top stack element.
Retract	Returns the stack minus its top element.
IsEmpty	Returns true if there are no elements on the stack.

Signatures

Create **return** STACK of V
Push (STACK of V, V) **return** STACK of V
Top (STACK of V) **return** (V, ERROR_STATUS)
Retract (STACK of V) **return** (STACK of V, ERROR_STATUS)
IsEmpty (STACK of V) **return** BOOLEAN

Equations

-- If Top is applied to Create, the result is undefined.
-- Indicated by setting error indicator
Top (Create) = (Create, Error)
-- Top returns the last item pushed on to the stack
Top (Push (S, X)) = (X, Ok)
-- If Retract is applied to a newly created stack, the result is undefined
Retract (Create) = (Create, Error)
-- Retract applied to push operation leaves the stack as if the Push had
-- not occurred
Retract (Push (S, X)) = (S, Ok)
-- A newly created stack is empty
IsEmpty (Create) = **true**
-- After a push operation, the stack is not empty
IsEmpty (Push (S, V)) = **false**

end STACK of V

Example 4.8 A specification of a stack including error indicators.

---

specification for STACK. In Example 4.9, the stack is defined as a generic package with the type of element and maximum size specified as generic parameters.

In Example 4.9, we have explicitly returned an error variable and this has meant that neither Top nor Retract may be implemented as Ada functions because such functions may not have **out** parameters. However, we have simulated the functional notation in the specification by specifying the values of all of the **out** parameters of the Top and Retract procedures. Notice that **in** parameter values need not be specified as they may not be changed in the procedure.

```
generic
      type E is private ;
      Max: NATURAL := 200 ;
package STACK is
      type T is limited private ;
      type ERROR_STATUS is (Ok, Error) ;
      function Push (Stck: T ; Val: E) return T ;
      procedure Retract (Stck: in T ; Nstck: out T ;
                              Status: out ERROR_STATUS ) ;
      procedure Top (Stck: in T ; Val: in out E ;
                              Status: out ERROR_STATUS ) ;
      function Is_empty (Stck: T ) return BOOLEAN ;
      function Create return T ;
private
      type ST_ARRAY is array (1.. Max ) of E ;
      type T is record
        ST: ST_ARRAY ;
        SP: NATURAL ;
      end record ;
--:   St : T ;
--:   V, Tval : E ;
--:   R: ERROR_STATUS ;
--|   axioms
--|     Top ( Push (St, V), Tval, R) => (Tval = V and R = Ok) ;
--|     Top ( Create, Tval, R) => (Tval = Tval ' and R = Error) ;
--|     Retract ( Push (St, V), Nstck, R ) => (Nstck = St and R = Ok) ;
--|     Retract ( Create, Nstck, R) => (Nstck= Create and R = Error) ;
--|     Is_empty (Create) = TRUE ;
--|     Is_empty (Push (S, V) ) = FALSE ;
end STACK ;
```

Example 4.9   An algebraic specification of a stack using Ada.

Notice also that parameters of type **in out** are not used as this implies that the parameter itself is changed by the procedure. Rather we have directly simulated functional operation with the results of the functions returned as **out** parameters. The notation Tval = Tval ' used in the definition of Top means that the output value of Tval is whatever its input value (specified by priming the name) was. As this is undefined for an Ada **out** parameter, this effectively means that the result of a Top operation which returns an error status has no meaning.

The key to effective algebraic specification is, obviously, the construction of a set of equations that is both consistent and complete. If a set of axioms is consistent, no one axiom should contradict any other axiom. If an axiom set is complete, it should specify all of the properties of the abstract data type. It is also desirable (although not essential) that the set of equations should be minimal – it should not be possible to deduce any axiom from the others in the set. A full discussion of this topic is very mathematical in nature and is outside the scope of this book. Interested readers are referred to the paper by Goguen *et al.* (1977) for a formal, rigorous discussion of algebraic specification.

Let us now look at some other examples of algebraic specification. Assume a graphics system is being implemented which makes use of abstract data types representing a coordinate in some space and a rectangle of pixels (called a Zone). Zones are made up of a coordinate representing the top-left corner of the rectangle, a height and a length. Examples 4.10 and 4.11 show how simple abstract types may be used in the specification of more complex types.

The abstract type Zone is defined in a similiar way with access

---

```
package Coord is
    type T is limited private ;
    function Create (X, Y: INTEGER) return T ;
    function Get_x (C: T) return INTEGER ;
    function Get_y (C: T) return INTEGER ;
    function Equals (C1, C2: T) return BOOLEAN ;
private
    type T is record
        Xval: INTEGER ;
        Yval: INTEGER ;
    end record ;
--:      C1, C2: T ;
--:      X1, Y1, X2, Y2: INTEGER ;
--|   axioms
--       Informally, Get_x returns the X coordinate
--|      Get_x (Create (X1, Y1)) = X1
--       Get_y returns the Y coordinate
--|      Get_y (Create (X1, Y1)) = Y1
--       Equals is only true if both the X and Y coordinates are equal
--|      Equals (Create (X1, Y1), Create (X2, Y2)) = (X1 = X2) and (Y1 = Y2)
end Coord ;
```

Example 4.10   Specification of abstract type Coord.

operations for each component of Zone, an operations called Includes which is true if a coordinate lies within a zone, and an operation called Overlaps which is true if one zone overlaps another.

The next example in this section shows how the abstract data type 'binary tree' may be defined. Informally, the operations that might be allowed on a binary tree are the Create operation to bring a null tree

```
package Zone is
    type T is private ;
    ' function Create return T ;
    function Get_coord (Z: T) return Coord.T ;
    function Get_height (Z: T) return NATURAL ;
    function Get_length (Z: T) return NATURAL ;
    function Includes (Z: T; C: Coord.T) return BOOLEAN ;
    function Overlaps (Z1, Z2: T) return BOOLEAN ;
private
    type T is record
        C: Coord.T ;
        Height: NATURAL ;
        Length: NATURAL ;
    end record ;
--:     Z1, Z2: T ;
--:     C1, C2: Coord.T ;
--:     Ht, Len: NATURAL ;
--| axioms
--|     Get_coord (Create (C1, Ht, Len)) = C1
--|     Get_height (Create (C1, Ht, Len)) = Ht
--|     Get_length (Create (C1, Ht, Len)) = Len
--     Essentially, the next axiom defines that the zone coordinate
--     represents the top-left hand corner of the zone
--|     Includes (Create (C1, Ht, Len), C2) =
--|         Coord.Get_x (C2) >= Coord.Get_x (C1) and
--|         Coord.Get_x (C2) <= Coord.Get_x (C1) + Len and
--|         Coord.Get_y (C2) <= Coord.Get_y (C1) and
--|         Coord.Get_y (C2) >= Coord.Get_y (C1) -Ht
--     Zones overlap if they at least one coordinate is included in each
--|     Overlaps (Z1, Z2) = exists C: Coord.T =>
--|         Includes (Z1, C) and Includes (Z2, C)
end Zone ;
```

Example 4.11 Specification of abstract type Zone.

```
generic
      type DATA is private ;
package Binary is
      type TREE is private ;
      type ERROR_STATUS is (Ok, Error) ;
      function Create return TREE ;
      function Add_in_order (T: TREE ; V: DATA)
              return TREE ;
      function Is_empty (T: TREE) return BOOLEAN ;
      function Left (T: TREE) return TREE ;
      procedure Eval (T: TREE; Val: out DATA;
                      Status: out ERROR_STATUS ) ;
      function Right (T: TREE) return TREE ;
      function Is_in_tree (T: TREE ; V: DATA) return BOOLEAN ;
private
      type BIN_TREE ;
      type TREE is access BIN_TREE ;
--:      L, R : TREE;
--:      X, V : DATA ;
--:      Status: ERROR_STATUS ;
--:      function Add (L: TREE ; V: DATA ; R: TREE) return TREE ;
--| axioms
--|      Is_empty (Create) = true ;
--|      Is_empty (Add (L, V, R )) = false ;
--|      Left (Create) = Create ;
--|      Left (Add (L, V, R )) = L ;
--       If an attempt is made to access the data in a newly created tree, the
--       result parameter has its input value (indicated by D')
--|      Eval (Create, X, Status) => ( X=X' and Status = Error ) ;
--|      Eval (Add (L, V, R ), X, Status) => ( X = V and Status = Ok ) ;
--|      Right (Create) = Create ;
--|      Right (Add (L, V, R )) = R ;
--|      Is_in_tree (Create, V) = FALSE ;
--|      Is_in_tree (Add (L, V, R), X) =
--|          if V = X then true else Is_in_tree (L, X) or Is_in_tree (R, X) ;
--|      Add_in_order (Create, X) = Add (Create, X, Create) ;
--|      Add_in_order (Add (L, V, R), X) = if V > X then Add_in_order (L, X) ;
--|              else Add_in_order (R, X) ;
end BINARY ;
```

Example 4.12   An algebraic specification of a binary tree.

into existence, the Add_in_order operation which adds an element to the tree, and the field selector operations Data, Left and Right which return a node's value, its left subtree and its right subtree respectively. Tree membership is tested using the Is_in_tree operation which returns true if its parameter has been entered into the tree. The Add_in_order operation is the familiar function operation used to create a binary tree representing a sorted list. However, Add_in_order is not really a primitive constructor operation and a more general Add operation which adds a single node to the tree is used as a constructor operation in the specification in Example 4.12. The specification again makes use of generics to emphasize that this is a generalized tree specification.

This binary tree specification illustrates a technique that is regularly used in abstract data type specification. This technique is the definition of primitive constructor operations that are distinct from those normally available to users of that type. There is no requirement that these operations be made available through the package specification when the abstract data type is actually implemented, although, obviously, they must be implemented in the body of the package.

Let us now apply this algebraic specification technique to some of the abstract data types that might be used in an electronic mail system. The packages defining abstract data types described in Chapter 3 were User, Mail_list and Mail_item. Of these, User and Mail_item are

```
package Mail_list is
   type INSTANCE is limited private ;
   -- create makes a new list
   function Create return INSTANCE ;
   -- Add adds an element to the front of the list
   function Add (List: INSTANCE ; Item: Mail_item.INSTANCE )
           return INSTANCE ;
   -- head returns the first item on the list
   function Head (List: INSTANCE) return Mail_item.INSTANCE ;
   -- tail returns the 'rest' of the list
   function Tail ( List: INSTANCE ) return INSTANCE ;
   -- Is_empty checks if the list has any members
   function Is_empty (List: INSTANCE) return INSTANCE ;
private
   type MAIL_ELEMENT ;
   type INSTANCE is access MAIL_ELEMENT ;
end Mail_list ;
```

Example 4.13 Package specification of a Mail_list.

concealments of record types and it is more appropriate to specify these types using type constraints as described above. Mail_list is an abstract type representing a list of mail items. The package specification for this abstract type was discussed in Chapter 3 and is repeated as Example 4.13.

The axioms to specify the actions on a mail list may be written as follows:

```
— —:      L : INSTANCE ;
— —:      M: Mail_item.INSTANCE ;
— —|   axioms
— —|      Head (Create) = ERROR ('empty list') ;
— —|      Head (Add (L, M)) ) = M ;
— —|      Tail (Create) = Create ;
— —|      Tail ( Add (L, M)) ) = L ;
— —|      Is_empty (Create) = true ;
— —|      Is_empty (Add (L, M) ) = false ;
```

Notice that these axioms make clear that applying the operation Head to an empty list results in an error whereas applying Tail to the empty list simply results in the return of the empty list. This reveals an important weakness in our original specification, which did not set out what should happen if Head and Tail were applied to empty lists. One of the advantages of formal rather than informal specifications is that exceptional cases such as this are less likely to be forgotten by the specifier. To cater for the error situation, the Head function above should really be specified as a procedure with the error indicator returned as a result. Thus, a revised specification of Mail_list is as shown in Example 4.14.

The waste-bin manager subsystem in the EM system is concerned with managing all of the system's waste bins. The operations defined by the waste-bin manager on waste bins are:

- Put an item into a user's waste bin.
- List the contents of a user's waste bin.
- Take an item from a user's waste bin.
- Empty a particular user's waste bin.

The waste-bin manager makes use of a local abstract data type called Wastebin.INSTANCE. The operations that are allowed on objects of this type are not necessarily those visible through the interface to the waste-bin manager. Rather, a set of more fundamental operations is presented by this abstract data type and the waste-bin manager interface is implemented in terms of these operations.

Items in a waste bin are referenced by the user using some identifier which is derived (interactively) by the Retrieve function provided in the waste-bin manager. Extraction of an item is accomplished by

```
package Mail_list is
      type INSTANCE is private ;
      type ERROR_STATUS is (Ok, Error) ;
      function Create return INSTANCE ;
      function Add (List: INSTANCE ; Item: Mail_item.INSTANCE )
             return INSTANCE ;
      procedure Head (List: INSTANCE ; M: out Mail_item.INSTANCE ;
                   Status: out ERROR_STATUS ) ;
      function Tail ( List: INSTANCE ) return INSTANCE ;
      function Is_empty (List: INSTANCE) return INSTANCE ;
private
      type MAIL_ELEMENT ;
      type INSTANCE is access MAIL_ELEMENT ;
--|   axioms
--:   L : INSTANCE ;
--:   M1, M2: Mail_item.INSTANCE ;
--:   Status: ERROR_STATUS ;
--|   Head (Create, M2, Status ) => ( M2 = M2' and Status = Error ) ;
--|   Head (Add (L, M1), M2, Status ) => ( M2 = M1 and Status = Ok);
--|   Tail (Create) = Create ;
--|   Tail ( Add (L, M)) ) = M ;
--|   Is_empty (Create) = true ;
--|   Is_empty (Add (L, M) ) = false ;
end Mail_list ;
```

Example 4.14   Revised specification for Mail_list.

specifying the item identifier which, in practice, may be derived from the Date.STAMP associated with each mail item (see Chapter 5).

The waste-bin abstract data type may thus be defined as shown in Example 4.15.

Notice that, in this example, the item identifier for waste-bin items has been defined as a local abstract data type within the package Wastebin. This is accessed by using the conjunction of package names, for example, Wastebin.Item_id.Create. The realization of this abstract type is straightforward and we do not include it here.

The other abstract data types that might be defined in the electronic mail system can be specified in a comparable way. It is not really worth providing other examples from this system as their operations are very similar to those operations defined for the waste-bin abstract data type.

```
package Wastebin is
    type INSTANCE is private ;
    type RESULT is (Ok, Error) ;
    package Item_id is
        type T is private ;
        function Create (D: Date.STAMP) return T ;
        function Get (Item: Mail_item.INSTANCE) return T ;
    private
        type T is new Date.STAMP ;
    end Item_id ;
    function Create return INSTANCE ;
    function Put (Bin: INSTANCE ; Item: Mail_item.INSTANCE )
            return INSTANCE ;
    procedure Get (Bin: INSTANCE ; Identifier: Item_id.T ;
                    Item: out Mail_item.INSTANCE ; Status: out (RESULT);
                        function Size (Bin: INSTANCE) return NATURAL ;
    function Clear (Bin: INSTANCE) return INSTANCE ;
private
    type INSTANCE is new Mail_list.INSTANCE ;
--:     W : INSTANCE ;
--:     Id : Item_id.T ;
--:     M1, M2: Mail_item.INSTANCE ;
--:     Status: ERROR_STATUS ;
--| axioms
--|     Get (Create, Id, M2, Status ) = (M2 => M2 ' and Status = Error )
--|     Get ( Put (W, M1), Id, M2, Status) => if Item_id.Get (M1) = Id then
--|             (M2 = M1 and Status = Ok)
--|                 else Get (W, M2, Id, Status )
--|     Size (Create) = 0 ;
--|     Size (Put (W, M1)) = Size (W) + 1 ;
--|     Clear (Create) = Create ;
--|     Clear (Put (W, M1)) = Create ;
end Wastebin ;
```

Example 4.15   Algebraic specification of a waste-bin type.

4.5 Summary

This chapter has been concerned with the activity of software
specification which we see as a critical stage of the software design
process. During specification, the operations of the components making

up a system are specified precisely and we emphasize that the precision of a specification is more important than the notation used for that specification.

The most effective specification techniques are those that make use of formal methods, but these are still the subject of a great deal of research effort and that no consensus on the most cost-effective formal specification techniques has emerged. In particular, full-scale systems specification is probably not yet cost-effective for most companies, so formal specification is unlikely to be widely used for some years.

However, we believe that formal interface specification is cost-effective now, and we demonstrated how interface definitions in Ada may be augmented with semantic descriptions to improve their clarity and precision. We started by showing how predicate calculus may be used to associate constraints with types and objects defined in an Ada system.

The majority of the chapter was concerned with the specification of abstract data types and we concentrated on the algebraic approach here as we have used it successfully in the specification of a graphics system. This approach involves defining the signatures of the operations on a type and a set of axioms which define the effect of these operations on entities of that type. The notation we use is based on augmenting Ada with formal specification annotations expressed as comments. This approach is similiar to that taken by the specification language Anna.

4.6   Further reading

IEEE Transactions on Software Engineering. SE-10, (2), 126–178 (1984).

> This special issue contains several papers on formal specification. Refreshingly, the authors mostly discuss examples of real systems rather than the relatively small 'toy examples' that are used in many specification papers.

Jackson, M. I. (1985). 'Developing Ada Programs using the Vienna Development Method (VDM)' *Software – Practice and Experience*, **15**, (3), 305–318.

> An interesting and (relatively) easy to read paper showing how VDM may be used in conjunction with Ada.

Gehani, A. D. and McGettrick, A. D.; Eds. (1985). *Software Specification Techniques*. London: Addison-Wesley.

> A collection of papers on software specification which covers background to specification techniques, approaches to specification, case studies and specification systems. The book includes a number of papers referenced in this chapter which were originally published elsewhere.

Chapter 5 Detailed Software Design

Following the architectural design stage and the construction of formal or informal specifications, the final stage of software design is detailed algorithm design. During this stage of the life cycle, the abstract software definition is refined and detail is introduced. The software design is expressed in such a way that it may be readily translated into a system programming language.

The level of detail that must be introduced at this stage is dependent on the programming language to be used for system implementation. If this is a high-level language with powerful inbuilt abstraction facilities (Ada is such a language), the software design need not be expressed in such detail as is necessary when a low-level language is chosen. In the latter the detailed software design must be developed to approximately the same level of detail as an Ada implementation.

The construction of a detailed software design is far from being a mechanical process. It requires understanding and creativity on the part of the designer and cannot be reduced to a formula to be followed in a slavish way. Although we describe different methodologies for software design later in this chapter (and we believe that these are important), they are not universally applicable. The designer must understand when to follow the route implied by a particular methodology and when to diverge from that route. As in earlier chapters, we illustrate the activity of detailed software design by example. We have chosen a number of different examples but, as before, examples from the electronic mail system described in Chapter 3 are our linking theme.

The aim of this chapter is to describe different design methodologies. First we look at the use of Ada and Ada-based notations for describing the details of a software design. This is followed by a general overview of three important design methodologies – namely data-driven design, top-down functional decomposition and object-oriented design. We then go on to cover two of these methodologies, top-down decomposition and object-oriented design, in more detail. We illustrate both these with examples from the electronic mail system and suggest that each has a place in large software systems design.

5.1   Using Ada as a PDL

The notion of using some form of program description language (PDL) to describe a software design has been accepted since the mid-1970s. Various PDLs have been described in the literature (Van Leer, 1976; Linger *et al.*, 1979), but a good deal of current thinking in this area is based around the idea of using Ada or an Ada variant as a universal PDL.

Ada has sufficient expressive power to act as a starting point for an effective PDL, and we have used a notation that is close to Ada for describing software design. However, using a programming language as a basis for a design description language has some disadvantages.

There are two opposing schools of thought on the question of whether Ada should be used as a basis for a PDL. One school argues that Ada is an implementation language and that describing a design in an Ada-like notation involves the introduction of excessive implementation detail. The other extreme view argues that Ada itself is sufficiently expressive to be an effective PDL and that there is no need for the development of a PDL with additional features. These opposing views are succinctly summarized by Taylor (1983) and by Youll (1983).

Our own view lies between these extremes. We believe that Ada, on its own, does force the designer to include unnecessary detail which tends to clutter the design description. For example, in the early stages of a design interface details are often unclear and the designer should not be forced to specify the parameters of sub-programs in detail. Similarly, the need to specify the dependencies between program units contradicts the principle of top-down design and there should be no need to require the designer to include **with** clauses during the design phase.

On the other hand, there seems to be little merit in introducing a new syntax for constructs that are adequately expressible in Ada. Thus, in this chapter, we use a description language whose control and structuring facilities are those of Ada, but which has a more relaxed approach to implementation detail. We believe that this approach adds to the expressiveness of the PDL and allows designs to be described more clearly than is possible with 'pure' Ada.

The disadvantages of using Ada as a PDL may be summarized as follows:

1. The use of Ada forces the designer to think in terms of an implementation rather than a design. For example, say the designer wishes to express that all members of some collection T should be set to zero. In Ada, this might be expressed by:

```
for J in T ' RANGE loop
   T (J) := 0 ;
end loop ;
```

The problem with this description is that it implies that a sequential process is used to zero each object in T. Thus T(1) should be set to zero before T(2), T(2) before T(3), etc. In fact, the order in which the elements of T are zeroed might be quite irrelevant and there may be implementations where it is convenient to make the assignments in a non-sequential way. Thus, a more abstract expression of this operation might be:

for all E **in** T **do**
T.E := 0 ;

2. Ada is not sufficiently expressive to describe some design abstractions. In fact, requirements for an Ada/PDL suggested by Lindley (1983) specify that an effective Ada-based PDL should allow the inclusion of English or some other natural language narrative in situations where comments are illegal. For example, an expressive form of a design might be:

if *messages available and user wishes immediate delivery* **then**
...

An alternative description in Ada involves introducing details of how available messages should be detected and how user wishes are communicated. Again, unnecessary implementation details must be introduced:

if not Empty (Message_queue) **and**
Immediate_delivery_required (User) **then**

3. Ada is designed to be machine processable. This may be seen as an advantage in that it allows some automatic checking of the design to be carried out by the Ada compiler. However, we believe that this benefit is sometimes outweighed by the fact that the design must always conform to Ada's punctuation conventions, must always follow Ada's syntax rules (such as the separation of local declarations and statements), must develop procedure and function parameters to fine detail, must specify all dependencies and must observe Ada's strict typing rules.

Whilst Ada's rules are an essential safety feature for an implementation language, they sometimes make the expression of a design in Ada a tedious business. The designer is forced to express all of the design at the same level of detail at the same time. This certainly does not reflect the practical reality of the design process where software designs are usually developed in an incremental way from a high level of abstraction to a detailed design.

However, there are advantages in using Ada as a PDL. Firstly, the design team need not develop automated tools for processing the design language. Such tools (syntax checkers, cross-referencers, etc.)

exist as Ada language processing tools. Secondly, Ada does have an effective encapsulation mechanism, which is a necessity in any PDL, as well as data and control structuring facilities. Finally, the boundary between designs and implementations becomes very blurred, so that designs may act as prototypes allowing assessment and evaluation of the system at an early stage.

Most uses of 'pure' Ada as a PDL have been in situations where available implementation languages have precluded the use of Ada as a system programming language. At the time of writing, many validated Ada compilers do not produce object code as efficiently as some other language processors, and this excludes Ada as a viable programming language for some classes of computer system. Using Ada as a PDL makes for an easy transition to an Ada-based system once efficient code generators from Ada become available.

However, we believe that the use of a PDL that has Ada constructs where appropriate, but which is not rigidly constrained by Ada's rules is the most effective notation for software design. In particular, we find it essential to be able to introduce names without declaration and to rely on the reader to deduce the operation of a sub-program or utility of a type from its name. This allows us to develop a design in a top-down way, so that objects are introduced, used intuitively and then defined at a later stage. We also find it useful to be able to introduce English language narrative when this makes the design clearer, to be able to postpone the definition of sub-program interfaces by leaving out the complete parameter list, and to be able to leave out compilation unit dependencies.

A factor that dramatically affects the understandability of a design is effective style in the use of the design language. This means that meaningful identifiers should be used always, design descriptions should be formatted in such a way that their parts are clearly distinguished and unnecessary detail avoided wherever possible. Although hard and fast style rules are not always appropriate, each organization should have its own style standards for design description. A good starting point for establishing these standards is given by Nissen and Wallis (1984), and the style guidelines in Chapter 7 are derived from there.

5.2 Design methodologies

A large number of methodologies have been described to control and constrain the activity of software design. These include methodologies based on the structure of the data to be processed by the system (Jackson, 1975; Warnier-Orr, 1977), those based on functional decomposition (Wirth, 1971; Constantine and Yourdon, 1979) and those based on information hiding (Parnas, 1972; Booch, 1983).

There is no single 'best' methodology, and all of the proposed approaches to software design work well in some situations and for some classes of application. However, no one methodology is ideal for all situations, and the pragmatic software engineer should not concentrate on any one technique to the exclusion of all others.

Furthermore, we believe that large software systems are such complex entities that they encompass sub-application areas where many different types of methodology are applicable. Thus, in the design of large systems, the software designer may make use of different techniques for different subsystems. Although we present a description of each methodology separately in this section, the reader should bear in mind that an integrated approach is often the most apt for large systems design.

5.2.1 Data-driven design

This approach to the design of software systems was first proposed by Jackson (1975), although comparable work was being done at the same time by Warnier-Orr (1977). Jackson's work was targeted at data processing systems, and as a result, this approach has had most use in the business DP community. However, Jackson (1982) has produced a revised and extended version of this methodology which seems to be more suitable for embedded systems design. This is more concerned with system specification than with software design and we do not discuss it here.

The basis of a data-driven methodology is that the data processed by a system have an inherent structure. This should be reflected in the structure of the programs that are involved in the processing of the data. For example, a program reads a sequence of characters which make up a message, and messages are made up of sentences and are terminated by a special message termination character. The program might output the sentences in the message with sentence numbers on some output device.

The structure of the input might be described graphically as shown in Figure 5.1. Note that left to right organization of boxes implies sequentiality, a box with an embedded circle (not shown) means an alternative and a box with an embedded star means an iteration. The output data structure that is produced may be represented as shown in Figure 5.2.

The structure of a sentence is shown in Figure 5.1. Jackson argues that the structure of the program should reflect the structure of the data. Thus, the design shown as Example 5.1 might be derived for part of the system.

Jackson's methodology appears to be most suitable for small or medium-sized systems, or subsystems of large systems where the data

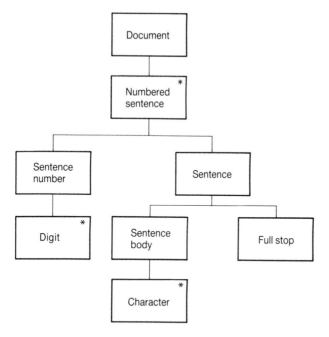

Figure 5.1   A Jackson data structure diagram.

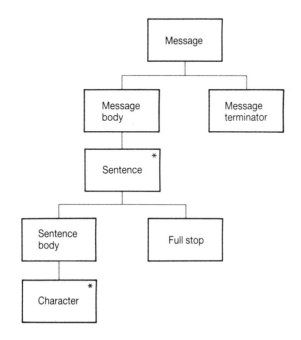

Figure 5.2   Output structure diagram.

```
N : INTEGER := 1 ;
loop
  declare
    – –Initialize sentence and token to the null string. Not valid Ada, but
    – –Ada's string handling is weak and higher level constructs are best
    – –used in a PDL
    Sentence: STRING := " " ;
    Token: STRING := " " ;
  begin
    – –get sentence
    Token := Get_token ;
    exit when Token is a message end token ;
    loop
      Sentence := Sentence + Token ;
      exit when Token is a full stop ;
      Token := Get_token ;
    end loop ;
    Output (N, sentence) ;
    N := N + 1 ;
  end ;
end loop ;
```

Example 5.1   JSP message processor.

to be processed have a clearly defined structure. In large system design, it is most useful when designing those subsystems which are concerned with input and output.

5.2.2   Top-down functional decomposition

This approach to software design is probably the most widely used design methodology. Although it has almost certainly been practised ever since programming began, it was brought to prominence in papers by Dijkstra (1968) and Wirth (1971). Since then, a number of authors (for example Linger *et al.* (1979) and Constantine and Yourdon (1979)) have developed and described this fundamental technique.

The top-down functional decomposition approach to software design assumes that the system may be represented as a hierarchy of functions. The level of detail expressed in any particular function is dependent on the level of that function in the hierarchy. The top-most functions are fairly abstract whilst those at the lowest levels deal with concrete system details.

For example, consider a patient monitoring system in an intensive care unit in a hospital. The system collects patient heart rate readings, checks them against some norm and, if the reading is potentially unsafe, triggers an alarm. In all cases, the heart rate reading is saved in database and displayed on a monitor at the patient's bedside. The highest, most abstract description of this system is a single statement:

Monitor_patients

This must then be decomposed to introduce more detail (see Example 5.2).

```
procedure Monitor_patients is
   Switched_off : EXCEPTION ;
begin
   loop
      for all patients loop
         Get_heart_rate ;
         if unsafe heart rate then
            Trigger_alarm (Current patient) ;
         end if ;
      end loop ;
   end loop ;
exception
   - -Assume the Switched_off exception is raised elsewhere
   when Switched_off =>
   Close_down_gracefully ;
end Monitor_patients ;
```

Example 5.2   A functional view of a patient monitoring system.

The Monitor_patients process has been expanded, but the operational description remains at an abstract level. Notice that the design description specifies that the process should cycle around the patients until the Switched_off exception is raised. As this is not raised explicitly in this description, it is assumed that it is propagated from some other lower-level function which interfaces with the system hardware.

The next stage in the top-down development process is to express the abstractions used in Monitor_patients in more detail. This process continues, level by level, until a complete, detailed design description has been created.

Whilst top-down functional design has been used successfully in the design of many large systems, very few of these systems exhibit the true hierarchical structure demanded by 'pure' top-down functional design. Rather, many procedures are shared so that there are cross-links in the hierarchy and there are procedure and function calls that span more than a single hierarchy level. The reality of large system structure means that it is very difficult indeed to construct a truly hierarchical design without a great deal of procedure duplication. However, as long as the design is first constructed hierarchically and then optimized, this is not a contradiction of the principles of top-down functional design.

5.2.3   Information hiding as a basis for software design

In 1972, Parnas published an important paper in which he questioned the functional approach to software design. Rather, he proposed an alternative scheme whereby the aim of the designer was to conceal as much representational information as possible. He argued that this technique led to software designs which were both easier and cheaper to maintain.

Although Parnas did not use the term, this was probably the first published account of abstract data types and was followed by important work by Zilles (1975), Liskov and Zilles (1974) and others. We have already discussed abstract data type specification, and the implementation of abstract data types is discussed in Chapter 6. Using information hiding as a starting point, a design methodology called object-oriented design has evolved. This is supported directly by the Smalltalk system (Goldberg and Robson, (1983)), and Booch (1983) describes how object-oriented design may be used with Ada.

An object-oriented approach to software design considers the software system to be made up of objects that may communicate by passing messages to each other. The object-oriented approach does not distinguish between functions (operations) and data (operands). Rather, an object is a collection made up of data and descriptions of permitted operations on that data. A message passed between objects specifies which operation or operations are to be initiated.

The important distinction between sending a message to invoke an operation and calling a procedure is that, in an object-oriented system, the details of how the operational data are represented are concealed from the invoker of the operation. It is possible, in principle, for the same message to invoke different operational implementations, although, obviously, their effect must ultimately be the same.

The reader will probably have noticed that there is a similarity between objects and abstract data types. It is important to realize that an abstract data type is not exactly the same thing as an object. Rather, an abstract data type is a more general construct which describes a class of objects. The objects themselves come into existence when they are declared to be of some particular type exported from a package defining an abstract data type (see Example 5.3).

```
generic
    type E is private ;
package Linked is
    type LIST is limited private ;
    function Add (Elem : E; Lst : LIST) return LIST;
    function Head (Lst : LIST ) return E ;
    function Tail (Lst : LIST) return LIST ;
private
    − − Details of list representation are not relevant to this example
    ...
end Linked ;
− −Now define an object class Integer_list

package Integer_linked is new Linked (INTEGER) ;

with Integer_linked ;
Numbers : Integer_linked.LIST ;

− −Now we have created a form of object called Numbers
− −Send a message to it indicating an addition to the list

Integer_linked.Add (Elem => 5, Lst => Numbers) ;
```

Example 5.3   An Ada implementation of list objects.

Booch (1983) suggests that Ada is a suitable language for expressing and implementing an object-oriented design, but this is only partially correct. The Ada package mechanism is sufficient to define abstract data types (or object classes); but if individual objects are defined as separate packages which maintain their own state they do not have full 'civil rights' and cannot be passed as parameters to other packages. Rather, variables must be declared and associated with particular abstract data types to simulate objects. A true object-oriented language allows the declaration of individual objects (data and operations) and allows these to be passed as parameters to other objects. We return to the use of Ada in object-oriented design later in this chapter.

We have already seen a functional view of a patient monitoring system where we identified operations such as Get_heart_rate, Add_heart_rate_to_database, Trigger_alarm, and so on. An object-oriented approach to the design of such a system would not start with this functional view, but would first attempt to identify the system objects and object classes.

Object classes that might be identified in such a system are *Patients* and *Heart_monitors*. Objects might be *The_alarm*, *The_display*, and *The_database*. Object operations might be *The_alarm (Trigger)*,

The_database(Add, Heart_rate) and *Heart_rate (Unsafe)*. Using this object-oriented view, part of the patient monitoring system (excluding the exception handler) is shown in Example 5.4. We have deliberately avoided using an Ada-based PDL here as a less familiar notation allows us to highlight the differences between an object-oriented and a functional approach to systems design.

---

for *P* **in all** *patients* **loop**
    – –send a message to a patient object P asking
    – –for heart rate to be returned as object H
    P ("Get heart rate", H)
    – –Now send message to heart monitor object to
    – –check rate
    Heart_monitor ("Check for safety", H, P)
    if *H ("Unsafe")* **then**
        – –trouble! trigger the alarm
        The_alarm ("Trigger", P)
    end if
    – –display heart rate and add to the database
    The_display ("Show", P, H)
    The_database ("Add", P, H)
end loop

Example 5.4   An object-oriented view of a patient monitoring system.

Although this description of the monitoring system looks quite unlike the functional description, examination reveals that the differences are relatively superficial from the designer's point of view. Top-down and object-oriented approaches to software design are complementary rather than opposing methodologies, and each has a role to play in large systems design. Neither approach should be excluded, but each should be used where it is appropriate to do so. This will be discussed in more detail in the following two sections.

5.3   Top-down functional decomposition

The principle underlying this design methodology was introduced in the previous section. The overall software system is viewed as a hierarchy of functional abstractions with the functions at level *n* in the hierarchy defined in terms of the functions provided by the deeper level *n + 1*. A top-down functional decomposition of a software design starts by identifying the functions at the top of the hierarchy and successively works its way down, decomposing each level into its more detailed sub-levels. By contrast, a bottom-up approach to design tries to identify useful functions at lower levels in the function hierarchy and defines higher level functions using these components.

As we have already suggested, a strict top-down approach should result in the creation of a tree-structured design with no cross-links between the branches of the tree. This implies that, if different branches of the tree make use of the same operation, this operation should be provided separately in each tree branch. In practice, sharing is essential and cross-links almost always exist between different parts of the design tree.

It might be argued that the designer should not be concerned with the fact that duplicate operations might exist in different branches of the tree. After all, it is the implementor's job to produce as efficient an implementation as possible from a design. Reduction of duplicate operations might be an activity to be carried out during system implementation rather than system design.

This point of view does have some merit, but the practicalities of large system construction mean that the designer rather than the implementor should be responsible for this type of optimization. The system designer has the ability to view the system as a whole and to identify possible duplications. The programmer, on the other hand, may be concerned with only a single branch in the design tree. Some other individual may be responsible for the implementation of another branch where a duplicate function may exist.

Let us now look at how the design of our example system (the electronic mail system) might be developed using top-down functional decomposition. In this study, we not only present part of the design; we also examine design decisions made during the design process and explain why these particular decisions seem to be the most appropriate.

We have already seen the first stages of the design of the EM system in Chapter 3 where a top-level view of the system and designs for the send and receive subsystems were developed. For the convenience of the reader, the definition of these components is repeated in Examples 5.5, 5.6 and 5.7.

From the system description, the major functions are identified along with how they might be initiated. This is then expressed as a high-level design which takes no account whatsoever of how these functions might be built. We have already seen that the major subsystems of the EM system are Send_mail, Receive_mail, Help, etc. We must re-emphasize that putting together this high-level design is a creative process that is dependent on the skill, experience and intuition of the designer.

```
– – Appropriate with declarations should appear here
procedure EM_system is
    type TM_INDEX is range 1..7 ;
    type TOP_MENU is array (TM_INDEX) of STRING (1..16) ;
    type OPTIONS is (Help, Send, Receive, Cancel, Edit, What_mail, Quit) ;
    type MENU_ERROR is range 1..4 ;
    Command_menu_file: constant STRING := "Command_file" ;
    – – Instantiate the generic menu manager package to create a menu
    – – manager for the top level menus used by EM_system
    package Command_menu is new Menu_manager (
                        INDEX => TM_INDEX ,
                        A_MENU => TOP_MENU ,
                        A_MENU_SELECTION => OPTIONS ,
                        STATUS => MENU_ERROR ,
                        Setup_filename => Command_menu_file) ;
    Action : OPTIONS ;
    Error: MENU_ERROR ;
    The_user : User.ID :=User.Get_uid ;
    Blank_form : Mail_item.INSTANCE ;
begin
    Command_menu.Setup (Error) ;
    loop
        Command_menu.Get_choice ( Action, Error);
        case Action is
            when Send => Send_mail (Blank_form, The_user) ;
            when Receive => Receive_mail (The_user) ;
            when Help => Help_me (The_user) ;
            when Edit => Profile_editor (The_user) ;
            when Cancel => Cancel_mail (The_user) ;
            when What_mail => Find_unread_mail (The_user) ;
            when Quit =>   exit ;
        end case ;
    end loop ;
    Close_down_the_EM_system ;
end EM_system ;
```

Example 5.5 The top-level design of the EM system.

In the first development of the design, each of these distinct functions is refined. At this stage, the system requirements definition still acts as a guide to the designer as it should set out detailed descriptions of subsystem facilities that must be provided. For example, it might be set out in the requirements that users may send the same mail to more than

```
procedure Send_mail (Mail_sender: User.ID ;
                         Mail_form: in out Mail_item.INSTANCE) is
   type SM_INDEX is range 1..3 ;
   type SEND_MENU_TYPE is array (SM_INDEX) of STRING (1..16 ) ;
   type OPTIONS is (Edit_mail, New_mail, Quit) ;
   type MENU_ERROR is range 1..4 ;
   Send_menu_file: constant STRING := "Send_file" ;
   package Send_menu is new Menu_manager (
                     INDEX => TM_INDEX ,
                     A_MENU => SEND_MENU_TYPE ,
                     A_MENU_SELECTION => OPTIONS ,
                     STATUS => MENU_ERROR,
                     Setup_filename => Send_menu_file) ;
   Action: OPTIONS ;
   Error: MENU_ERROR ;
   Blank_form: Mail_item.INSTANCE ;
begin
   Display_the (Mail_form)   ;
   Mail_form := Get_form_filled_in_by (Mail_sender, Mail_form) ;
   Put_into_receivers_mailbox (Mail_form) ;
   Send_menu.Setup (Error) ;
   Send_menu.Get_choice (Action, Error) ;
   case Action is
     when Edit_mail =>
        Send_mail (Mail_sender, Mail_form) ;
     when New_mail =>
        Send_mail (Mail_sender, Blank_form) ;
     when Quit => return ;
   end case ;
end Send_mail ;
```

Example 5.6   The Send_mail subsystem design.

one other user, and this must be reflected in the design of the Send_mail subsystem. Notice that this is a refinement of the design that was originally expressed as Example 3.3.

The top-down functional design process guides the designer in selecting which abstraction to refine, but does not inhibit the designer's creativity. For example, consider the design of the Send_mail subsystem (Example 5.6). Here, a decision has been made to implement mail preparation as a form-filling operation. This implies that the mail

```
procedure Send_mail is
begin
    loop
        Get_mail_text ;
        Get_receiver_list ;
        Fill_in_sender ;
        Fill_in_date ;
        for all receivers loop
            Put_mail_into_mailbox ;
        end loop ;
        User_info.Ask ("more mail?") ;
        exit when no more mail ;
    end loop
end Send_mail ;
```

Example 5.7   An alternative design for Send_mail.

form has sender and receiver fields. If the same message is to be sent to a number of users, this may be accomplished by editing the receiver field in the mail form.

This approach was chosen because it seems to be an elegant one which supports possibilities such as sending slightly different messages to different receivers. However, as with most software designs, the design was not immediately apparent and iteration through several intermediate stages was necessary before the final design was formulated.

Naturally, if the only requirement is for the same item of mail to be sent to different receivers, alternative designs for the Send_mail subsystem are possible. An outline of one possibility expressed at a very abstract, non-detailed level is shown as Example 5.7.

We believe that the design that we have formulated is a more elegant and general-purpose design than that shown in Example 5.7. However, there is no way of quantifying the 'goodness' of a software design or deciding objectively whether some program A is 'better' than some other program B. We tend to rely on aesthetics, intuition, prejudice and experience to judge which is the best design.

To illustrate the top-down functional decomposition process, let us continue the design of the Send_mail subsystem and examine the decomposition of Put_into_receivers_mailbox. This is of more interest than the form display and input routines which are lengthy, but straightforward input/output routines.

Recall that each user has an associated profile which is applied to incoming mail and which may cause mail to be redirected or may change mail priorities. This must be taken into account by the

```
procedure Put_into_receivers_mailbox (Form: in out
                            Mail_item.INSTANCE) is
   Recipient: User.ID ;
   Profile_name: Profile.NAME ;
begin
   - -Get the receiver of the mail and the name of the profile to be applied
   Recipient := Mail_item.Get_receiver (Form) ;
   Profile_name := Profile.Get_name (Recipient) ;
   - -the next operation applies a profile to the form and may modify some
   - -fields of the form
   Form := Profile.Apply (Form, Profile_name) ;
   - -if the receiver has been changed by instructions in the profile then
   - -call Put_into_receivers_mailbox recursively to put the form into the
   - -new receiver's mailbox. Otherwise, execute a Mailbox_manager.Put
   if Mail_item.Get_receiver (Form) /= Recipient then
       Put_into_receivers_mailbox (Form) ;
   else
       Mailbox_manager.Put (Form, Recipient) ;
   end if ;
end Put_into_receivers_mailbox ;
```

Example 5.8   Procedure to put mail into a mailbox.

Put_into_receivers_mailbox routine. One possible design for this procedure is shown in Example 5.8.

The design of this routine is still expressed in abstract terms and the representations of the manipulated objects (forms, mailboxes and profiles) have not been taken into account. It is important that software designers should delay making decisions on representations until as late as possible in the design process. The reason for this is that such decisions inevitably constrain the freedom of choice of the designer, and such constraints are undesirable in the early stages of top-down functional decomposition. In fact, we believe that it is around the level of decomposition represented by Put_into_receivers_mailbox that the functional approach to system design should normally change to an object-oriented approach so that decisions on representation may be delayed.

Let us now consider the procedure Put_into_receivers_mailbox and examine the design decisions that were made in formulating its design.

It is clear that the general operation 'put mail into a receivers mailbox' must identify the receiver's mailbox and enter the mail in that mailbox. This is achieved in Example 5.8 by identifying the receiver, finding the name of that receiver's mailbox and using the Mailbox_manager.Put procedure to enter the mail in the appropriate mailbox. However, in our system, the function is complicated by the fact that mail receivers may specify in their profile that mail that is originally destined for them may be redirected elsewhere.

We have decided that this profile application, which may change the receiver of the mail, and possible redirection should be part of the Put_into_receivers_mailbox function. If the receiver is changed, Put_into_receivers_mailbox is called recursively to direct the mail to the new receiver. It might be argued that the operation of entering mail in a mailbox should be kept separate from mail redirection and that before Put_into_receivers_mailbox is called from Send_mail, the 'true' receiver should be computed.

We disagree with this argument. The Send_mail operation is concerned with handling input mail and sending it to the destination specified by the user. The fact that this destination may be changed by the receiver is a lower-level decision and of no concern to the Send_mail operation. We believe that our decision is justified by the fact that multiple profile application and redirection (*A* redirects to *B* who redirects to *C*) is easily handled by recursive calls of Put_into_receivers_mailbox.

Another, less apparent design decision has been made in formulating this procedure. Recall that the user may specify that mail should be discarded by redirecting that mail to the user wpb (waste paper basket). Redirection to wpb is not the same as redirection to another user's mailbox, for two reasons:

- Each user has his or her own waste-bin, so redirection to wpb is a form of self-redirection.
- Waste-bins are not mailboxes – they have a different set of permissible operations and constraints.

We have decided in designing Put_into_receivers_mailbox that the handling of this special redirection should not be the responsibility of that procedure. Rather, we assume that it will be handled by the Mailbox_manager.Put operation and that the Profile.Apply procedure is also aware of possible redirections to waste baskets.

At this stage, it is not clear whether our decision on this matter is a correct one. A case may be made for handling waste-bin redirections explicitly in Put_into_receivers_mailbox, but we feel it is more effective to conceal the fact that waste-bin redirection is distinct from mailbox redirection at this level in the design. After all, it is conceivable that a future change to the system might be such that waste-bins have the same operations as mailboxes. Such a change could be incorporated without requiring modifications to Put_into_receivers_mailbox.

The general rule to be adopted in making design decisions is to make them as late as possible. That is, if the design is considered as a hierarchy, it is best to make decisions that are liable to subsequent change as near to bottom of the hierarchy as possible. The reason for this is that, in general, change to a member of a hierarchy impacts all submembers. By forcing likely changes to the lowest possible level, the number of other units to be changed is minimized.

Let us now further illustrate top-down design by considering the decomposition of the Receive_mail subsystem (Example 5.9). Notice that Example 5.9 is a refinement of Example 3.4. We deliberately delay further decomposition of Put_into_receivers_mailbox because the next level in the decomposition process involves making decisions about object representations. As we have already suggested, an object-oriented view may be the most appropriate at this stage, so we return to this decomposition in the following section.

The Receive_mail subsystem has a more complex set of user options than the Send_mail subsystem. After initiating a receive mail operation, the user may read an item of mail, call for a summary (titles and senders) of her mail, redirect mail to another user, file the mail, reorder her mail list or retrieve an item of mail from the waste bin.

A design decision which has been made here is to extract all mail from the mailbox at once rather than item by item in the course of the receive mail operation. This decision was made by analogy with manual systems where most of us take all the mail from our mailbox, glance at everything and then roughly sort the mail so that we may first read what appear to be the most interesting items.

Another decision made in designing this subsystem was that two distinct mail lists should be maintained. These are a list of unread mail, which holds mail items not yet presented for reading, and a list of mail that has been read. As items of mail are presented to the user, they move from one list to the other.

The decision to maintain two mail lists is an important one as it allows the design of the other receive subsystem functions to be fairly straightforward. Unless redirection is specified, all the mail removed from the user's mailbox is accessible until the user explicitly quits the Receive_mail subsystem and returns to the higher-level routine. Because all mail is always available within Receive_mail, there is no requirement that operations must take place in a specific order. Items of mail may be filed before reading, several messages may be read and some redirected, some can be read and the unread mail may then be reordered, and so on, as long as the routines responsible for these activities are aware that two mail lists must be processed.

Alternative mechanisms, such as presenting a list of optional operations after a message has been read, force the user to carry out actions in an order that is defined by the system and not necessarily in the order which best suits his or her way of working.

```ada
procedure Receive_mail ( Mail_receiver: User.ID ) is
   type RM_INDEX is range 1..6 ;
   type RECEIVE_MENU_TYPE is
           array (RM_INDEX) of STRING (1..16 ) ;
   type OPTIONS is (Read, Summary, Redirect, Reorder, File, Quit) ;
   type MENU_ERROR is range 1..4 ;
   Receive_menu_file: constant STRING := "Receive_file" ;
   package Receive_menu is new Menu_manager (
                   INDEX => RM_INDEX ,
                   A_MENU => RECEIVE_MENU_TYPE ,
                   A_MENU_SELECTION => OPTIONS ,
                   STATUS => MENU_ERROR,
                   Setup_filename => Receive_menu_file) ;
   Action : OPTIONS ;
   Error: MENU_ERROR ;
   Unread_mail: Mail_list.INSTANCE := Mail_list.Create ;
   Examined_mail: Mail_list.INSTANCE := Mail_list.Create ;
   End_of_receive: BOOLEAN := false ;
begin
   Receive_menu.Setup (Error) ;
   Unread_mail := Mailbox_manager.Empty (Mail_receiver) ;
   Unread_mail := Discard_expired_mail_from (Unread_mail) ;
   Unread_mail := Sort_on_priority (Unread_mail) ;
   loop
      Receive_menu.Get_choice (Action, Error) ;
      case Action is
        when Read =>
           Present_mail (Unread_mail, Examined_mail) ;
        when Summary =>
           Present_summary (Unread_mail, Examined_mail) ;
        when Redirect =>
           Redirect_mail (Mail_receiver, Unread_mail, Examined_mail) ;
        when File =>
           File_mail (Unread_mail, Examined_mail) ;
        when Reorder =>
           Reorder_mail (Unread_mail, Examined_mail) ;
        when Quit => exit ;
      end case ;
      exit when Mail_list.Is_empty (Unread_mail) ;
   end loop ;
   Return_to_mailbox (Unread_mail) ;
   Place_in_pending_tray (Examined_mail) ;
end Receive_mail ;
```

Example 5.9   The receive subsystem design.

As an example of a refinement of part of the Receive_mail subsystem, Example 5.10 shows the design of the Present_mail routine. Notice how natural language text is used to describe actions in this procedure.

The important design decision made here is that the user may choose to look at the mail in the order decided by the EM system or may explicitly request items of mail for presentation. Notice that this routine is solely concerned with the presentation of mail and with the movement of items from Unread_mail to Examined_mail once they have been presented. It is not concerned with and need not be aware of the existence of other options such as mail redirection or mail filing. Notice, in this routine, the use of the User_info subsystem for communications with the system user. This exports the type YES_OR_NO and functions Affirmative, Negative, Ask, Tell and Get_number.

We make extensive use of narrative text at this level in the design description so that the design is more understandable. In general, at high levels in the design, the design is mostly a list of abstractions and these are easily represented as calls to other components. Once a more detailed design stage is reached, distinct actions are more likely to be implemented as a sequence of statements, and these are sometimes best expressed as narrative where unnecessary detail is excluded.

As an illustration of how these other receive subsystem options use Unread_mail and Examined_mail, the refinement for the Redirect_mail routine is shown as Example 5.11.

Notice how the use of two mail lists makes it easy to redirect the last item of mail that has been read. It also means that the redirection of mail that has been examined and mail that has not been read may be handled in exactly the same way.

The major design decision to be made in this routine is how to handle the redirection of mail. We have chosen simply to invoke the Send_mail subsystem which displays the item to be redirected and the normal procedure for sending mail is followed. This approach was adopted for two reasons:

1. It means that the user is always presented with a single consistent way of passing mail to a receiver.

2. It allows redirected mail to be edited, if so desired by the sender. To redirect mail involves editing the receiver field, but the text of the message, the expiry date or any other information may also be edited at the same time.

Until now, we have taken a functional approach to the design of the EM system. We have designed the system so that the user selects a function and then identifies the object on which that function is to operate. An alternative approach would have been for the user to identify an object and then select the function of interest – we illustrate how this technique affects the design in the following section.

```
with Mail_list, Mail_item, User_info ;
procedure Present_mail ( Unread_mail: in out Mail_list.INSTANCE ;
                    Examined_mail: in out Mail_list.INSTANCE) is
   - - User_info is the subsystem used to
   - - communicate with the EM system
   - - user . We assume its definition. YES_OR_NO is a type
   - - defined in the visible part of User_info
   Reply: User_info.YES_OR_NO ;
   The_item: Mail_item.INSTANCE ;
   Status: Mail_list.ERROR_STATUS ;
begin
   Reply := User_info.Ask ("Default presentation order?") ;
   if User_info.Affirmative (Reply) then
      while Unread_mail is not empty and User answers "yes" loop
         Mail_list.Head (Unread_mail, The_item, Status) ;
         Present_mail_item (The_item) ;
         Examined_mail := Mail_list.Add ( Lst => Examined_mail,
                                   Item => The_item) ;
         Unread_mail := Mail_list.Tail (Unread_mail) ;
         Reply := User_info.Ask ("More mail?") ;
      end loop ;
      if User answers "yes" and Mail_list.IsEmpty (Unread_mail) then
         User_info.Tell ("All mail presented") ;
      elsif
```

(cont.)

Example 5.10   The Present_mail procedure.

At this stage in the refinement process, our consideration of the objects used in the electronic mail system has been completely abstract. We have not discussed their representation in any way, nor have any representation-dependent features been used in the design description.

However, further refinement using functional decomposition must necessarily take object representation into account. Because representations are subject to change, we prefer to delay representation decisions so, at this level of decomposition, it is useful to change our approach to system design. Rather than consider this level of the system as interacting functions, we view it as a set of interacting objects. The design of these objects should be carried out in accordance with the principles of object-oriented design discussed in Section 5.4.

```
declare
      Presenting_items: BOOLEAN := true ;
      Mail_number: NATURAL := 1 ;
begin
      - - Show user what is available associating a number with each
      - - mail item
      Display_headers (Mail_number, Unread_mail, Examined_mail) ;
      while Unread_mail not empty and Presenting_items loop
          Mail_number := User_info.Get_number ;
          if the mail item whose number is input is in Unread_mail then
              Present (The mail item identified by the Mail_number) ;
              Add the mail item presented to Examined_mail ;
              Remove that item from Unread_mail ;
          elsif the mail item whose number is input is in Examined_mail
          then
              Present (The mail item identified by the Mail_number) ;
          else
              User_info.Tell ("No item with this number?") ;
          end if ;
          Reply := User_info.Ask ("More mail?") ;
          Presenting_items := User_info.Affirmative (Reply) ;
      end loop ;
    end ;
  end if ;
end Present_mail ;
```

Example 5.10 (cont.)

5.4 Object-oriented design

We have already introduced the notion of object-oriented design. This approach to software design considers the software system to be made up of a set of objects which interact by passing messages to each other. Each object has its own internal state and the messages passed to an object determine what operations on that state are to be activated. Thus, we can define as object as follows:

An object is an entity that has a state and an associated set of operations which may modify or make public all or part of that state. The state should not be modified by any operation apart from those defined as part of the object.

```
procedure Redirect_mail ( Unread_mail: in out Mail_list.INSTANCE ;
                          Examined_mail : in out Mail_list.INSTANCE
                          Sender: User.ID) is
   Reply: User_info.YES_OR_NO ;
   The_item: Mail_item.INSTANCE ;
   Status: Mail_list.ERROR_STATUS ;
begin
   - -Mail may be redirected before or after reading.
   - -The default is to redirect the last item read
   - -which is the first item on Examined_mail. Otherwise the
   - -user must provide a mail identifier to identify the item
   - -which is to be redirected.
   Reply := User_info.Ask ("Redirect last item read?") ;
   if User_info.Affirmative (Reply) then
      Mail_list.Head (Examined_mail, The_item, Status) ;
      - - at this level of refinement, we assume that the Status is Ok
      Send_mail (Sender, The_item) ;
      Examined_mail := Mail_list.Tail (Examined_mail) ;
      Reply := User_info.Ask ("More redirections?") ;
      if User_info.Negative (Reply) then
         return ;
      end if ;
   end if ;
   - -Handle redirections by mail number
   declare
      Mail_number: NATURAL := 1 ;
```

(cont.)

Example 5.11 The Redirect_mail procedure.

It is quite possible to take an object-oriented view of a software system at any design level from the most abstract to the concrete. For example, the electronic mail system might be viewed as a set of abstract objects (The_mail_sender, The_profile, etc.) rather than a set of functions as described in the previous section. Authors such as Abbott (1983) and Booch (1983) argue that this is a 'better' methodology of software design than functional decomposition.

Their argument is based on two precepts. Firstly, they claim that object-oriented designs are easier to modify than designs produced by top-down functional decomposition because the representation of objects is always hidden and may be modified without the need to change other objects. Secondly, they argue that an object-oriented view is a more 'natural' way to view a system. By this we presume they mean it is more

```
begin
   - -Show the user what mail is available by displaying the header of
   - - each message
   Display_mail_headers (Mail_number, Unread_mail,
                         Examined_mail) ;
loop
      - -Get the message to be redirected. The user may either type
      - - a number or may direct the screen cursor over the item
      - - header to be redirected
      Mail_number := User_info.Get_number;
      if the item whose number is input is in Unread_mail then
         Send_mail (Sender, That mail item) ;
         Remove (The mail item sent) ;
      elsif the item whose number is input is in Examined_mail then
         Send_mail (Sender, That mail item ) ;
         Remove (The mail item sent) ;
      else
         User_info.Tell ("No item with this number?") ;
      end if ;
      Reply := User_info.Ask ("More redirections?") ;
      exit when User_info..Negative (Reply) or
                ( Mail_list.IsEmpty (Unread_mail) and
                  Mail_list.IsEmpty (Examined_mail) ) ;
   end loop ;
   end ;
end Redirect_mail ;
```

Example 5.11 (cont.)

in accord with how we actually tackle everyday problems like getting to work, making coffee, etc.

There is no doubt that delaying decisions on representation and hiding as much information as possible makes systems easier to change and, in this respect, the proponents of object-oriented design have a good argument. Whether or not an object-oriented view is more natural is perhaps more contentious. There is obviously not a definitive answer to this. We believe that functional and object-oriented views of a software system are equally useful depending on the level at which the system is viewed. At very high levels, a functional view is most appropriate; at intermediate levels, an object-oriented view is appropriate; at the lowest levels within objects a functional view again becomes appropriate. A discussion of this is given in Sommerville *et al.* (1985).

5.4.1 Object implementation using Ada

We have defined an object as a state and a set of operations that are exclusively used for manipulating that state. Therefore, to implement an object in Ada we must have a way of representing both the state and these private operations. In addition, we must recognize that in any system there are often several objects of the same class or type that have common operations but different states, and it is clearly desirable to have some way of defining these object classes and instantiating instances of these classes. Furthermore, the notion of an object class hierarchy should be supported where classes may be viewed as sub-classes of some more general class. Operations defined for the general class should be inherited by the sub-classes. Finally, an object should have full 'civil rights', in that it ought to be possible to create and destroy objects and to pass them as parameters to other objects or sub-programs.

In this section, we illustrate two techniques of object implementation using Ada. The reader should note that extensive use of generics is made here with the assumption that this concept is understood. The principles underlying generics are discussed in Chapter 8. Ada is only partially suitable for object implementation as it does not permit the definition of objects that can always be passed as parameters to other objects.

An object is an encapsulated entity and the Ada package construct in conjunction with Ada's typing mechanisms allow many of the desired features to be provided. We have already seen the abstract data type approach, which relies on defining an object class as a type exported from a package in which the operations on the object are defined. Example 5.12 shows the specification of a package implementing the abstract data type Sequence.

Of course, there are other functions which might be considered necessary for the complete implementation of sequences, but those set out in Example 5.12 will suffice for this discussion. Notice how we have defined the Sequence abstract type as a generic package with the type of the objects in the sequence and the maximum sequence length defined as generic formal parameters. Where appropriate, it always makes sense to define abstract data types as generic packages as this provides a consistent implementation for all types.

It is now possible to instantiate this generic abstract type and to declare objects of that type:

```
package Integer_sequence is new
          Sequence (ANY_TYPE => INTEGER, Max => 500) ;
Sequence1, Sequence2: Integer_sequence.T ;
```

This defines two objects called Sequence1 and Sequence2 and the permissible operations on these objects are those set out in the generic package Sequence. The state of an object defined in this way is held in

```
generic
   type ANY_TYPE is private ;
   Max: NATURAL := 100 ;
package Sequence is
   type T is private ;
   – –Create brings a sequence into existence
   function Create (Seq: T) return T ;
   – –Put adds an item to the end of the sequence
   function Put (Val: ANY_TYPE; Seq: T) return T ;
   – –Get returns an item from the sequence at the position referenced by
   – –some notional sequence pointer
   function Get (Seq: T) return ANY_TYPE;
   – –Reset sets the notional sequence pointer to refer to the beginning of
   – –the sequence
   function Reset (Seq: T) return T ;
   – –AtEnd determines if the notional pointer refers to the last sequence
   – –member
   function AtEnd (Seq: T) return BOOLEAN ;
   – –IsEmpty determines if the sequence has any members
   function IsEmpty (Seq: T) return BOOLEAN ;
private
   type SEQ_ARRAY is array (1..Max ) of ANY_TYPE ;
   type T is record
      Pointer: NATURAL ;
      Values: SEQ_ARRAY ;
   end record ;
end Sequence ;
```

Example 5.12   Sequence abstract data type.

the object itself, although, because the object type is private, its representation cannot be accessed directly. Thus, when the private part of the package is declared, it is essential that provision is made for maintaining state information. Almost inevitably, this involves representing the object as a record type with each field of the record holding some component of the state information.

In the majority of cases, this is an acceptable approach; but there are some applications (simulation is an example that comes to mind) where the state of an object may be updated asynchronously by several tasks. For example, say the object being implemented represents a ship entering harbour. The position of the ship may be updated by tasks simulating the ship's engines, the state of the tides at that time and the current wind direction and speed. Thus, the position state is a shared

```
generic
    type ANY_TYPE is private ;
    Max: NATURAL := 100 ;
package Sequence is
    – –Put adds an item to the end of the sequence
    procedure Put (Val: ANY_TYPE) ;
    – –Get returns an item from the sequence at the position referenced by
    – –some notional sequence pointer
    procedure Get (VAL: in out ANY_TYPE) ;
    – –Reset sets the notional sequence pointer to refer to the beginning
    – –of the sequence
    procedure Reset ;
    – –AtEnd determines if the notional pointer refers to the last sequence
    – –member
    function AtEnd return BOOLEAN ;
    – –IsEmpty determines if the sequence has any members
    function IsEmpty return BOOLEAN ;
end Sequence ;
```

Example 5.13   An alternative implementation of object class Sequence.

variable and must be protected by implementing it as a task.

An alternative implementation of objects, that allows the state to be held completely within the package implementing the object, involves representing the object class as a generic package and instantiating that package for each object that is required. Example 5.13 illustrates how this is accomplished for the Sequence object class as defined in Example 5.12.

Of course, this implementation is very similiar to that shown in Example 5.12, with the difference that there is no type information made visible in the package specification. In addition, the access operations do not take an entity of type Sequence as a parameter, and in some cases are implemented as procedures rather than functions. The state information is concealed completely within the package body, part of which is shown as Example 5.14.

Notice that the state information for the sequence (the array and the sequence pointer) are held separately here and need not be packaged together into a record. Individual instances of sequences are brought into existence by instantiating the package as follows.

```
package Sequence1 is new Sequence (ANY_TYPE => INTEGER,
                                    MAX => 500) ;
```

```
package Sequence2 is new Sequence (ANY_TYPE => INTEGER,
                                    MAX => 500) ;
```

These sequences are updated by calling the procedures defined in the generic package Sequence.

```
Sequence1.Put (Some_value) ;
Sequence2.Reset ;
Sequence1.Get (The_value_required) ;
```

There are two circumstances where this is the most appropriate way to implement objects in Ada. As discussed above, one of these is where the state information is such that it is not convenient to export it from the Ada package defining the object. The other is where we wish to have similiar objects with the same operations, but where the operations themselves are to be implemented in quite a different way.

For example, say we have a number of menu objects with an operation called Display on each of these objects. Some menus we may wish to display as a set of icons (pictures), others might be permanent text menus, and others pop-up menus on a bit-mapped screen. It is possible to define a menu package and pass an indicator into it indicating the type of display that is required, but this is somewhat artificial. It is better to implement the objects as packages with a different implementation for each function. This is illustrated in the EM system example in Section 5.4.2.

In other circumstances, we recommend that objects should normally be implemented by defining an abstract data type and then creating object instances by declaring variables of that type. This approach allows us to make use of Ada's derived type mechanisms to construct type hierarchies, where a general object class is declared. Sub-classes may then be derived from the general class and inherit the operations defined for that class. Thus we might define a general object class TEXT_OBJECT with operations such as Display, Put_on_disk, Get_from_disk and Edit. We might then define a sub-class PROGRAM_TEXT which inherits these operations, but which has additional operations such as Compile, Analyse,

---

```
package body Sequence is
    type SEQ_ARRAY is array (1..Max ) of ANY_TYPE ;
    SEQUENCE_POINTER: NATURAL ;
    --Sequence function definitions here
end Sequence ;
```

Example 5.14   Part of the package body for Sequence.

```
generic
    type ANY_TYPE is private ;
    Max: NATURAL := 100 ;
    --assignment procedure
    with procedure Assign (T1: in ANY_TYPE ; T2: in out ANY_TYPE ) ;
    --equality function
    with function Equals (T1, T2: ANY_TYPE) return BOOLEAN ;
    --There may be other functions defined here, but they may not be defined
    --for all types
package Sequence is
    type T is private ;
    --The operations on the type are as specified in Example 5.12
private
    --The private part of the package is as specified in Example 5.12
end Sequence ;
```

Example 5.15   Sequence abstract data type.

etc. Space does not permit a full discussion of the use of derived types here – we return to this topic in Chapter 6.

When objects are declared as generic packages with parameters that are types, there is an implicit requirement that the operations defined on these types are known to the generic package where the object operations are provided. In practice, this means that only assignment and equality operations should be taken for granted. Unfortunately, this means that types that are themselves abstract data types and are defined as **limited private** types may not be used as the generic parameter as the assignment and equality operation need not be defined for these types. The existence of these operations is assumed for all generic types.

This illustrates one of the drawbacks of Ada as an object-oriented language. True hierarchical systems of objects are not allowed because it is not possible for a generic package to take another package (defining an abstract data type) as its parameter. Thus, to be completely general, the objects should be defined with generic function parameters setting out the permitted operations on the generic type parameter. These functions must be instantiated to the actual abstract type operations when the generic package is instantiated. Thus, the sequence example might be rewritten as shown in Example 5.15.

5.4.2   An object-oriented EM system design

In this section, we redesign part of the electronic mail system using an object-oriented approach and compare that design with the functional design set out above. Of course, this exercise is somewhat artificial as we have already designed the system from a functional viewpoint and it is impossible for us to avoid allowing this to influence our design. Nevertheless, we hope that the examples below illustrate the fundamental differences between the object-oriented approach and the functional approach to software design.

In order to provide a true picture of object-oriented design, we must start at the highest level and view the system as a set of objects rather than a set of functions. Therefore, rather than identifying functions such as 'send mail', 'receive mail', 'get help', we must identify the objects and object classes that are of interest to the system user. A provisional list is as follows:

    A_mail_message
    A_mail_message_list
    A_help_message
    A_mail_profile
    A_menu
    All_mail

Whilst most of these objects are obvious, notice that we need a 'global' object which we have called All_mail. This represents all of the mail that is known to the system and is necessary because the Cancel and Find_unread_mail facilities may actually need to access every piece of mail that is known to the EM system.

In order to provide a true object-oriented approach, the user interface must be redesigned so that the user first selects the class of object that is to be manipulated, instantiates a particular object (the mail message from Fred, say) and then chooses the operations on that particular object. We do not describe the actual form of this interface here. Indeed, it is actually unlikely that we would explicitly ask the user to choose an object by typing its name. Indeed, the user may select a function and the system will work out what object is implied, or alternatively may point at a screen icon representing the object.

A possible implementation of the EM system is shown as Example 5.16.

If the user chooses a mail message as the object of interest, a further menu is presented asking what operation on the message is to be initiated; if a help message is chosen, a help message is displayed and this is set up to an initial help frame giving information on how to get further help; if a profile object is chosen, the user's current profile is displayed; and if the entire mail object is chosen, find and cancel options are displayed.

We have used both of the techniques of object implementation discussed earlier. Objects of class Mail_message, Help_text and Profile are implemented as instances of abstract data types; whereas the All_mail object and menus are implemented as packages. This goes against

```
procedure EM_system is
begin
  loop
    case Object_menu.Get_choice is
      when Mail_message =>
        - -Mail_message.Create brings a blank form into existence
        - -Display a blank form (the object). This is then filled in either
        - -by the user or by operations on the mail message
        Message_form := Mail_message.Create ;
        Mail_message.Display (Message_form) ;
        case Mail_message_menu.Get_choice is
          when Send =>
              Mail_message.Send (Message_form) ;
          when Receive =>
              Mail_message.Receive (Message_form) ;
        end case ;
      when All_mail =>
        case All_mail_menu.Get_choice is
          when Cancel => All_mail.Cancel ;
          when Find_unread_mail => All_mail.Find ;
        end case ;
      when Help_message =>
        Help_text.Retrieve (How_to_get_help, Start_frame_text) ;
        Help_text.Display (Start_frame_text) ;
        while Help_text.NotEnded loop
          Help_text.Get_frame_id (Frame_id) ;
          Help_text.Retrieve (Frame_id, Help_frame_text);
          Help_text.Display (Help_frame_text) ;
        end loop ;
      when Profile =>
        Profile.Display (User.ID) ;
        Profile.Edit (User.ID) ;
        Profile.Save (User.ID) ;
      when Quit => exit ;
    end case ;
  end loop ;
end EM_system ;
```

Example 5.16   An object-oriented EM system design.

our earlier guidelines. However, there is only a single All_mail object and it does not make sense to have an All_mail object class; and we may wish quite different operation implementations for different menus. For example, the object menu might be displayed as a menu of icons and the mail message menu as a pop-up menu beside the appropriate icon.

Notice that this system design is not really very different from the functional design shown in Example 5.5. This is to be expected as, at the most abstract level, it often makes sense to view any system as a set of functions with the objects on which these functions operate being defined in a later refinement. Indeed, attempting to use an object-oriented approach at a very early stage in the design process may actually force decisions on objects to be made before it is really necessary to make such decisions. As we have suggested, good design involves delaying such decisions for as long as possible, so a functional approach at the most abstract levels may lead to a better software design.

Let us continue the design, assuming that the user has indicated that a mail message is the object of interest. The next stage in the design is to attempt to identify the operations that are associated with the object class 'mail message'. Some of these operations are used in the top-level design and others (such as Get_summary) are required by the Receive operation. A possible list of operations is as follows:

Mail_message
    Create
    Send
    Receive
    Display
    Edit
    Put_into_mailbox
    File
    Get_summary

This class of object can be represented as an Ada package as specified in Example 5.17.

Notice how this object class definition includes the definition of the sub-object class Summary which represents mail summarizations. In addition to the operations defined in Example 5.17, it is probably necessary to include access functions and update functions (Get and Put) for each of the components of a mail message such as the sender, receiver, message text, etc. For brevity, these have not been included in the example.

The process of object-oriented design continues in the same way for the remainder of the system: each object is defined and then expanded in terms of its operations and sub-objects. However, as we have already suggested, we believe that the optimum approach to software design involves integrating a functional and an object-oriented approach.

5.4.3   Integrating object-oriented and function-oriented design

The most effective approach to software design is to view the system as a hierarchy of functions built on a base of objects. It may be useful to gather these functions into packages when the system is implemented but,

```
package Mail is
  type MESSAGE is private ;
  package Summary is
    type T is private ;
    function Get (The_mail: MESSAGE) return T ;
    - - Precis is supplied by the user and associated with The_mail
    procedure Make (The_mail: in out MESSAGE ; Precis: STRING) ;
  private
    type T is new STRING (1..512) ;
  end Summary ;
  function Create return MESSAGE ;
  procedure Send (The_mail: MESSAGE) ;
  procedure Receive (The_mail: MESSAGE) ;
  procedure Display ( The_mail: MESSAGE ) ;
  procedure Edit ( The_mail: in out MESSAGE ) ;
  procedure Put_into_mailbox (The_mail: MESSAGE;
                              Receiver: User.ID ) ;
  - - Notice the use of object File with type attribute NAME
  procedure Filer (The_mail: MESSAGE ; In_file: File.NAME ) ;
    - - Get_summary is provided via a call Mail.Summary.Get
private
- -The representation details are not relevant to this example
end Mail ;
```

Example 5.17   The Mail.MESSAGE object class definition.

during design, a functional view is often the most natural one for the higher levels of system design.

However, there comes a stage in the functional decomposition of a software system where further decomposition depends on the representation chosen for data manipulated by the system's functions. It is at this stage that it is useful to move to an object-oriented rather than a functional view of the system.

The reason why it is useful to switch to an object-oriented methodology is that this allows object representation decisions to be delayed or modified. If a strictly functional approach is adopted and the wrong decision on representation is made, changing that decision may involve changing all functions that depend on that representation. By concealing a representation within an object, however, representation changes simply involve a change to the object implementation rather than changes to other functions or objects.

For example, the Present_mail procedure shown as Example 5.10 makes use of a list of items of unread mail. We have used operations Head and Tail on this list which select the 'first' and the 'rest' of the list respectively.

Further functional decomposition would force us to make a decision about list representation, and we may decide that lists of mail are to be presented as arrays. To do so, we might define an array type as follows:

```
type MAIL_LIST_INDEX is range 1..Mail_list_size ;
type MAIL_LIST is array (MAIL_LIST_INDEX) of Mail_item.INSTANCE ;
– –Now define the actual list
Unread_mail_pointer, Examined_mail_pointer: MAIL_LIST_INDEX ;
Unread_mail, Examined_mail: MAIL_LIST ;
```

To access the head of the unread mail list (say), we would use an array access Unread_mail (Unread_mail_pointer), and to access the tail of the list, the array slice Unread_mail (Unread_mail_pointer + 1..Unread_mail'LAST) would be used. This provides very efficient access and might be built into all routines which make use of the list of mail. However, let us assume that in some other implementation space is at a premium and unused array space cannot be afforded. The list representation may change to that of a linked list, represented as follows:

```
type MAIL_LIST_INSTANCE ;
type MAIL_LIST is access MAIL_LIST_INSTANCE ;
type MAIL_LIST_INSTANCE is record
   Item: Mail_item.INSTANCE ;
   Next: MAIL_LIST ;
end record ;
– –Now define the entities Unread_mail and Examined_mail
Unread_mail, Examined_mail: MAIL_LIST ;
```

The head of the unread mail list is now accessed as Unread_mail.Item and the tail of this list is accessed as Unread_mail.Next. Had the array representation been widely used, this change would have required all functions that use entities of type MAIL_LIST to be modified.

However, if we define Mail_list as an abstract data type, it describes a class of objects rather than a simple type and the list representation is local to the package in which it is declared. Access is via functions called Head and Tail, so that changing the representation from an array to a linked list (or vice versa) does not affect other functions. A definition of this abstract type which makes use of an array representation for lists is shown as Example 5.18. The alternative linked list representation is shown as Example 4.14 and this is, in fact, the representation we have used in the EM system.

In line with our thinking that an object-oriented view is most appropriate when further functional decomposition requires decisions

```
- -Mail list abstract data type specification
with Mail_item ;
generic
    - -The list size is a generic parameter
    Size: NATURAL ;
package Mail_list is
    type INSTANCE is private ;
    type STATUS is (Ok, Error) ;
    function Create return INSTANCE ;
    function Add (List: INSTANCE; Item: Mail_item.INSTANCE)
            return INSTANCE ;
    procedure Head (List: INSTANCE ; Item: out Mail_item.INSTANCE ;
                    Result: out STATUS) ;
    function Tail (List: INSTANCE) return Mail_item.INSTANCE ;
    function Is_empty (List: INSTANCE) return BOOLEAN ;
private
    type LIST_ARRAY is array (1..Size) of Mail_item.INSTANCE ;
    type INSTANCE is record
        Current_position: NATURAL ;
        The_list: LIST_ARRAY ;
    end record ;
end Mail_list ;
```

Example 5.18 Mail list abstract data type.

on representation, let us continue our EM system design example by
examining the objects that might be introduced at this stage of the design
after the major functions have been identified.

To identify these objects, it is useful to return to the notion of
resource management subsystems which was introduced in Chapter
3. Recall that we identified the following resource management
subsystems:

Menu_manager
Wastebin_manager
Mailbox_manager
Profile_manager

These are actually subsystems for managing system objects which might
be thought of as All_menus, All_waste bins, All_mailboxes and
All_profiles. Because there is only ever a single instance of these objects,
they should not be implemented as object classes, but as Ada packages
which include state information. Because there is some similarity in their

implementations, we consider only a single example here, namely the waste-bin manager.

Recall that users each have a waste bin into which they may consign unwanted mail. Expired mail may also be sent to a user's waste bin by automatic procedures. The user may look at what items are in the waste bin and may retrieve them if they have been sent there by mistake.

The waste-bin manager is responsible for looking after all user waste bins, so its principal object is All_wastebins. This object is made up of a collection of waste bins, so it has a sub-object class which is A_wastebin and which we have discussed in Chapter 4 as the package Wastebin. The waste-bin manager makes use of a user identifier to identify the waste bin of interest but, clearly, there must be some mapping between this user identifier and a particular waste-bin identifier. Thus, the operations associated with the object called All_wastebins may be set out as follows:

```
Object:
    All_waste bins
Sub_object_classes:
    A_waste bin
Operations:
    Empty_the_waste bin,
    List_waste bin_contents
    Put_item_in_waste bin,
    Get_item_from_waste bin
```

In all cases, these operations are applied to a particular waste bin, namely that belonging to some user U. Thus, the operations take as a parameter the identifier of U, so that the appropriate waste bin object within all objects may be identified. The entity All_wastebins can be defined in an Ada package specification as shown in Example 5.19. Notice that we do not adopt the naming convention used in an object-oriented approach of calling the package the name of the managed objects, but use what we feel is the more descriptive name Wastebin_manager.

The Put procedure adds an item to the waste bin, Retrieve interacts with the user to determine which item is to be retrieved from the waste bin, Clearout clears all items from a waste bin and List shows what items are contained in the waste bin. The sub-object class A_wastebin is defined in another Ada package as shown in Example 5.20.

This package would normally be declared within the Wastebin_manager subsystem package and would not be visible outside that package. Perhaps the most interesting feature of the definition is the use of derived types to represent waste bins. Waste bins in the system are actually represented as lists of mail items with permitted operations as set out in the Mail_list abstract type definition. Similarly, the waste-bin package makes use of an identifier for each mail item and

```
package Wastebin_manager is
   procedure Put ( Bin: User.ID ; Item: Mail_item.INSTANCE ) ;
   procedure Retrieve (Bin: User.ID ) ;
   procedure Clearout (Bin: User.ID) ;
   procedure List (Bin: User.ID) ;
   - - Wastebin package declared here, but set out below
end Wastebin_manager;
```

Example 5.19   The Wastebin_manager subsystem interface.

this is a derivation of the type Date.STAMP. We thus assume that no two items in the waste bin can have been entered in the bin at exactly the same time.

In summary, then, we are convinced that object-oriented and

```
with Date, Mail_list ;
package Wastebin is
   type INSTANCE is private ;
   type RESULT is (Ok, Error) ;
   package Item_id is
      type T is private ;
      function Create (D: Date.STAMP) return T ;
      function Get (Item: Mail_item.INSTANCE) return T ;
   private
      type T is new Date.STAMP ;
   end Item_id ;
   function Create return INSTANCE ;
   function Put (Bin: INSTANCE ; Item: Mail_item.INSTANCE )
            return INSTANCE ;
   procedure Get (Bin: INSTANCE ; Identifier: Item_id.T ;
                    Item: out Mail_item.INSTANCE ; Status: out RESULT) ;
   function Size (Bin: INSTANCE) return NATURAL ;
   function Clear (Bin: INSTANCE) return INSTANCE ;
private
   type INSTANCE is new Mail_list.INSTANCE ;
end Wastebin ;
```

Example 5.20   The Wastebin abstract data type.

function-oriented approaches to design work well together and should both be used in the design of any large system. The attraction of an object-oriented approach to software design is that it provides firewalls around representations and thus localizes required changes caused by a change to representations; whereas a functional approach to design at the top-most abstract levels allows us to delay decisions on what objects are needed in the system. Both techniques allow the application of probably the most important design principle – which is to delay decisions as long as possible so that the locus of a system change is minimized.

5.5 Summary

This chapter has been concerned with the process of software design and has devoted most space to a discussion of two complementary design methods – namely top-down functional decomposition and object-oriented design.

We started off by examining the role of Ada as a basis for a program design language in which to express software designs. Ada is a reasonable basis for such a language, but requires additional facilities and a relaxation of its rules if it is to be truly useful in this area.

An overview of three approaches to software design – top-down functional decomposition, data-driven design and object-oriented design – showed that none of these approaches, on its own, was ideal for large system design. The designer should use experience and judgement in selecting the appropriate technique for whichever part of the system is under consideration.

A more detailed look at top-down functional decomposition was illustrated by example. The design of the EM system was developed to a greater level of detail to show how functional decomposition is applied. However, we did not simply show designs in isolation, but examined alternative design decisions and justified why a particular decomposition strategy was adopted.

Finally, object-oriented design is an approach to software design based on information hiding. We showed two alternative ways of implementing objects in Ada – namely by the use of abstract data types to define object classes and the use of generic object packages. We then went on to look at the design of the EM system from an object-oriented point of view and contrasted this with the functional view of the system design. We suggested that the optimal design strategy is to switch from a functional view to an object-oriented view part-way through the design process, and illustrated how this might be done in the EM system by considering the design of some of the system objects.

5.6   Further reading

As this chapter is really a continuation of the general topic of software design, the most appropriate further reading is that set out in Chapter 3. Booch's book in particular is a very useful exposition of an object-oriented approach using Ada.

Chapter 6 **Data Types**

The type system of a programming language defines the nature of the data objects that may be modelled using the language. In mathematical terms this is called the universe of discourse of the language. The power of the Ada type system is derived from the fact that we can combine the basic types, a method of constructing multiple structured types and a powerful abstraction mechanism. This allows almost any problem to be modelled.

There are two main reasons for using a type mechanism in a programming language. The first is descriptive where the actions of the components of a system may be described in terms of the data objects that they use, manipulate or produce. These components may be subsystems or modules, functions or sub-programs, or even simple variables. The descriptive power of the type system determines how easy or how difficult it is to specify these components. This means that the descriptive power of the type system has implications for life cycle costs, since well-described systems are cheaper to specify, design, implement and maintain.

The second reason for using a type system is protection. In order to detect faults in a system there must be rules that may be violated. The type system specifies the set of rules for the legal manipulation of data objects. Again this has implications for software life cycle costs since the earlier that errors can be detected in the life cycle the cheaper it will be to correct them.

The type mechanism of the language forces users to face up to certain issues about how information in the proposed system should be organized. These issues centre around protection, programming discipline and life cycle costs. From the chaos of total freedom, a structure can be imposed on the data by constraining the manner in which data objects may be combined or manipulated.

The three issues of protection, programming discipline and life cycle costs with regard to data, are interrelated. A good rule of thumb that can be used when enforcing a general protection scheme on data is to ensure that each data object has the minimum necessary visibility. That is, the data can only be used in certain parts of the program or system and then only in the manner designated by the designer. Such security is extremely important in the structuring and design of large systems, especially when more than one person is involved, since it prevents accidental misuse of the data. Using a type system we can define how data objects are modelled and how they may be accessed and manipulated. Once defined the programming language ensures automatically that the data is used in the correct manner.

Enforcing a discipline on the use of data through the protection mechanism should also reduce the life cycle costs of the software produced. Typical figures show (Boehm, 1975) that stage-five costs of the software life cycle – operation and maintenance – exceed the development costs of the software by a factor ranging from 2 to 100 times. To reduce the total life cycle costs we must concentrate on reducing the cost of the operation and maintenance phase of the software produced. Indeed, as discussed in Chapter 1, Ada is specifically designed to reduce maintenance costs even if this means some increased development costs.

This has some consequences for the design of a programming language type mechanism. Leaving the automatic checking of the use of data types until program execution is liable to increase the cost of the software, since a type error will increase the cost of operation. In embedded systems, a run-time overhead in checking a type may be unacceptable in terms of performance. However, as we shall see later, it is not always convenient to check the use of data objects before the program runs and a reasonable compromise is to perform the checking as soon as is convenient, whatever that means in the context of the total system.

We see, therefore, that the type system of a programming language can play an important part in the software engineering process by providing descriptive power and protection and ultimately reducing software costs.

The aim of this chapter is to discuss the problems of types from the point of view of both the language designer and the applications programmer. Ada provides a powerful type system, allowing comprehensive protection and modelling. We study this here and also look at abstract data types and Ada packages and their relation to object-oriented programming. Task types will be discussed in Chapter 9.

6.1 Type systems

There are many definitions of 'data type' available in the literature and we propose the following as a working definition. A data type is a set of values with an associated set of operations on these values. The set of values characterizes the domain of the data type and the set of operations the mappings from one value in the domain to another. The operations may consist of constructors (how to create the object), selectors (how to get at its components) and predicates (how to find out facts about the object). For example, the type BOOLEAN in Ada has the value set [False, True] and the operations = and ≠ among others. Thus to define a data type the user must specify the set of values that objects of the type may take along with a set of operations for manipulating the values.

The type system of a programming language is the mechanism for declaring, using and manipulating types rather than the data objects themselves. The power of the type system depends on the flexibilty of this mechanism.

There are almost as many data type mechanisms as there are programming languages. The variations are caused by language designers placing different emphasis on different aspects of the type system. The central issues around which the variations take place can be identified as:

- Is there a fixed or extensible set of types?
- When is type checking performed?
- What is the meaning of type equivalence?
- Are data types objects themselves?
- What syntactic devices are used for types?
- What are the appropriate abstraction mechanisms for types?

We shall discuss each of these issues in turn with particular reference to the Ada type system.

6.1.1   Fixed or extensible set of types?

In early programming languages, such as Algol60, there is a predefined set of data types from which the programmer can model an application. A consequence of such a type system is that, sometimes, two logically separate entities may have to be represented by the same data type in a program. For example, in a payroll system the employee's number and the employee's age may be represented by integers. The danger with such a system is that the two entities may be combined or manipulated as integers without the type system detecting an error, even though the programmer may not desire such combinations or manipulations. This is unsafe since invalid data can accidentally or deliberately impersonate valid data.

To avoid undetected misuse it is essential to have finer grain control of the data space. To enforce the minimum necessary visibility on data objects it is necessary to place each data object in a separate type if required. Thus the user must have the facility to extend the type system with user-defined types to suit the needs of the application.

In a language such as Ada, with user-defined types the method of modelling the abstract data objects of the system's design is quite different from a language with a fixed set of data types. In the latter the implementor splits the problem into a set of abstract objects and chooses the most suitable fixed type for each of these abstract objects. Much care in programming is then necessary to preserve the integrity of the data objects.

The method is reversed in a language with user-defined types where each abstract object is given a separate type and then legal combinations of the objects are defined. Each data object has the minimum possible range and therefore the maximum possible protection. Unlike the former method, the programming language ensures this protection, giving the user a higher level of confidence in the integrity of the program.

The goal of minimum necessary visibility is most important in large systems that are written by many different people. While it may be possible to keep within one's intellectual grasp all the combinations of types in a small program, it is certainly less likely in large programs or in programs written by many people. By using the technique of data modelling outlined above, and a language with user-defined types, the possibility of undetected accidental misuse of data is greatly reduced.

The facilities of Ada which enable the user to obtain fine grain control of the data space are enumeration types, derived types, subtypes, compound data types and packages. We shall start with enumeration types.

In Ada the user may extend the type system using enumeration types. This allows the user to define a set of values that objects of the type may take. For example, in a program for controlling traffic lights the user may wish to restrict the colours that the lights may take. In defining the type

```
type TRAFFIC_LIGHT_COLOUR is (Red, Amber, Green) ;
```

then objects of this type, for example

```
Traffic_light: TRAFFIC_LIGHT_COLOUR ;
```

may only take the literal values Red, Amber and Green. Thus the statements

```
Second_traffic_light: TRAFFIC_LIGHT_COLOUR := Red ;
Traffic_light := Second_traffic_light ;
```

are legal, whereas any statement giving the variable values other then those defined is illegal. For example:

```
Traffic_light := 32 ;
```

All data types defined by enumeration are considered to be ordered. The user is given a number of operations on enumerated types automatically which generally exploit the ordering of the literals of the type. Some of the operations are selecting the first, last, successor and predecessor element of the type plus the relational operations. For example, with

type DAY **is** (Monday, Tuesday, Wednesday, Thursday,
                Friday, Saturday, Sunday) ;

then:

DAY ' Last = Sunday
DAY ' Pred (Tuesday) = Monday
Monday $<$ Tuesday = True

The enumeration type facility combined with the predefined types INTEGER, BOOLEAN and CHARACTER form the discrete types of Ada. Indeed the type BOOLEAN is predefined by

type BOOLEAN **is** (False, True) ;

This is a predefined type in the package Standard, defined by enumeration. The difference between the predefined types and the enumerated types is that the former have a rich set of predefined operations defined on them, whereas enumeration types have not.

Augmenting the type system by enumeration types allows the user to define types as sets of values with a limited number of operations. In itself this is not powerful enough for our needs but, as we shall see later, it can be used in conjunction with packages to define new operations on the objects.

The second method of defining new types in Ada is by using a derived type. In this, a new type is established that has the same properties – that is values and operations – as the parent type. For example:

type PAYROLL_NUMBER **is new** NATURAL ;
type AGE **is new** NATURAL ;

defines two new types PAYROLL_NUMBER and AGE which have the same set of values and operations as type NATURAL but are separate types from it and each other. This allows objects that act like natural numbers to be declared. For example:

Employee_number: PAYROLL_NUMBER ;
Employee_age: AGE ;

allows such statements as

Employee_age := 32 ;
Employee_number := 10_000 + 42 ;

but not

Employee_age := Employee_number ;

They are separate types even though they have the same set of values and operations. The facility to derive types is probably more important than enumerated types since it allows the traditional method of fragmenting the data space with the security of type checking on the logical objects. That is, instead of having to model different entities by the same data type, as in Algol60 for example, we can use the security of separate types. The problem described earlier, of accidentally combining two logically separate entities, can be avoided by giving them separate derived types. However, as with enumerated types this facility alone is not sufficient for all our needs as new operations on the types cannot be defined.

There is one minor drawback to derived types which is to do with the user's expectation of how the real world acts. For example, if we define types for length and area by

```
type LENGTH is new INTEGER ;
type AREA is new INTEGER ;
```

and define variables of these types by

```
A: AREA ;
L, B: LENGTH ;
```

we might expect the statement

```
A := L * B ;
```

to be a valid use of the types. This, of course, is unreasonable as it assumes that the language will have some knowledge of the semantics of the identifiers LENGTH and AREA. We can overcome this minor difficulty by defining a suitable function such as

```
function Times (L, R: LENGTH) return AREA is
begin
    return AREA (L * R) ;
end Times ;
```

which allows two lengths to be coerced into an area when they are multiplied together.

The third facility of Ada that allows the user to segment the data space is the subtype. A subtype does not create a separate type from the parent but restricts the values that objects of the subtype may take. For example:

```
subtype WEEKDAY is DAY range Monday..Friday ;
```

will restrict objects of subtype WEEKDAY to the values of type DAY between Monday and Friday inclusive. The important difference between derived types and subtypes is that the subtype does not create a new type, and therefore objects of type DAY and WEEKDAY above are type compatible. This may seem to be splitting hairs. How can two types be the same if they do not have exactly the same domain of values and set of operations on the values? We shall see later that the definition of 'same' with regard to type is quite a difficult one to resolve. For the present, it can be pointed out that with derived types we can have two types with exactly the same set of values and operations but which are still considered as separate types.

Indeed it is debatable whether a subtype and its parent are the same or not. The decision in Ada is influenced by whether a type error can be detected statically by a compiler or dynamically at run time. Consider the following example:

```
subtype SMALL_INTEGER is range 0..15 ;
First: INTEGER ;
Second: SMALL_INTEGER ;
```

The assignment

```
First := Second ;
```

will always be legal, whereas

```
Second := First ;
```

will be legal only if First has a value between 0 and 15. In general we cannot tell whether this will be a legal assignment until it is performed at run time when the value of First is known. When we use a derived type we wish the use of the objects always to be checked statically. With a subtype we wish objects of the subtype and the parent type, and indeed other subtypes of the parent, to be freely mixed until the checking can be done which, in the worst case, is when the program executes. This is the problem of when to perform type checking that was referred to earlier and will be expanded later.

The final part of the fine grain control in Ada type mechanism is the package. So far, we have seen how to extend and constrain the range of values a data object may take. In each case the set of operations available for the new data type was predefined. In order to have a fully flexible type mechanism it is necessary to have the ability to extend the set of operations as well as the set of values for a data type.

The Ada package facility is a rather powerful device that provides two separate mechanisms. The first is name control where the package acts rather like a declaration abstraction. A group of declarations can be grouped together in a package and then introduced whenever the package is used. The names are then visible in the package calling context (see Example 6.1).

The second major mechanism provided by the Ada package is to define an abstract data type. We have already discussed this in Chapters 3 and 5 but reintroduce it here in considerably more detail. Used as an abstract data type the package may or may not export the representation of the data type but will export the operations on the type. In Example 6.2 a package to create and define the operations 'add' and

```
package Wastebin_manager is
   procedure Put (Bin: User.ID ; Item: Mail_item.INSTANCE) ;
   procedure Retrieve (Bin: User.ID) ;
   procedure Clearout (Bin: User.ID) ;
   procedure List (Bin: User.ID) ;
end Wastebin_manager ;
```

Example 6.1   The waste-bin manager package.

```
package Comp is
   type COMPLEX is private ;
   function Create (A, B: REAL) return COMPLEX ;
   function Add (A, B: COMPLEX) return COMPLEX ;
   function Subtract (A, B: COMPLEX) return COMPLEX ;
private
   type COMPLEX is record
      R_part, I_part: REAL ;
   end record ;
end Comp ;

package body Comp is
   function Create (A, B: REAL) return COMPLEX is
   begin
      return (R_part => A, I_part => B) ;
   end Create ;

   function Add (A, B: COMPLEX) return COMPLEX is
   begin
      return (R_part => A.R_part + B.R_part,
              I_part => A.I_part + B.I_part) ;
   end Add ;

   function Subtract (A, B: COMPLEX) return COMPLEX is
   begin
      return (R_part => A.R_part - B.R_part,
              I_part => A.I_part - B.I_part) ;
   end Subtract ;
end Comp ;
```

Example 6.2   A complex number package.

'subtract' on complex numbers is given. The representation of the type COMPLEX for complex numbers is private so that the representation is not known outside the package itself (anything in the private part of the package specification is not visible outside the package). The operations Create, Add and Subtract are defined on the type and the names are visible outside the package. Thus we have a method of constructing new data types in terms of sets of values and sets of operations.

It is possible to regard both array and record data types as abstract data types defined by inbuilt packages. When an aggregate is declared the data type required is given a representation and a set of operations. The representation, for example, of an array, is not private and operations such as indexing are predefined. It is perhaps wise not to carry the analogy too far but comforting that nearly all the data types can be defined by one simple abstraction mechanism.

6.1.2 When is type checking performed?

A data type mechanism forces the user to face the issues of protection, programming discipline and life cycle costs when designing large programming systems. A very necessary part of the type mechanism which influences these issues is its ability to detect errors, and when this detection is performed. It is unforgivable to have a type mechanism that does not detect all type errors but the issue of when type checking is performed is not so clear cut. A balance has to be struck between the expressive power of the language and the need to detect errors as early as possible. This can be seen from the program segment:

```
declare
    N: INTEGER range 0..15 ;
begin
    Get (N) ; - - requires a run time check - -
    .
    .
    .
    N := True ; - - is illegal - -
end ;
```

In this we cannot check that the Get statement will receive a value in the range 0 to 15, or even worse that the value is an INTEGER at all until the program is executed. On the other hand, assigning the BOOLEAN value to the integer variable is always illegal and can be detected by the compiler. In the interests of reducing the operation and maintenance costs of a large system, it is sensible to do such checking by a static analysis.

It is a design feature of Ada that it is a strongly typed language. That is, all uses of data in programs can be checked by a compiler. There are a number of advantages to strong type checking. Detecting errors at compile time means that we shall be aware of such errors sooner than if they were discovered at run time. The mechanism is safer. Imagine the consternation of an airline pilot on being told there was a type error in the fuel monitoring system when the aeroplane is 30 000 feet in the sky and has perhaps run out of fuel. The situation is also critical when programs are used in embedded systems, such as in the control of nuclear power stations or military devices.

A second advantage of strong typing is that, since less run-time checking is required, the programs should be smaller and run faster. Code for run-time type checks is not necessary and therefore not generated. This factoring out of type errors from the produced code should lead to more efficient execution of Ada programs.

One aspect of strong typing which is often overlooked is that if the compiler can statically check the use of data types then so can anyone else reading the program. Thus it can be used as a form of self-description or program documentation. This ties in very neatly with one of the design aims of Ada – that the readability of programs is important even at the expense of some verbosity.

Ada provides a discipline for data types by enforcing the protection of separate types. The third aim of reduced life cycle costs is achieved by removing from the operation and maintenance phase of the cycle all type errors. The programs are more efficient, as are the programmers, since type errors are discovered earlier and validation costs are therefore reduced.

Strong typing has some disadvantages in that we cannot capture all checks statically and thus must consider them outside the type system. Hence the distinction between type and subtype. Some subtype checks can be made at compile time, but not all, whereas all of the type checks can be made. Also, as we shall see later, we cannot have data types as data objects since if they could be manipulated we could generate types at run time requiring a run-time check. Given that Ada is intended for use in embedded systems, the designers have reached a sensible compromise on what is checked by the compiler. The payoff is in safety and reduction of life cycle costs.

6.1.3   Type equivalence

A consequence of allowing programmers the facility to define their own types in a programming language is the problem of knowing when two types are equivalent. Two programmers working on the same project perhaps separated by thousands of miles in distance and several years in time, must have the ability to share types. More importantly they must also have the ability to avoid accidentally inventing the same one.

Consider, for example, the programmers wishing to invent a type to represent a sorted array of integers. In Ada they might write

type SORTED_ARRAY **is array** (INTEGER **range** <>) **of** INTEGER ;

If both programmers made this type declaration in separate parts of the program, then there is a need for a type rule to indicate whether the types are the same or not. That is, are objects created from these definitions of the same type?

One method of evaluating type equivalence, called structural equivalence, would evaluate the two types as the same. If the types have the same shape then, by structural equivalence, they are of the same type.

In Ada, the type equivalence mechanism is called name equivalence which means that for two types to be the same they must have the same name. Ironically this means that the above types would be different because, although they have the same name, the names are declared in different scopes and hence they are considered different. With name equivalence two objects have the same type only if their type names refer to the same type declaration.

It is a matter of some research interest as to whether structural equivalence or name equivalence is more appropriate in programming languages. In practice it makes little difference, although the above example highlights one problem of name equivalence in Ada in that two objects of the different array types are assignment incompatible. The designers of Ada obviously feel that name equivalence is more appropriate for the types of applications that the language is designed.

6.1.4   Are data types objects themselves?

Some programming languages allow the user to manipulate types as data objects themselves. There are some advantages to this. Consider, for example, a procedure to sort an array of elements of some type, T say. To perform this it is necessary for the type to be ordered and to have an operation < which will decide the ordering. Example 6.3 shows such a program. It is not written in Ada but something very like it. The program is given for comparision with the Ada solution provided later.

If this were an Ada procedure the type of Left, Right and A would be fixed at compile time. If we required a vector of REALs and a vector of INTEGERs to be sorted, then we would require two different procedures. A shorthand mechanism for just this is provided using the generic package defined in Example 6.4. Generics are discussed more fully in Chapter 8.

In Example 6.4 the data type is itself not an object, the generic merely being a shorthand method of providing the two versions of the sort procedure required. In order to use the generic it has to be

```
procedure Sort_array (Left, Right, A) is
begin
    if Left < Right then
        let V := A (Right) ; let I := Left ;
        let J := Pred (Right) ; let T := A (Right) ;
        while I < J loop
            while A (I) < V loop I := Succ (I) ; end loop ;
            while I < J and then V < A (J) loop
                J := Pred (J) ;
            end loop ;
            T := A (I) ; A (I) := A (J) ; A (J) := T ;
        end loop ;
        T := A (I) ; A (I) := A (Right) ; A (Right) := T ;
        Sort_array (Left, Pred (I), A) ;
        Sort_array (Succ (I), Right, A) ;
    end if ;
end Sort_array ;
```

Example 6.3   A polymorphic sort procedure.

instantiated. Every instantiation causes the compilation system to generate a specific version of the procedure. Different instantiations of the generic cause separate versions of the procedure to be generated. There is no notion of programming with a type 'type' here, which means that certain types of operation are unavailable to us by this approach. For example, it is impossible to read the type of the objects from a file followed by the objects themselves, and sort them. Thus, we cannot write a generalized file sort that is independent of the type of the objects in the file.

The Ada generic facility is a special form of polymorphism (Strachey, 1967) where different code is generated by the compiler for every possible type. It is possible for the Ada compiler to determine these types since they must be explicitly instantiated by the programmer. Another form of polymorphism is where the generic procedures all execute the same code. This is called parametric polymorphism and is found in the language ML (Milner, 1983). In both cases types are very definitely not data objects and cannot be manipulated in the same manner as data objects.

It is a matter of very active research interest as to whether we require languages that allow types themselves to be manipulated as data objects. Certainly such languages have greater expressive power than those without; but at some expense. In such languages it is often not

```
generic
   type VALUE is private ;
   type INDEX is (<>) ;
   type SORT_ARRAY is array (INDEX range <>) of VALUE ;
   with function "<" (L, R: VALUE) return BOOLEAN is <> ;
procedure Quicksort (Left, Right: INDEX ;
          A: in out SORT_ARRAY) is
begin
   if Left < Right then
      declare
         V: VALUE := A (Right) ;
         I: INDEX := Left ;
         J: INDEX := INDEX ' Pred (Right) ;
         T: VALUE ;
      begin
         while I < J loop
            while A (I) < V loop
               I := INDEX ' Succ (I) ;
            end loop ;
            while I < J and then V < A (J) loop
               J := INDEX ' Pred (J) ;
            end loop ;
            T := A (I) ; A (I) := A (J) ; A (J) := T ;
         end loop ;
         T := A (I) ; A (I) := A (Right) ; A (Right) := T ;
         Quicksort (Left, INDEX ' Pred (I), A) ;
         Quicksort (INDEX ' Succ (I), Right, A) ;
      end ;
   end if ;
end Quicksort ;
```

Example 6.4   An Ada generic sort procedure.

possible to check if a data object is being used correctly until it is actually used. Languages such as Pebble (Burstall and Lampson, 1984) allow types to be manipulated in order that system interfaces may be captured by the type system. For example, the type of the compiler itself or the binder mechanism can only be expressed in such a type system. Ada does not include such objects in its typed universe. However, most but not all of the expressive power of languages with data types as objects can be obtained by Ada generics. The Ada designers argue that it is much safer to check statically all uses of data.

6.1.5   What syntactic devices are used for types?

In any programming language with a type mechanism like Ada's, the designer is faced with the task of inventing a suitable syntactic form for types. In Ada types can be defined; for example:

    (Monday, Tuesday, Wednesday)

is a type definition. They can be declared:

    type ABC **is new** INTEGER ;

that is, given a name in a declaration. Types usually have names, but occasionally as a shorthand they can be anonymous. For example:

    A: **array** (1..6) **of** T ;

is short for

    type B **is** INTEGER ;
    subtype Ba **is** B **range** 1..6 ;
    type Baa **is array** (Ba **range** <>) **of** T ;
    A: Baa (1..6) ;

all of which can be confusing. Although the shorthand version is sometimes convenient, the presence of anonymous types can lead to some unexpected results. For example:

    A, B: **array** (1..6) **of** INTEGER ;

is short for

    A: **array** (1..6) **of** INTEGER ;
    B: **array** (1..6) **of** INTEGER ;

and means that A and B are of different types even although they look as if they are declared with the same type definition. The only solution to this is to insist that all types have names, which is tedious but leaves no doubt as to the meaning of the equivalence of two types in a name equivalence scheme.

Since the type system allows the introduction of new types, the syntax must accommodate the definition of new literals and operations for the type. We have already seen how to define new literals of an enumerated type; the main syntactic issue is the overloading of names of literals. For example:

    type COLOUR **is** (Red, Yellow, Blue, Green) ;
    type PRIMARY_COLOUR **is** (Red, Green, Blue) ;

defines two types with the common literals Red, Green and Blue. As long as there is no ambiguity in the context of their usage, then the literal names can be used freely. However, if a possibility of an ambiguity exists then the names can be extended to

    COLOUR ' (Red) and
    PRIMARY_COLOUR ' (Red)

---

procedure A ; – – subprogram specification declare A – –
procedure B **is**
begin

   .

  A ;   – – **call** A – –

   .

end B ;
procedure A **is**
begin

   .

  B ;   – – **call** B – –

   .

end A ;

Example 6.5   Declaration of mutually recursive procedures.

to distinguish them. Such an ambiguity might arise if we had two procedures with the same name defined on these types. For example:

```
procedure Paint (This: COLOUR) ;
procedure Paint (This: PRIMARY_COLOUR) ;
```

In this case Paint (Red) is ambiguous, whereas Paint (COLOUR ' (Red)) is not.

We shall see in detail in Section 6.2 how to define packages of operations on types, but it is perhaps interesting to note here how to define literals for private types. For example:

```
package Semaphore is
   type SEM is private ;
   Init: constant SEM ;
   procedure Wait (S: in out SEM) ;
   procedure Signal (S: in out SEM) ;
private
   type SEM is new INTEGER ;
   Init: constant SEM := 0 ;
end Semaphore ;
```

With this definition we can write

```
Buffer_control: Semaphore.SEM := Semaphore.Init ;
```

and later we can use an equality test such as

```
if Buffer_control = Semaphore.Init then...
```

Init is called a deferred constant in Ada but is in effect a method of defining a literal for the type SEM.

```
type NODE ; – – incomplete type definition – –
type LINK is access NODE ;

type NODE is record
    Value: INTEGER ;
    Left, Right: LINK ;
end record ;
```

Example 6.6   An incomplete record definition.

The final syntactic issue of a type system is how objects are declared. In Ada all declarations must precede the use of the object. This of course presents no problem except when definitions are mutually dependent, as can be the case with mutually recursive procedures or record type declarations. In both cases this can be overcome by using a sub-program specification or an incomplete type definition. An example of each is given in Examples 6.5 and 6.6.

All declarations for a block must precede the code for the block. It is illegal to use an object before it is initialized and the initialization can be done at the declaration. It is interesting to note that the designers of Ada did not force initialization of every object either implicitly, as they do for **access** types, or explicitly. The advantage of forced initialization is that it eliminates one possible source of error, that of the uninitialized variable. To force explicit initialization would probably mean allowing declarations to be mixed freely with statements in order to avoid senseless initializations. In that case declarations would only be made where the object is first used and initialized to the first value (Morrison, 1979). However, this is not possible in a language with **goto** statements as declarations may be skipped.

6.1.6   Type hierarchies

A type hierarchy exists where there is a general method of defining a group of types from which a particular type may be generated. The generated type inherits all or part of the properties of the general type, except where this is specifically excepted. Derived types and subtypes in Ada allow new types to be generated from others with a range of values or operations. Not so obvious type hierarchies are also present with discriminated types and generic packages with type substitution. Type hierarchies are important in modelling since they allow similar objects to be defined even though in particular instances these objects may be different.

The concept of inheritance was first seen for object-oriented programming in the language Simula and has become an important modelling technique, particularly in databases and artificial intelligence systems (Brachman, 1983). Inheritance is based on the notion of subtype where a particular type inherits attributes from its supertype. For example, we may have a type CAR which has some attributes such as engine, body, tyres, etc., and types such as RENAULT, JAGUAR, TOYOTA which inherit the attributes of CARs and add some of their own. Thus we can say that TOYOTA is a subtype of CAR since operations available on CARs are also available on TOYOTAs.

Inheritance can be single, where the attributes are derived from one supertype, or multiple where they may be inherited from many supertypes. For inheritence to be general it must be available for all types, and Cardelli (1984) has devised such a type system with multiple inheritance. The main issues of inheritance with regard to a type system are whether types may be modified to provide generalization, that is fewer attributes, or specialization (more attributes), and how this is integrated with the type system.

Ada has limited facilities for inheritance and it has been argued that it is not a true object-oriented programming language because of this lack. However, as we shall see later, derived types and packages together do give some form of inheritance.

6.2   Abstract data types and Ada packages

In designing and building large systems it is important to keep the task firmly under intellectual control. The process of ignoring non-essential detail to concentrate on the task in hand is called **abstraction**. The most familiar form of abstraction in programming languages is the procedure or subroutine which allows a collection of statements to be gathered together and given a name. The user needs only to know what the procedure does and not how it does it.

The style of programming developed using the procedure as the main abstraction mechanism is called **top-down functional decomposition** (Wirth, 1971). At any level in the analysis the inessential details of the lower levels may be ignored in order to completely understand the current level.

As well as facilities for abstracting over statements, a programming language requires methods for other abstractions, including abstractions over data types. Data type abstractions allow a style of programming called programming with abstract data types, or **object-oriented programming**, to be used. The system is decomposed into the the major data components which are defined by abstract data types. Procedural abstractions are then used to manipulate the abstract types. With each abstract data type the process is repeated by defining the abstract type in terms of other types, abstract or not, and using procedural abstraction to define the legal operations on the refined abstract types. This style of programming can only be effectively used in languages that have both procedural and data abstractions as well as an extensible type systems. In Ada, data type abstractions are supported by packages.

Given a powerful type mechanism such as Ada's it is possible to consider using programming methodologies other than functional decomposition. Object-oriented programming, originated from use of the languages Simula (Birtwistle *et al.*, 1973), Smalltalk (Goldberg and Robson, 1983) and Clu (Liskov *et al.*, 1974, 1977) among others and was first proposed by Parnas (Parnas, 1972). The technique is to consider any problem to be a manipulation of the data space. Since the method is based on abstraction, at any level in the refinement of the solution there will be abstract objects formed from abstract data types that will be realized at a lower level. An abstract data type is a specification of the domain of values for the type and the set of operations on the type. Thus the refinement process is not unlike functional decomposition, the main difference being the view of the system at any particular level as a view of the data objects. We have already discussed abstract data types and object-oriented design in Chapter 5, but we shall discuss it here in more detail since it is such an important and powerful modelling tool.

An abstract data type specifies a set of values and a set of operations for the type. This specification is published to the rest of the system so that objects of the abstract type may be created and manipulated. For any abstract data type the specification should enforce the minimum necessary visibility of the components of the data type. It must also be possible to hide the internal representation of the abstract data type if required. That is, the implementation of the type at a lower level should be hidden to avoid accidental or malicious misuse. Morris (1973) specified three ways in which a data object may be used in a manner not intended. They are:

1. **Alteration**. An object that involves references may be changed without use of the primitive functions provided for the purpose.

2. **Discovery**. The properties of an object may be explored without using the primitive functions.

3. **Impersonation**. An object, not intended to represent anything in particular, may be presented to a primitive function expecting an object representing something quite specific.

A major advantage of protecting and hiding the representation of a data object is that the representation may be altered without alteration to the published interface. New implementations may be tried without having to identify every use of the data in the system.

It should be noted, however that it is not always convenient to hide completely the representation of data objects, and therefore the language should allow hiding or not and should, if possible, support the functionally different aspects of specification and implementation of data types.

6.2.1   Ada packages

The package mechanism in Ada allows the user to define abstract data types. It is a powerful device and some care in programming style must be exercised to ensure that Morris' three evils of alteration, discovery and impersonation do not take place. Of course, the freedom in the package mechanism is there specifically to allow the user the flexibility of breaking one of the rules when it is convenient to do so.

The package of Ada acts more like an abstraction over declarations rather than type. A group of declarations may be gathered together, parameterized and given a name. Using the separate compilation facility the package (abstraction) may be used (called) wherever declarations are appropriate. Thus we have an abstraction mechanism for declarations.

As an example of this consider the following package which specifies the data type INTERVAL and functions to perform interval arithmetic on the objects:

```
package Interval_globals is
    type INTERVAL is record
        Inf, Sup: REAL ;
    end record ;
    function " + " (A, B: INTERVAL) return INTERVAL ;
        .
        .
        .
end Interval_globals ;
```

When the package definition is encountered the elaboration of the declarations makes all the package names available in the current scope. Thus the declaration

```
X: Interval_globals.INTERVAL := (0.0, 0.0) ;
```

would declare a variable X with the stated type. Notice, however, that the name is rather long-winded, and Ada offers a device, the **use** clause to overcome this difficulty. The equivalent definition could be made by

```
use Interval_globals ;
X: INTERVAL := (0.0, 0.0) ;
```

The **use** clause can be used in a declarative part of the program and simply allows the package name to be dropped from the full name. Of course, this may lead to two names that are the same being used for different definitions in the same scope. Ada makes a very sensible ruling on this name overloading which states that the shorthand notation may be used when there is no ambiguity as to the meaning of the name. Otherwise the full name must be used. In the above example package the function + only refers to an operation on objects of type INTERVAL. We refer to this rule as sensible since it allows us to define the package specification without worrying about the context in which the names will be used. We may, for example, use interval arithmetic and complex arithmetic in the same program segment, each having its own distinct operations with similar names, without concerning ourselves about such a combination when we specify the packages.

In the above example the representation of the type INTERVAL is completely open and not protected in any way. The user can create objects of type INTERVAL, assign values to them, interrogate them and even change their components by assignment. For example,

    X.Inf := 13.2 ;

would be a legal assignment. The representation of the data type can be altered (by assignment), discovered (by inspection) but not impersonated. The name equivalence rule of Ada does not allow impersonation of data types at all. There is no way in which anything other than an object of type INTERVAL can be passed to the function + defined in the package.

There is one important sense in which the Ada package acts more like an abstract data type than a declaration abstraction. This is where a new type is derived from one defined in the package. Normally derived types inherit all the values and operations of the parent type but not any additional sub-programs with parameters or results of the type. For example, with

    function Golf_day (D: DAY) **return** BOOLEAN ;
    type WORK_DAY **is new** DAY ;

the type WORK_DAY will not have the function Golf_day defined on it. When a type is defined in a package, the sub-programs with parameters or results of the type are considered operations on the type. Types derived from the package type therefore inherit all the operations of the package. With the package Interval_globals defined above, if we have

    type NEW_INTERVAL **is new** INTERVAL ;

then the + operation will be defined on the new type NEW_INTERVAL.

It is a matter of design as to whether the user wishes to publish the representation of the type or not. Almost certainly there will be cases where it is reasonable to inspect the internal values, but it is nearly always unsafe to allow alteration.

To hide the representation of the type and make it a true abstract data type, we must use the private facility of Ada. A private type can be declared, assigned, tested for equality or inequality and be used by any of the operations in the defining package. Consider the following package specification for defining a picture data type in Ada. The specification is based on the Outline system (Morrison, 1982), which allows line drawing in an infinite two-dimensional space. Operations on pictures include joining the last point of one picture to the first point of a second by a straight line, including one picture in another and the mathematical transformations of shifting, scaling and rotation. Pictures

```
package Picture is
  type PIC is private ;
  function Point (A, B: REAL) return PIC ;
  function " + " (A, B: PIC) return PIC ;
  function "&" (A, B: PIC) return PIC ;
  function Rotate (A: PIC ; B: REAL) return PIC ;
  function Scale (A: PIC ; B, C: REAL) return PIC ;
  function Shift (A: PIC ; B, C: REAL) return PIC ;
  procedure Draw (A: PIC) ;
private
  type PICT ; – – defined in the package body – –
  type PIC is access PICT ;
end Picture ;
```

Example 6.7   Outline graphics package specification.

are built from sub-pictures and the system is lazy in that the pictures are constructed as a data structure before they are drawn. The package in Example 6.7 specifies the user interface.

There are a number of points of interest in this package. When a type is made private only its name and not its representation is published. The declarations in the private part of the package specification are hidden from the outside world. Notice that using an **access** type to represent the **private** type in the package means that the declaration of its representation can be delayed until the package body. It is perhaps a criticism of Ada that in general the package specification makes the user specify the representation of the private type. The whole point of having a separate specification is that the representation can be ignored as a level of detail in the implementation. It is, of course, understandable from the compiler's point of view in that code generation would be impossible from a specification that did not give the representation. However, it is not desirable from every other point of view. The use of the above coding technique, that is using an **access** type, overcomes this problem. With the **private** declaration types cannot be impersonated, or have their internal representation discovered or altered.

When a type is made **limited private** then the only operations available on the type outside the package are the ability to declare objects of the type and to apply the operations provided for the type by the package. These are the primitive functions of Morris (1973), and a **limited private** type would be used when we do not wish assignment of the abstract objects or when predefined equality is not appropriate. Of course, equality may be defined explicitly in the package. The rules for limited types have a number of consequences, as Morris stated:

1. An explicit initialization is not allowed in an object declaration if the type of the object is limited.
2. A default expression is not allowed in a component declaration if the type of the record component is limited.
3. An explicit initial value is not allowed in an allocator if the designated type is limited.
4. A generic formal parameter of mode **in** must not be a limited type.

Notice the rules do not exclude a formal parameter of a limited type having a default expression.

As an example of a limited type consider the problem of a symbol table in a compiler. The main reason for using an abstract data type is to hide the representation of the object at the specification level of abstraction. To illustrate this we shall give two methods of implementing the symbol table, one using a binary tree and the other a linked list. The important point is that for both implementations the package specification that is published to the world is the same.

The problem of the symbol table is to store identifiers and their addresses and release this information when requested. This is, of course, a simplified view of symbol tables, but the problem is analogous to any other dictionary system. The package will define a type for identifiers and addresses, a type to represent the symbol table, and the procedures lookup and insert to search the table and to insert entries. The specification of the package is given in Example 6.8.

```
package Symbol is
    type IDENT is new STRING (1..20) ;
    type ADDRESS is new INTEGER ;
    type TABLE is limited private ;
    procedure Create (Result: out TABLE) ;
    procedure Insert (Key: IDENT ; Addr: ADDRESS ;
                        S_table: in out TABLE) ;
    procedure Lookup (Key: IDENT ; Addr: out ADDRESS ;
                        S_table: TABLE) ;
    Duplicate_name, Not_in_table: exception ;
private
    type TABLE_NODE ;
    type TABLE is access TABLE_NODE ;
end Symbol ;
```

Example 6.8   A symbol-table package specification.

By making the representation of the symbol table **limited private** we completely constrain it to use the operations defined in the package. We now have the ability to alter the representation without changing the specification. The two implementations of the symbol tables are quite different, as can be seen from the package bodies. First the linked-list version is given in Example 6.9, and then the binary-free version is as shown in Example 6.10.

```
package body Symbol is
  type TABLE_NODE is record
    Name: IDENT ;
    Add : ADDRESS ;
    Link: TABLE ;
  end record ;
  procedure Create (Result: out TABLE) is
  begin
    Result := null ;
  end Create ;
  procedure Insert (Key: IDENT ; Addr: ADDRESS ;
                    S_table: in out TABLE) is
  begin
    if S_table = null or else Key < S_table.Name then
      S_table := new TABLE_NODE ' (Key, Addr, S_table) ;
    elsif Key = S_table.Name then
      raise Duplicate_name ;
    else
      Insert (Key, Addr, S_table.Link) ;
    end if ;
  end Insert ;
  procedure Lookup (Key: IDENT ; Addr: out ADDRESS ;
                    S_table: TABLE) is
  begin
    if S_table = null or else Key < S_table.Name then
      raise Not_in_table ;
    elsif Key = S_table.Name then
      Addr := S_table.Add ;
    else
      Lookup (Key,Addr, S_table.Link) ;
    end if ;
  end Lookup ;
end Symbol ;
```

Example 6.9 A linked-list symbol-table package body.

```
package body Symbol is
   type TABLE_NODE is record
      Name: IDENT ;
      Add : ADDRESS ;
      Left, Right: TABLE ;
   end record ;

   procedure Create (Result: out TABLE) is
   begin
      Result := null ;
   end Create ;

   procedure Insert (Key: IDENT ; Addr: ADDRESS ;
                     S_table: in out TABLE) is
   begin
      if S_table = null then
         S_table := new TABLE_NODE ' (Key, Addr, null, null) ;
      elsif Key = S_table.Name then
         raise Duplicate_name ;
      elsif Key < S_table.Name then
         Insert (Key, Addr, S_table.Left) ;
      else
         Insert (Key, Addr, S_table.Right) ;
      end if ;
   end Insert ;

   procedure Lookup (Key: IDENT ; Addr: out ADDRESS ;
                     S_table: TABLE) is
      Temp: TABLE := S_table ;
   begin
      while Temp /= null and then Key /= Temp.Name loop
         if Key < Temp.Name then
            Temp := Temp.Left ;
         else
            Temp := Temp.Right ;
         end if ;
      end loop ;
      if Temp = null then
         raise Not_in_table ;
      else
         Addr := Temp.Add ;
      end if ;
   end Lookup ;
end Symbol ;
```

Example 6.10   A binary-tree symbol-table package body.

By keeping the type TABLE **limited private** we guarantee that no impersonation, no alteration and no discovery of the internal structure of the type can take place. Thus the three conditions for an abstract data type specified by Morris are met, and this is therefore available as a possible programming method to the Ada programmer.

When a data type is defined by encapsulation in a package, only the set of operations is exported to the outside world. This abstract view of the type represents the values by operations on the type. The procedure Insert transforms the initial value into another in the possibly infinite domain of values for the type TABLE. Notice that the infinite domain does not come from the operations but the nature of the composite types in Ada, of which there are infinitely many. Viewing the types in the above abstract manner leads to the expression 'abstract data type'.

6.2.2 The electronic mail system

In Chapter 3 we undertook the high-level design of an electronic mail system. We are now in a position to fill in some of the details that were left at that time. We do this by writing the package bodies for some of the abstract data types. Because of lack of space we shall only take one of these types – the Mail_list package given as Example 3.10. We encourage the reader to adopt the same technique in writing the others.

The mail list abstract data type is specified by the Mail_list package given in Example 6.11.

```
package Mail_list is
    type INSTANCE is private ;
    type ERROR_STATUS is (Ok, Error) ;
    procedure Head (List: INSTANCE ; M: out Mail_item.INSTANCE ;
            Status: out ERROR_STATUS ) ;
    function Tail (List: INSTANCE) return INSTANCE ;
    function Add (List: INSTANCE ; Item: Mail_item.INSTANCE)
            return INSTANCE ;
    function Create return INSTANCE ;
    function Is_empty (List: INSTANCE) return BOOLEAN ;
private
    type MAIL_ELEMENT ;
    type INSTANCE is access MAIL_ELEMENT ;
end Mail_list ;
```

Example 6.11 The Mail_list package specification.

```ada
package body Mail_list is
  type MAIL_ELEMENT is record
    Item: Mail_item.INSTANCE ;
    Next: INSTANCE ;
  end record ;
  procedure Head (List: INSTANCE ; M: out Mail_item.INSTANCE ;
                  Status: out ERROR_STATUS ) is
  begin
    if List = null then
      Status := Error ;
    else
      Status := Ok ; M := List.Item ;
    end if ;
  end Head ;
  function Tail (List: INSTANCE) return INSTANCE is
  begin
    if List = null then
      return List ;
    else
      return List.Next ;
    end if ;
  end Tail ;
  function Add (List: INSTANCE ; Item: Mail_item.INSTANCE)
                return INSTANCE is
    Result: INSTANCE   ;
  begin
    Result := new MAIL_ELEMENT ' (Item, List) ;
    return Result ;
  end Add ;
  function Create return INSTANCE is
  begin
    return null ;
  end Create ;
  function Is_empty (List: INSTANCE) return BOOLEAN is
  begin
    return List = null ;
  end Is_empty ;
end Mail_list ;
```

Example 6.12   The Mail_list package body.

Notice how we again use an **access** type in order that we do not have to specify the actual representation until the package body. One possible implementation of the package is given as Example 6.12.

We shall return to this example in Chapter 8 and show how it may be generalized by using generics.

6.3 Summary

We have outlined the issues on which type systems in programming languages vary. Two key goals in the design philosophy of Ada determine the nature of its type system (the types available are summarized in Figure 6.1). The first is that Ada is primarily designed for use in embedded systems where it is unsafe to allow errors to occur when the system is live. The second is the need to provide data abstraction facilities.

The first of these aims leads to a strong typing regime where all uses of types are resolved at compile time. It is entirely possible to design a type system that may be used to enforce all the constraints on the use of data (Jones and Liskov, 1978), even those of sharing and order of use (Campbell and Habberman, 1974). While Ada does not address all of these problems, it nevertheless encapsulates most of them in its type and subtype mechanism. When a constraint is not checkable at compile time it is implemented by a subtype, forcing the user to be aware of the inherent lack of safety. A generalized type scheme cannot be anything but dynamic in nature; but Ada very neatly distinguishes what can be checked at compile time, and is therefore safe in some sense, from what cannot. A consequence of this is that types are static and are not data objects themselves.

The aim to provide data abstraction facilities leads directly to

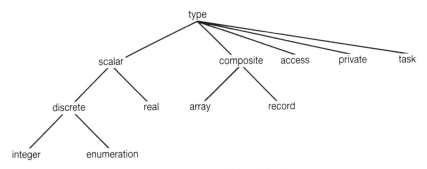

Figure 6.1   A summary of the Ada data types.

enumeration types, and packages. Enumeration types allow types to be specified as sets of values and when combined with packages may be used to provide new operations on these values. Derived types allow further decomposition and fine control of the data space. However,the data types are still finite in nature. Composite types and access types give us the ability to create a type with an infinite number of values in its domain.

The power and flexibility of the Ada type mechanism is derived directly from the integration of the above type facilities.

6.4   Further reading

Wirth, N. (1971). 'Program development by stepwise refinement' *Communications of the ACM*, **14**, (4), 221–227.

Parnas, D.L. (1972). 'A technique for software module specification with examples' *Communications of the ACM*, **15**, (5), 330–336.

> These papers are the seminal papers on top-down and object-oriented programming. They are worth reading for more than just historical purposes.

Milner, R. (1979). 'A theory of type polymorphism in programming' *JACM*, **26**, (4), 704–818.

> This is the seminal paper on polymorphism and describes the mechanism and an algorithm that may be used for type checking.

Cardelli, L. (1984). 'A semantics of multiple inheritence' In *Lecture Notes in Computer Science*, Vol. 173, Springer-Verlag, 51–67.

> The issue of inheritence in programming language has been highlighted by the database and AI community. This paper describes how multiple inheritence may be incorporated into a suitable type scheme.

Chapter 7 **Programming Style**

It is a major design goal of Ada that programs written in the language should be easy to read. This recognizes that programs are read more often than they are written, and that the first step in maintaining a fragment of a large collection of software is to understand the existing code, which involves reading the program as well as the documentation. A major cause of the so-called 'software crisis', which can be seen in the operation and maintenance costs in the life cycle of systems, is the inability to maintain large software systems cheaply. One contributing factor to this cost is the lack of readability in the programs being maintained.

The designers of Ada recognized the problem of readability in programs and set about trying to solve the problem. The difficulty is that, given any reasonably powerful notation that is convenient to use, it is almost always possible to write obscurely in the notation. Giving programmers the power to express themselves freely also gives them the power to write incomprehensibly.

There is a balance between expressive power and safety in programming notations. For example, most computer scientists would agree that APL (Iverson, 1962), is a very powerful notation. However, it is terse to a point of being so unreadable that even the author of a program can often have difficulty in deciphering it. Other examples of this terseness can be seen in Chapter 6, where the polymorphic sort routine (Example 6.3), which has no mention of type, is a very powerful notation, but is difficult to read. Experiments using predicate calculus (logic systems) and lambda calculus (functional systems) as programming languages have also run into this difficulty. The main problem with these notations is that they have little or no redundancy in them. This means that, no matter what is written down, it is almost always a legal program. However, is it the one that was intended?

Notations are not new, and neither is the problem of achieving the balance between power and safety. The problem is one for the large system only, since for small notational descriptions the users can overcome the inherent lack of safety in a terse notation by keeping it within their intellectual grip. As an example of this, mathematical and logical proofs are rarely long since the level of confidence in the proof diminishes with its length. If we regard a program as a proof of the specification of the system, we can see that terse notations, which may be adequate for small programs, are often totally unsuitable for large systems.

Achieving a notation is easier said than done. The designers of Ada have provided abstraction mechanisms, sub-programs and packages, which along with generics help overcome the problems of scale. Redundancy in the syntax to clearly delimit the scope of some statement, the forcing of declarations at certain parts of the program, and the ability to write comments all lean towards safety. However, it is quite clear from the definition of Ada that the programmer will have to exercise a great deal of self-control on how the program is written and laid out, if the final version is to be readable and maintainable.

Unfortunately programmers often find redundancy in syntax and a preferred style of layout a distraction in the creative process of writing software. The programmer's skill is often regarded as how well a particular algorithm is implemented in terms of speed and space efficiency, rather than the total efficiency of the product life cycle. Some re-education of both programming and management staff is usually required to achieve readability. It should be a maxim in any organization that sloppiness in program layout is sloppiness in program documentation and will cause a reduction in the total efficiency of the product. It should be further stated that program documentation is required throughout the life cycle of the system and should never be added as an afterthought.

In this chapter we look at programming style and practice with a view to achieving better software products. The aim is to highlight the problems of programming style and to suggest a number of solutions.

7.1   Program layout

Some problems of program documentation can be alleviated by the use of syntax-directed editors and prettyprinters. A syntax-directed editor reduces the number of keystrokes required to input or change a program segment. It achieves this by using a shorthand version of each keyword. The keyword can never be changed incorrectly and layout based on the keyword can be enforced. By ensuring that the only manner in which programs can be entered or altered is by the use of a syntax-directed editor, standard forms of layout can be enforced without too much effort. We shall suggest such a standard for Ada later. Prettyprinters tidy up a program to a preferred style. Before releasing a segment of code it is first passed through the prettyprinter to establish the preferred style.

There are some problems in readability that syntax-directed editors cannot solve, and the programmer must take on the responsibility for these. Let us start with the choice of identifiers. Identifiers in Ada start with a letter and can be made up of letters, digits and single underlines. The case of the letters is not significant, but the position of the underline character is. There is no restriction on the length of an identifier. It seems almost too obvious to say that identifiers should be chosen to reflect the real world object they are modelling. To model a light switch we could use the name Light_switch and for a bus wheel we could use Bus_wheel, and so on. The point is that identifiers should be *meaningful*. With no restriction on length, plus the fact that by using packages the scope of the name is reduced to its minimum visibility, thus reducing the chance of a duplicate, not using meaningful identifiers constitutes criminal negligence on the part of the programmer. A good test in the selection of names is for the programmer to ask another what the code does and is used for: from the identifiers the second programmer should be able to make a good guess at the application. Bad use of identifiers can easily be spotted. Consider Example 7.1.

This is a very simple function, and no doubt everyone could eventually work out what it is doing. The point is that the use of identifiers gives no help in this process where it so easily could. If this program is read many times then the cost of deciphering it is multiplied many times. Another version of the same function is shown in Example 7.2. Although this is easily recognizable as exactly the same program,

```ada
generic
   type A is private ;
   type B is (<>) ;
   type C is array (B range <>) of A ;
   with function ">" (AA, BB: A) return BOOLEAN is <> ;
function D (E: C) return B is
   F: A := E (E ' First) ;
   G: B := E ' First ;
begin
   for I in E ' range loop
      if F > E (I) then
         F := E (I) ;
         G := I ;
      end if ;
   end loop ;
   return G ;
end ;
```

Example 7.1   An example of the use of bad identifiers.

for very little cost – that of choosing and typing more appropriate identifiers – the program has become more readable and understandable and therefore a better software component.

```
generic
   type ELEMENT is private ;
   type INDEX is (<>) ;
   type VECTOR is array (INDEX range <>) of ELEMENT ;
   with function ">" (Aa, Bb: ELEMENT) return BOOLEAN is <> ;
function Find_index_of_smallest_element (A: VECTOR)
                 return INDEX is
   Low_element: ELEMENT := A (A ' First) ;
   Low_index: INDEX := A ' First ;
begin
   for I in A ' range loop
      if Low_element > A (I) then
         Low_element := A (I) ;
         Low_index := I ;
      end if ;
   end loop ;
   return Low_index ;
end Find_index_of_smallest_element ;
```

Example 7.2   An example of use of good identifiers.

The sensible use of names is particularly important where the scope of the name extends beyond its immediate surrounding unit. We shall see in Chapter 8 that this can happen in packages, records, inner scope levels, entry declarations, procedure parameters, generic parameters and discriminant specifications. For example:

Mail_item.INSTANCE

is the name of the type of a mail item declared in the package Mail_item. Care must be taken with names where the name does not have an obvious meaning in the surrounding scope.

The second obvious point in making programs more readable is in the use of comments. A comment in Ada starts with two hyphens and continues to the end of the line. Of course, comments can be on lines by themselves. Just as identifiers can be used badly, so can comments. Consider

J := J + 1   – – add one to J

This is a bad comment because it is obvious what the statement does and the comment is merely noise in the system to distract the reader. A more useful rule of thumb for comments is to use them to describe the units that have already been defined in the program. Thus we might use a comment to describe what a procedure or package does rather than how it does it. Or we might use it to describe a formula or method that is not easily discernible from the code. In Chapter 4 we saw how comments could usefully be used for specifications. The comments should enhance the documentation of the code and not merely duplicate it.

One final problem with comments is that they often get out of step with the code over the lifetime of the system. It is part of the discipline of good programming to update the comments when the code is altered. The use of a code and comment control system could help to prompt the programmer here; but, as with identifiers, the final responsibility rests with the programmer.

7.1.1 Syntax-directed formatters

We mentioned earlier that it would be possible to enforce a strategy for program layout by using a syntax-directed editor through which programs are initially entered and altered. To ensure that the layout is uniform no other method of entering or updating the source should be allowed. A syntax-directed editor must have a built-in set of rules for program layout, and we propose the following. Indeed the layout we propose by example is the one used for the layout of programs in this book. They are not meant to be the only such set of rules and can be modified to suit individual tastes. Over a whole project, however, only one set of rules should be used.

1. Reserved words should be lower case, type identifiers in upper case and all other uses of identifiers start with an upper case letter followed by the rest in lower case. This makes it easy for the reader to distinguish between reserved words, type identifiers and others. The only real danger is with duplicates. The compiler will soon find these if there are any. An example of the different use of names can be seen in the following function specification:

    function Empty (The_user: User.ID) **return** Mail_list.INSTANCE ;

2. Procedures should be laid out with the specification on a line by itself, followed by declarations indented by tab characters, **begin** on its own line, statements indented by tabs and the **end** followed by the procedure identifier. This is shown informally by:

    procedure Swap (I, J: INTEGER ; A: **in out** SORT_ARRAY) **is**
        Temp: INTEGER := A (J) ;
    begin
        A (J) := A (I) ;

```
   A (I) := Temp ;
end Swap ;
```

Functions can be laid out in a similar manner. For example:

```
function Sign (N: INTEGER) return INTEGER is
begin
   if N > 0 then
      return 1 ;
   elsif N = 0 then
      return 0 ;
   else
      return -1 ;
   end if ;
end Sign ;
```

Similarly for packages:

```
package Comp is
   type COMPLEX is private ;
   function Create (A,B: REAL) return COMPLEX ;
   function Add (A,B: COMPLEX) return COMPLEX ;
   function Subtract (A,B: COMPLEX) return COMPLEX ;
private
   type COMPLEX is record
      R_part,I_part: REAL ;
   end record ;
end Comp ;
```

3. and generics:

```
generic
   type ELEMENT is private ;
   type INDEX is (<>) ;
   type SWAP_ARRAY is array (INDEX range <>) of ELEMENT ;
   procedure General_swap (I, J: INDEX ; A: in out SWAP_ARRAY) is
   Temp: ELEMENT := A (J) ;
begin
   A (J) := A (I) ;
   A (I) := Temp ;
end General_swap ;
```

The effect of the above formats is to highlight the different sections of code. The user can then easily see to which part of a program a particular statement belongs. To make this workable it should of course be extended to all Ada constructs.

We continue in the knowledge that a law of diminishing returns applies to specifying rules too precisely, since most users will wish to adapt them to their own taste. The important points are in the use of indentation, tab symbols, to delimit declaration sequences, statement sequences, visible and invisible sections of the package.

This would, of course, be extended for generics and exceptions. An important part of the above is always repeating the sub-program or package name at the end.

4. Blocks:

```
Level_1: declare
   I: INTEGER := 32 ;
   J: INTEGER := 1 ;
begin
   .
   Level_2:
   declare
      I: INTEGER := J ;
      J: INTEGER := Level_1.J ;
   begin
      - - The names I and Level_2.I, J and Level_2.J
      - - refer to the same object respectively
      - - the outer objects can be referred to by the
      - - names Level_1.I, Level_1.J
   end Level_2 ;
end Level_1 ;
```

5. **if** statements:

```
if a < 3 then
   a := 3 ;
elsif a > 4 then
   a := 4 ;
else
   a := 0 ;
end if ;
```

6. **case** statements:

```
case Day is
   when Monday..Friday =>
      Go_to_work ;
   when Saturday =>
      Play ;
   when Sunday =>
      Rest ;
end case ;
```

7. Loops:

```
for I in 2..N loop
   Factorial := Factorial * I ;
end loop ;
while I < N loop
   Factorial := Factorial * I ;
   I := I + 1 ;
end loop ;
```

```
loop
    Text_io.Get (Char) ;
    exit when Char = ASCII.EOT ;
    Text_io.Put (Char) ;
end loop ;
```

7. Record types:

```
type CELL is record
    Name: STRING (20) ;
    Addr: INTEGER ;
    Next: LINK ;
end record ;
```

There are a number of other layout issues and the solutions we have chosen are:

- Surround operators by a space either side.
- Put a space after a colon, but not before.
- Put a space before a left parenthesis and after a right one.
- Put a space after a comment.
- If two spaces are adjacent they may be made into one.

These rules are not meant to form an exhaustive set for Ada programs and can be broken in sensible cases, such as fitting on to a line of text. Rather they are intended to give the reader the idea that consistency of layout can be achieved at very little cost. The benefits of consistent layout are in the increased readability of the programs. Since the above proposed rules are used in the layout of programs in this book, readers can judge for themselves whether the resultant programs are readable or not.

Finally, Example 7.3 shows a badly laid out program with bad identifiers. It is left to the reader to work out what it does.

7.2   Programming practice

As with program layout, it is wise to establish some ground rules for the programming style that the members of the programming team will use. The rules should achieve a compromise between portability, efficiency and maintainability of the systems depending on the aims of the overall project. This subject has been extensively documented and could easily fill a book on its own. However, specifying how the programmer may program may be self-defeating if the quality of programs produced is reduced by the programmer being distracted from programming by the programming practice rules. Therefore the rules must be sensible in that a good programmer would choose the given method naturally if otherwise

```
task C is
entry A(N:inINTEGER);
entry S(N:inINTEGER);
entry I(N:outINTEGER);
end;
task body C is
Total: INTEGER := 0 ;
begin
  loop
    select
        accept A(N:in INTEGER)do
Total:=Total+N;
        end;
    or
        accept S(N:inINTEGER)do
Total:=Total-N;
end;
or
accept I(N:outINTEGER)do
N:=Total;
end I;
end select ;
end loop ;
end;
```

Example 7.3   Bad programming style (A well-laid-out version of
this program is given in Chapter 9).

unconstrained. Any particular rule that does not fall into this category
must be fully justified in terms of other overall system benefits, such as
greater efficiency or portability.

Of course it is best to instil good programming habits into
programmers when they are trained. However, even given that all
the programmers in a team are well trained and disciplined, it is a foolish
project leader who does not set up checks for irregularities in style. This
can be done by a mixture of code inspections and mechanical aids.

The advantage of having a set preferred style is that the programs
can be tuned to some criteria such as portability. A hidden benefit
is that the programmers in the team are more interchangeable since the
switching time is less when the new program style is consistent with the
old. Thus programmers leaving the project or being absent for long
periods of time have a less disastrous effect on the overall production.

These advantages may or may not be illusory. It is up to the system manager to decide for a particular system. Here we have broken down the Ada language into a number of components and hint at some aspects of good and bad programs. We do not think it is possible to get a definitive document for this, and it is up to the system manager to tailor these ideas to a particular system. Rather than state any hard and fast rules for programming practice, we shall make some recommend-ations that highlight the decisions that the project manager may wish to make. Readers are referred to Nissen and Wallis (1984) for a more comprehensive coverage of this topic.

7.2.1   Types and declarations

We have already discussed how to model a real-world situation in Ada. The type system offers us a protection mechanism and allows us to decompose the problem space into interactions between objects. The use of the object is protected by its type and we should ensure that we use the type system in full when manipulating these objects.

The first recommendation that we make is that separate types should be used for logically distinct objects, and the types should be defined as precisely as possible. This ensures that there is no accidental misuse of data objects via a type misunderstanding. If the types sometimes share values, then they can be derived from each other or a common ancestor. Defining the type as precisely as possible refers more to derived types or subtypes than to enumeration types, where it is more natural to be precise. For example, in a graphics system it is usually desirable to keep a drawing cursor and a text cursor. Furthermore we may wish the x and y coordinates to be quite separate types, although derived, since a combination of values may be required. Objects to represent the cursors could be defined as in Example 7.4. This ensures that the two objects can never be mixed in an expression.

In declarations, static forms should be used rather than dynamic forms wherever possible. Consider the following:

```
Get (N) ;
declare
    New_value: INTEGER range 0..N := 15 ;
    .
    .
    .
```

The initialization of the object New_value requires a run-time range check. Furthermore, the compiler does not know the value of N and has to generate more expensive code to deal with the range check than is often strictly necessary. For example:

```
New_value: INTEGER range 0..10 := 15 ;
```

is obviously illegal and can be detected by the compiler, whereas the

```
type TEXT_X_CO_ORDINATE is new INTEGER range 0..79 ;
type TEXT_Y_CO_ORDINATE is new INTEGER range 0..23 ;
type PLOT_X_CO_ORDINATE is new INTEGER range 0..511 ;
type PLOT_Y_CO_ORDINATE is new INTEGER range 0..255 ;

type TEXT_CURSOR_TYPE is record
   X: TEXT_X_CO_ORDINATE ;
   Y: TEXT_Y_CO_ORDINATE ;
end record ;

type PLOT_CURSOR_TYPE is record
   X: PLOT_X_CO_ORDINATE ;
   Y: PLOT_Y_CO_ORDINATE ;
end record ;

Text_cursor: TEXT_CURSOR_TYPE ;
Plot_cursor: PLOT_CURSOR_TYPE ;
```

Example 7.4   Text and plot coordinate types.

previous declaration of New_value could not. Thus errors are detected earlier in the static form and more efficient code can be produced. It is, however, not always possible to be both as precise as necessary and to use static forms, since using a static form would necessitate the type being less precisely defined. In Chapter 3 we also gave an example of where the dynamic form was necessary. This was with reference to configuration management, where we wished to configure dynamically according to the environment. However, in general static forms are safer than dynamic ones.

When declaring an object it always makes sense to initialize it if possible. This eliminates one type of error completely: namely the use of an uninitialized object and the possibility of writing nonsense like

```
M, N: INTEGER ;
begin
   M := N + 2 ;
   .
   .
   .
```

More complicated versions of this can be seen when uninitialized objects are used as **in** or **in out** parameters to sub-programs. Of course, in a language like Ada, it does not always make sense to initialize an object on declaration. This is because all declarations in a block are evaluated before any of the statements. An initial value that depends on the execution of one or more of the statements cannot therefore be calculated. To enforce an initial value would mean an arbitrary value being chosen, which is almost as bad as none at all. However, where possible, objects should be initialized when declared.

In well-written programs objects that never change their value should be declared as constant. Only those that require to be updated need to be variable. Some programming language designers have suggested that the default for objects should be constant rather than variable. It is another form of data protection – that of guarding against alterations – and it is perhaps a pity that the designers of Ada did not see fit to extend the constancy concept to all updatable objects such as fields of records and elements of arrays, as suggested by Gunn and Morrison (1979).

Finally, with regard to declarations, names of constants should be used in preference to literal values in the program. Consider the following segment of code:

```
Dictionary_limit: constant := 10000 ;
No_of_words: INTEGER ;
begin
    .
    .
    .
    Space_left_in_dictionary := Dictionary_limit – No_of_words ;
```

This last statement is more portable and maintainable, in that it is easier to change the value of the constants, than

```
    Space_left_in_dictionary := 10000 – No_of_words ;
```

since it is easier to find all the instances of literals when they are in the declaration part of the block.

7.2.2   Sub-programs

Procedures and functions are the abstraction mechanisms over program code available to the Ada programmer. The function is an abstraction mechanism over expressions and the procedure an abstraction over statements. Together with packages, which are abstractions over data objects, the three mechanisms provide the tools necessary to control the complexity of large programs. This being the case they are ideal units of program for annotation with comments. In any form of program construction, be it functional decomposition or object-orientated, the units of program are sub-programs and packages or their equivalent. Since the language designer has already seen fit to use these as units of program construction, it seems appropriate to use them as units of program documentation as well. In this way there is a greater chance that program and documentation may be kept in phase.

As a general rule a description of each sub-program should be given with its declaration. This description should include:

- the problem that the sub-program solves, including the method if necessary,

- the role of the formal parameters and non-local objects (especially side effects) used,
- exceptions raised that may have to be dealt with outside the sub-program.

An example of such a description with a procedure declaration is given as Example 7.5.

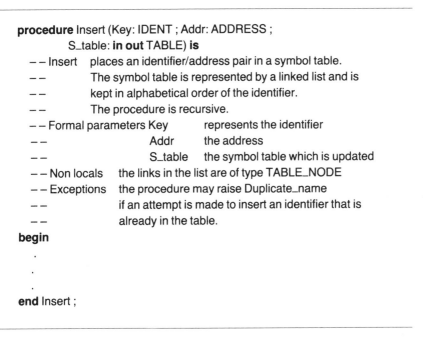

```
procedure Insert (Key: IDENT ; Addr: ADDRESS ;
         S_table: in out TABLE) is
  -- Insert    places an identifier/address pair in a symbol table.
  --           The symbol table is represented by a linked list and is
  --           kept in alphabetical order of the identifier.
  --           The procedure is recursive.
  -- Formal parameters Key      represents the identifier
  --                   Addr      the address
  --                   S_table   the symbol table which is updated
  -- Non locals   the links in the list are of type TABLE_NODE
  -- Exceptions   the procedure may raise Duplicate_name
  --              if an attempt is made to insert an identifier that is
  --              already in the table.
begin
  .
  .
  .
end Insert ;
```

Example 7.5   An annotated symbol-table procedure.

Notice that the commented description of the sub-program does not say very much about the program code. It is assumed that the code is well-written and will adequately document the method or algorithm used. The description tells what is being done and the code tells how it is done. Indeed, in Chapter 4 we saw how we could be very precise by making formal specifications into comments.

The problem with descriptions like the above, as with all comments, is that they get out of phase with the code. The above example has a rather ritualized style, and it would be a simple matter to provide a software tool to encourage the programmer to update the comment when the code is altered. However, care has to be exercised with these descriptions. A bad description or a wrong one constitutes noise in the system and makes it more difficult to maintain rather than less. We have an all-or-nothing situation where the comments are either all up to date and correct or are useless otherwise. That is, the user either trusts all the comments or none of them.

When programming with Ada the use of side effects should be avoided wherever possible. Updating a global variable directly in a sub-programs constitutes a source of potential programming error. Often it can be avoided by passing the global variable as a parameter to the procedure in a suitable mode. For example:

```
Stack_pointer: INTEGER ;
procedure Increment is
begin
    Stack_pointer := Stack_pointer + 1 ;
end Increment ;
```

would probably be better written as

```
procedure Increment (Value: in out INTEGER) is
begin
    Value := Value + 1 ;
end Increment ;
```

since it is more general-purpose and avoids a side effect.

With object-oriented programming it is not always possible or advisable to avoid side effects. Consider the random-number package given as Example 7.6. To avoid the side effect it *could* be written as in Example 7.7. However, the first solution is safer since the user of the package can have no influence over the stream of random numbers generated, whereas the second solution depends on the user never impersonating the value given to the function Next_random_number. Since the user has a stream of random numbers, one can always be substituted for another.

```
package Random_number is
    function Generate return INTEGER ;
end Random_number ;

package body Random_number is
    Random_value: INTEGER range 0..8191:= 2111 ;
    function Generate return INTEGER is
    begin
        Random_value := (519 * Random_value) mod 8192 ;
        return Random_value ;
    end Generate ;
end Random_number ;
```

Example 7.6   A random-number package.

```
package Random is
    type RAND is private ;
    Seed: constant RAND ;
    function Next_random_number (Value: RAND) return RAND ;
private
    type RAND is new INTEGER range 0..8191 ;
    Seed: constant RAND:= 2111 ;
end Random ;

package body Random is
    function Next_random_number (Value: RAND) return RAND is
    begin
        return (519 * Value) mod 8192 ;
    end Next_random_number ;
end Random ;
```

Example 7.7   Another random-number package.

In object-oriented programming the use of a side effect is sometimes necessary to maintain the state of the object while hiding it. It is of course a controlled side effect, since the only operations that can be performed on the hidden object are those of the primitive functions which collaborate with each other in maintaining the object. All other kinds of side effect are not as acceptable.

A related problem to side effects is the aliasing of data objects. An alias occurs in programming when a data object has two different names. This may happen in a number of ways, but the important point is that if the value of the object is altered through one name then the view of the object through the other name is also changed. An example of an alias is given in Example 7.8.

```
procedure Incorrect_program is
    procedure Alias_count (A,B: in out INTEGER) is
    begin
        A := 32 ;
        B := 106 ;
    end Alias_count ;
begin
    Alias_count (Count,Count) ;
end Incorrect_program ;
```

Example 7.8   An example of variable aliasing.

This program is in error since after the call of **procedure** Alias_count the value of Count could be 32 or 106, since the order of parameter updating is not specified by the language. Aliasing can be more subtle than this, especially where **access** types are involved, but should be avoided if at all possible since it reduces the understandability of programs.

The size of sub-programs should be kept relatively small. As we have said before, the sub-program is the main abstraction facility in Ada. The purpose of using abstractions is that the programmer or reader of the program can keep the complexity of the present part of the system under their intellectual control. Sub-programs form these units of program, and it follows that if they get too big themselves then they will be difficult to master. We suggest that a sub-program that covers more than one page or a screen on a VDU will cause problems in seeing all at once. It also turns out that this is a reasonable amount to master at once, and we suggest that this is a good maximum size for sub-programs.

Functions are abstractions over expressions and should therefore never be used to alter global variables since, in general, expressions cannot. It is for this reason that the designers of Ada restricted the parameter modes to **in** for functions. Procedures, on the other hand, are abstractions over statements which may manipulate the abstract store. Thus parameters may be **in**, **out** or **in out**. Thus we should use function sub-programs when we wish to calculate a value based on input parameters, and procedures otherwise.

7.2.3 Packages

Packages have two main uses in Ada. The first is to control the use of names (or visibility of objects), and the second is to implement abstract data types. In Chapter 6 we saw that there were three problems in implementing abstract data types – that of alteration, discovery and impersonation. To avoid these problems we suggested that packages be used to provide a restricted view of objects. This ties in well with the first use of packages for name control. Packages should therefore provide only the minimum necessary visibility to data objects.

The visibility of the objects within a package will depend on the use for which the package was designed. A package that is merely a named collection of data objects or types will usually not require information hiding. Example 7.9 shows a package that allows names to be grouped together in a program. Notice that, since there are no variables declared in the package, the package acts like a declaration abstraction. The one important difference is that no matter how many different **use** clauses are employed, objects declared of the same name in the package will be of the same type. The package Standard is an example of the use of the above type of package.

Packages used in the above manner can easily become cluttered. To

```
package Week_days is
   type WEEK_DAY is (Monday,Tuesday,Wednesday,Thursday,
                     Friday,Saturday,Sunday) ;
   subtype WORK_DAY is WEEK_DAY range Monday..Friday ;
   subtype WEEKEND is WEEK_DAY range Saturday..Sunday ;
   subtype MIDWEEK is WEEK_DAY range Tuesday..Thursday ;
end Week_days ;
```

Example 7.9 A package of types.

avoid this, only items that are logically related to each other should
be placed in the same package. This is most important with abstract data
types. When a package is used to implement an abstract data type there
are subtle variations on how that may be done.

One possibility is to use the package to provide access to one fixed
data object. In this the user is only provided with functions and
procedures which manipulate the object. The user does not have access
to the object itself and therefore cannot alter it without using one of the
primitive functions provided. An example of such a package is given in
Example 7.10. All that the user can do here is to find the next random
number in the sequence. The user is not allowed access to the random
value itself.

Alternatively, the package may be used to implement one abstract
data type. Many objects of the type may be created, but as in the
language CLU, (Liskov *et al.*, 1974) only one type of object can be created

```
package Random_number is
   function Generate return INTEGER ;
end Random_number ;

package body Random_number is
   Random_value: INTEGER range 0..8191:= 2111 ;
   function Generate return INTEGER is
   begin
      Random_value := (519 * Random_value) mod 8192 ;
      return Random_value ;
   end Generate ;
end Random_number ;
```

Example 7.10 A protected value in a package.

```
package Comp is
  type COMPLEX is private ;
  function Create (A,B: REAL) return COMPLEX ;
  function Add (A,B: COMPLEX) return COMPLEX ;
  function Subtract (A,B: COMPLEX) return COMPLEX ;
private
  type COMPLEX is record
    R_part,I_part: REAL ;
  end record ;
end Comp ;
```

Example 7.11 An abstract data type.

from the package. An example of such a package is given in Example 7.11. Again the package only contains related objects. The functions defined in the package all relate to type COMPLEX. This kind of package allows objects to be hidden, but the type of the object to be exported to the outside world. Thus the objects can be integrated into the type system without detailing the actual type.

The third use of the package is a combination of the above two. More than one abstract data type may be defined in the package. This power must not be misused; and therefore only when we wish two or more abstract data types to be distinct, but closely related should we use the package in this manner. An example is given in Example 7.12.

Irrespective of how the package is used, it is important that only logically related items are placed together. If data abstraction is to work as a programming methodology, it is important to identify clearly the separate abstractions. If they are mixed up in one package then problems of readability, maintenance and separate compilation will occur. It will also be difficult to write separate software tools if the abstractions are not clearly identifiable.

Returning to the visibility of data objects, Ada provides other hiding

```
package Morse is
  type DOT is ( ... ) ;
  type DASH is ( ... ) ;
  function " + " (A: DOT,B: DASH) return INTEGER ;
end Morse ;
```

Example 7.12 A package of mixed types and operations.

mechanisms. Names that are local to the packages should be declared in the package body. This means that types, objects, procedures, functions and other packages that we do not wish to export at all should be confined to the package body. Private types should be used to restrict the type of access given to objects that are exported. A good rule of thumb here is that all objects should be **private** unless specifically excepted. When programming with abstract data types confidence in the solution is increased if you know that the object being abstracted over cannot be altered 'on the fly'. Quite often this means using **limited private** types especially if we wish to redefine equality.

Constancy is another form of this type of protection and objects should be made constant wherever possible.

7.2.4 Control structures

There is a rich collection of control structures in Ada. These include **if**, **case**, **loop**, **exceptions**, **goto**, rendezvous and procedure call. All of these are considered safe constructs, except **goto** statements which should not be used. Well-structured programs do not contain **goto** statements. (A **goto** statement that jumps backwards in a program forms a loop). The problem, of course, is not that there is one well-understood **goto** statement in the program, but that through time others are added, causing overlapping loops and a sequence structure that is very hard to unravel. To understand programs written in Ada we have to understand their sequency. **Goto** complicates the sequencing. There are two other problems with **goto** statements. The first is that it sometimes inhibits the compiler's ability to generate efficient code. The second is that given the current state of the science, program verification is made more difficult.

The argument often put forward in favour of **goto** is in premature exit conditions from loops and from deeply nested blocks. Ada provides for both of these with exit statements and exceptions which, again, should always be used in preference to **goto**.

7.2.5 Exceptions

Exceptions can be used to simplify the logic of a program and are essential in event-driven programming. However, exception identifiers are bound by the dynamic evaluation of the program and are therefore unlike any other identifiers in Ada. Care should be taken with this, and exception handlers should be written so that each logical program section deals with its own exceptions. The advantage of this is that tidying up can be done at each logical level. Such tidying up may include closing files, giving reasonable values to **out** and **in out** parameters, and generally making the layer consistent with the rest of the system. We do not wish an inconsistent return to generate exceptions at lower levels endlessly.

```
package Symbol_table is
  type IDENT is new STRING (1..20) ;
  type ADDRESS is new INTEGER ;
  type TABLE is limited private ;
  procedure Create (Result: out TABLE) ;
  procedure Insert (Key: IDENT ; Addr: ADDRESS ;
                        S_table: in out TABLE) ;
  procedure Lookup (Key: IDENT ; Addr: out ADDRESS ;
                        S_table: TABLE) ;
  Duplicate_name, Not_in_table: exception ;
private
  type TABLE_NODE ;
  type TABLE is access TABLE_NODE ;
end Symbol_table ;

package body Symbol_table is
  type TABLE_NODE is record
    Name: IDENT ;
    Add : ADDRESS ;
    Link: TABLE ;
  end record ;

  procedure Create (Result: out TABLE) is
  begin
    Result := null ;
  end Create ;
```

(cont.)

Example 7.13   An example of exceptions.

Note that exceptions that cannot be dealt with at one level should be converted into exceptions for a lower-level handler.

A correct use of exceptions is given in Example 7.13, and we return to this subject in Chapter 10.

7.3 Summary

We have set out a number of recommendations for the layout and style of Ada programs. We do not suggest that these recommendations form a complete guide to programming with Ada. Rather we have included them in the book to give both programmers and managers an insight into the problem. Different criteria for programming style, such as portability which is covered in Chapter 12, may tailor the manner in which programs are written for a particular application. This we would accept and realize that the contents of this chapter may not be universally applicable. One thing is clear, however. That is, there are very good reasons for enforcing

```
procedure Insert (Key: IDENT ; Addr: ADDRESS ;
                  S_table: in out TABLE) is
begin
  if S_table = null or else Key < S_table.Name then
    S_table := new TABLE_NODE ' (Key, Addr, S_table) ;
  elsif Key = S_table.Name then
    raise Duplicate_name ;
  else
    Insert (Key, Addr, S_table.Link) ;
  end if ;
end Insert ;
procedure Lookup (Key: IDENT ; Addr: out ADDRESS ;
                  S_table: TABLE) is
begin
  if S_table = null or else Key < S_table.Name then
    raise Not_in_table ;
  elsif Key = S_table.Name then
    Addr := S_table.Add ;
  else
    Lookup (Key,Addr, S_table.Link) ;
  end if ;
end Lookup ;
end Symbol_table ;
```

Example 7.13 (cont.)

a preferred style on programmers. These centre about the adaptability and reuse of program components and on the interchangability of programmers themselves. If one preferred style is adopted, then programs and programmers may be exchanged with less disruption than if there is not a consistent style theme in the project.

In this chapter we have concentrated on programming types in Ada. The layout of Ada programs for readability and maintenance and programming practice using various aspects of Ada were discussed in detail.

7.4   Further reading

Nissen, J. and Wallis, P. (1984). *Portability and Style in Ada*. Cambridge: Cambridge University Press.

This is a major book on programming style in Ada. It contains many suggestions for good and bad programming practice.

Chapter 8 Large System Programming

The notion of programming in the large rather than programming in the small recognizes the fact that there are problems of scale associated with large software systems. These problems are concerned with the complexity of the large systems, where the systems developers can no longer keep the total problem within their intellectual grip. Indeed it is usually the case with large software systems that no one person completely understands the total system. This in itself leads to problems of who resolves difficulties when parts of the system are found to be in conflict.

Building and maintaining a large system is a difficult task. We have seen how to use abstraction in order to control the complexity of the system, but the abstraction mechanisms alone are not sufficient. Ada recognizes this problem and provides a number of facilities, which may be used along with its abstraction mechanisms, to combat complexity. These facilities are not different from abstraction, but rather support the mechanisms so that they can be used effectively to build and maintain large systems.

The first of these facilities is the provision of a library of units and for the separate compilation of program units. Programs may be built and maintained incrementally, allowing the system to be constructed and tested in parts. The facilities provide support for both top-down and bottom-up approaches to system development, and indeed envisage both methods being used together. This incremental system development is the usual method for constructing large systems since it is unlikely that the total system would be written all at once. The designers of Ada have combined this need with the need to change bits of the system incrementally and have provided a uniform solution. Indeed, they envisage a software tools industry where system components may be marketed for use in other systems. The reuse of Ada components is discussed in Chapter 12.

Another major problem in large systems is in the management of the name space. Accidental, but erroneous use of names must be detected. Facilities to hide names, overload names and rename objects are also required and are not usually available in programming languages.

Finally, the effort required to build and maintain a system is some function of the number of lines of code it contains. Although this is not the only factor in the total cost, it seems reasonable to assume for any given language that a reduction in the size of the code will also give a reduction in its costs. Packages and sub-programs help with this problem, and Ada augments these with generics. The generic is a template for similar sub-programs or packages. The generic is written once and the particular form of the generic generated when required. In Chapter 6 we saw the use of a generic for a general-purpose sort routine, and generic specifications are used extensively in Chapter 5 in the discussion of object-oriented programming. The use of generics shortens the total source code size and therefore reduces the cost of building and maintaining the system.

In this chapter we look at the facilities of Ada that are specially designed for programming in the large. These include incremental system development and separate compilation, name space management and generics. We have touched on some of these aspects of Ada in earlier chapters, but cover them in more detail here with special reference to programming in the large.

8.1   Incremental system development

Most languages in the past have ignored the need for incremental system development. FORTRAN, for all its deficiencies, is a notable exception and recognizes that large systems are made up of components that can be separately compiled. Large numbers of FORTRAN subroutine packages have been built and implemented on many sites, and some of the success of FORTRAN as opposed to Algol60, for example, can be attributed directly to this facility.

Ada also recognizes this need and supports both a top-down and bottom-up method of program development. To understand how this may be done we must look at the action of the compiler. Parts of systems that are submitted to the compiler are called compilation units. The compilation units of a program belong to a program library. It is outside the scope of this book to discuss the organization of program libraries,except to say that they exist and that everything the compiler processes will be placed in the program library.

Compilation units themselves can be one of two types – a library unit or a secondary unit. Library units are those with unique names in the library,whereas secondary units are separately compiled sections of library units or other secondary units. This recursive definition of the secondary unit allows the compilation units to be decomposed to any level. That is, there is a flat structure of library units within the library from which a tree of secondary units may hang. The syntax given in the language reference manual may help here (Figure 8.1).

```
compilation ::= {compilation_unit}

compilation_unit ::= context_clause library_unit |
                     context_clause secondary_unit

library_unit ::= subprogram_declaration | package_declaration |
                 generic_declaration | generic_instantiation |
                 subprogram_body

secondary_unit ::= library_unit_body | subunit

library_unit_body ::= subprogram_body | package_body
```

Figure 8.1   The syntax of compilation units.

From the syntax we can see that library units, which must have unique names, may be sub-program or package declarations or their generic form or a sub-program body. The bodies of these library units can also be compiled separately and constitute part of the original library unit. Thus we compose programs from sub-programs and packages at the top level. This is equivalent to bottom-up construction and is often used with software tool sets. We shall study later how sub-units are used in top-down program construction.

All compilation units must have unique names so that the compiler can combine the units with one another. This means that operators cannot be separately compiled unless they are given a unique name and redefined with a **renames** clause. Overloaded names are not allowed as library unit names. However, the effect of overloaded names can be obtained by renaming two distinct library units so that the user sees them as the same name.

Readers may have noticed the possible ambiguity with regard to sub-program bodies in the above syntax. They are interpreted as secondary units if the program library already contains their names and are regarded as providing the body. Otherwise they are interpreted as library units where the body is included. This allows a sub-program specification such as

procedure Insert (Key: IDENT ; Addr: ADDRESS ; S_table: TABLE) ;

to be compiled separately from its body, or that the whole sub-program can be compiled in one.

8.1.1   Context clauses

The Ada compiler provides the facilities to decompose large systems into sections that may be compiled separately. It also provides a method of constructing systems out of the separately compiled units. These units in turn must specify the context in which they operate.

For bottom-up construction of programs we can imagine a library of component parts which may have been written by many people. These components can be combined using **with** clauses. Notice, however, that the **with** clause can only be used at the outermost declarative level and can only name library units. An example of a **with** clause is given in Example 8.1.

```
with Text_IO ;
procedure Read_stream is
    .
    .
    .
end Read_stream ;
```

Example 8.1   An example of a **with** clause.

This specifies that the procedure Read_stream can operate with the names of the package Text_IO available to it. More than one library unit may be specified in the **with** clause. For example:

```
with Text_IO, Stream_text ;
procedure Write_stream is
    .
    .
    .
end Write_stream ;
```

8.1.2   An example of compilation units

In Example 8.2 the procedure Colours contains the package Primary_colours and the function Previous_colour.

To illustrate how this program may be constructed in a bottom-up manner, we assume that package Primary is a library unit compiled as in Example 8.3.

Notice that the package specification is the library unit that has its name in the library and that the package body is a secondary unit, which, although it may be separately compiled, depends on the specification in the library. The body is part of the compilation tree whose root is the library unit (the specification). It should also be noted

```
procedure Colours is
  package Primary is
    type COLOUR is (Red, Yellow, Blue) ;
    function Get_next_colour (C: COLOUR) return COLOUR ;
  end Primary ;

  D: Primary.COLOUR := Primary.COLOUR ' First ;

  package body Primary is
    function Get_next_colour (C: COLOUR) return COLOUR is
    begin
      if C = COLOUR ' Last then
        return COLOUR ' First ;
      else
        return COLOUR ' Succ (C) ;
      end if ;
    end Get_next_colour ;
  end Primary ;

  function Previous_colour (C: Primary.COLOUR)
                            return Primary.COLOUR is
  begin
    return Primary.Get_next_colour (Primary.Get_next_colour (C)) ;
  end Previous_colour ;
begin
  .
  D := Previous_colour (D) ;
  .
end Colours ;
```

Example 8.2   The procedure Colours.

that, unlike sub-program bodies, package bodies may not be library units on their own.

The function   Previous_colour is also assumed to be a library unit compiled as in Example 8.4. Since the function uses another in the package Primary_colours, it must be compiled after it, and must make use of a **with** clause to set its context. Notice that the function is dependent on the package specification (library unit) and not the body.

Finally the remains of the original procedure may be compiled in its context. This is given in Example 8.5.

Thus we now have as library units a package, Primary, a function, Previous_colour and a procedure, Colours. This example illustrates how to

```
package Primary is
  type COLOUR is (Red, Yellow, Blue) ;
  function Get_next_colour (C: COLOUR) return COLOUR ;
end Primary ;

package body Primary is
  function Get_next_colour (C: COLOUR) return COLOUR is
  begin
    if C = COLOUR ' Last then
      return COLOUR ' First ;
    else
      return COLOUR ' Succ (C) ;
    end if ;
  end Get_next_colour ;
end Primary ;
```

Example 8.3   The library unit Primary.

construct a program from library units. The technique is most suitable when a library of components is being used to construct programs. The components are often referred to as tools and the library as a software tool-kit.

A compilation unit should only mention in a **with** clause those library units which it uses directly. Thus if compilation unit A requires library unit B which uses library unit C, the A should only mention B leaving B to mention C. This allows greater flexibility for recompilation, as we shall see later.

```
with Primary ;
function Previous_colour (C: Primary.COLOUR)
                          return Primary.COLOUR is
begin
  return Primary.Get_next_colour (Primary.Get_next_colour (C)) ;
end Previous_colour ;
```

Example 8.4   The library unit Previous_colour.

```
with Primary, Previous_colour ;
procedure Colours is
   D: Primary.COLOUR := Primary.COLOUR ' First ;
begin
   .
   D := Previous_colour (D) ;
   .
end Colours ;
```

Example 8.5   The separate compilation of the main body.

8.1.3   Top-down program construction

Library units may be decomposed into sub-units as opposed to being
glued together with other library units. This style of program
development is top-down since the user starts with the top unit and
decomposes it. Sub-units of library units or other sub-units may be
defined and compiled separately. This is done by leaving a body stub in
place of the unit and allows the user to decompose the program from the
top. Body stubs may only be used for sub-program, package and task
bodies.

Consider again the Mail_list package given in Example 6.11. Example
8.6 now shows the package, and Example 8.7 shows how it may be
compiled.

Thus we have specified that the package body is to be compiled
separately. This may be done as in Example 8.8.

Now we specify the sub-unit dependencies, right back to the library
root and those internal procedures that are to be further decomposed
(see Example 8.9).

Each sub-unit mentions the name of its parent in the **separate** clause.
The name of the parent starts with the library unit and includes all
the intermediate sub-unit names. The only restriction on the name is that
it must be unique in the tree of names. Thus two sub-units of different
parents may have the same name since they will appear in different places
in the tree.

8.1.4   Order of compilation

To understand program construction from compilation units we must
understand the rules of compilation. We have seen how to construct
programs from the bottom-up and from the top-down but have not
considered what happens if one component is replaced. When the system

```ada
with Mail_item ;
procedure Main is
  package Mail_list is
    type INSTANCE is private ;
    type ERROR_STATUS is (Ok, Error) ;
    procedure Head (List: INSTANCE ;
          M: out Mail_item.INSTANCE ; Status: out ERROR_STATUS ) ;
    function Tail (List: INSTANCE) return INSTANCE ;
    function Add (List: INSTANCE ; Item: Mail_item.INSTANCE)
                  return INSTANCE ;
    function Create return INSTANCE ;
    function Is_empty (List: INSTANCE) return BOOLEAN ;
  private
    type MAIL_ELEMENT ;
    type INSTANCE is access MAIL_ELEMENT ;
  end Mail_list ;
  package body Mail_list is
    type MAIL_ELEMENT is record
      Item: Mail_item.INSTANCE ;
      Next: INSTANCE ;
    end record ;
    procedure Head (List: INSTANCE ;
        M: out Mail_item.INSTANCE ; Status: out ERROR_STATUS ) is
    begin
      if List = null then
        Status := Error ;
      else
        Status := Ok ; M := List.Item ;
      end if ;
    end Head ;

    function Tail (List: INSTANCE) return INSTANCE is
    begin
      if List = null then
        return List ;
      else
        return List.Next ;
      end if ;
    end Tail ;

    function Add (List: INSTANCE ;
      Item: Mail_item.INSTANCE) return INSTANCE is
      Result: INSTANCE ;
```

(cont.)

Example 8.6 The Mail_list package.

```ada
begin
   Result := new MAIL_ELEMENT ' (Item, List) ;
   return Result ;
end Add ;

function Create return INSTANCE is
begin
   return null ;
end Create ;

function Is_empty (List: INSTANCE) return BOOLEAN is
begin
   return List = null ;
end Is_empty ;
end Mail_list ;
begin
   null ;
end Main ;
```

Example 8.6(cont.)

```ada
with Mail_item ;
procedure Main is
   package Mail_list is
      type INSTANCE is private ;
      type ERROR_STATUS is (Ok, Error) ;
      procedure Head (List: INSTANCE ;
            M: out Mail_item.INSTANCE ; Status: out ERROR_STATUS ) ;
      function Tail (List: INSTANCE) return INSTANCE ;
      function Add (List: INSTANCE ; Item: Mail_item.INSTANCE)
                  return INSTANCE ;
      function Create return INSTANCE ;
      function Is_empty (List: INSTANCE) return BOOLEAN ;
   private
      type MAIL_ELEMENT ;
      type INSTANCE is access MAIL_ELEMENT ;
   end Mail_list ;

   package body Mail_list is separate ;
begin
   null ;
end Main ;
```

Example 8.7   Separate compilation of the Mail_list body.

```
separate (Main)
package body Mail_list is
   type MAIL_ELEMENT is record
      Item: Mail_item.INSTANCE ;
      Next: INSTANCE ;
   end record ;

   procedure Head (List: INSTANCE ;
                    M: out Mail_item.INSTANCE ;
                    Status: out ERROR_STATUS ) is separate ;
   function Tail (List: INSTANCE) return INSTANCE is separate ;
   function Add (List: INSTANCE ; Item: Mail_item.INSTANCE)
                    return INSTANCE is separate ;
   function Create return INSTANCE is separate ;
   function Is_empty (List: INSTANCE)
                    return BOOLEAN is separate ;
   end Mail_list ;
```

Example 8.8   The Mail_list package body.

is operational we may have to install updates and the compilation system must support this.

There is a very simple rule that governs the order in which programs are compiled in Ada. It states that any unit must be compiled after any other on which it depends. Thus:

1. A unit must be compiled after all library units named in its context clause.

2. A secondary unit must be compiled after the corresponding library unit in which it is specified.

3. A sub-unit must be compiled after its parent.

This defines a partial ordering for compilation, but has some disadvantages. For example, if a package specification is recompiled then so must be the package body, even although it is not altered. The same is true for all sub-units of library units and may cause considerable recompilation. However, the advantage of the system is that it is simple to understand and to automate.

We can now see that both the top-down and bottom-up methods of program construction would be used in the building and maintenance of a large system. Careful thought has to be put into the design of the system of how the maintenance will operate in order to minimize the disturbance caused by updating a particular unit. If this is ill-considered then the overheads of recompilation may become unacceptable.

```
separate (Main.Mail_list)
procedure Head (List: INSTANCE ; M: out Mail_item.INSTANCE ;
                  Status: out ERROR_STATUS ) is
begin
   if List = null then
      Status := Error ;
   else
      Status := Ok ; M := List.Item ;
   end if ;
end Head ;

separate (Main.Mail_list)
function Tail (List: INSTANCE) return INSTANCE is
begin
   if List = null then
      return List ;
   else
      return List.Next ;
   end if ;
end Tail ;

separate (Main.Mail_list)
function Add (List: INSTANCE ;
              Item: Mail_item.INSTANCE) return INSTANCE is
              Result: INSTANCE ;
begin
   Result := new MAIL_ELEMENT ' (Item, List) ;
   return Result ;
end Add ;

separate (Main.Mail_list)
function Create return INSTANCE is
begin
   return null ;
end Create ;

separate (Main.Mail_list)
function Is_empty (List: INSTANCE) return BOOLEAN is
begin
   return List = null ;
end Is_empty ;
```

Example 8.9   The separate compilation of the Mail_list functions.

8.2   Name space management

Another major problem of large systems is keeping control of the names that are used in the programs. We have already seen that in order to compile units into a library, they must have unique names. This ensures that there is no confusion over what name a compilation unit refers to. Thus one problem of naming is solved. However, there are others. We should remember that we wish to apply the principle of minimum visibility to names so that we can strictly control access to the objects the names denote. To understand how this can be done in Ada we must look at the rules for overloading names, renaming objects and the rules for the scope and the visibility of names.

8.2.1   Scope and visibility

Ada is essentially a block-structured language and the scope and visibility rules for names follow this block structure. Ada defines declarative regions and a name declared in such a region is in scope from its declaration to the end of the region. A block is such a region:

```
declare
    I: INTEGER := 0 ;
    J: INTEGER := 16 ;
begin
    .
end ;
```

When we exit from the block the names disappear. Notice that the name is not visible during its own declaration to avoid recursive declarations like

```
declare
    I: INTEGER := I ;
    .
```

In Ada's terminology the declarations are elaborated and then the statements in the block are executed. Furthermore the declarations are elaborated one at a time, linearly in Ada's parlance. This means that blocks such as

```
declare
    I: INTEGER := 32 ;
    J: INTEGER := I ;
begin
    .
end ;
```

are correct since I is in scope and elaborated when the declaration of J is elaborated.

```
declare
   I: INTEGER := 0 ;
   J: INTEGER := I ;
begin
   .
   declare
      I: INTEGER := J ; -- redefines I and sets it to old J
      J: INTEGER := I ; -- redefines J and sets it to new I
   begin
      .
   end ;
   -- old I and J visible again
end ;
```

Example 8.10 Redefining names in inner blocks.

The block structure of Ada is recursive in nature and we may have blocks within blocks. An inner block may redeclare a name, and in this case it is said that the outer name is no longer visible. Again notice the terminology. The scope of the name is the area of program throughout which the object exists. In that scope the name is visible unless it is redefined by an inner block. In Example 8.10 the inner declarations of I and J hide the old ones. However, the old ones are still in scope and are available if required. To make them available, we must label the blocks, use the dot notation and concatenate the block label and the object name. This ensures a unique name (see Example 8.11).

Sub-programs also form declarative regions, and the nesting of sub-programs brings the same problems as the nesting of blocks. The solutions are similar, which is just what we would expect in a well-designed language (see Example 8.12).

This notation also applies to operators. In Example 8.13, note the slightly different syntax. Also, "+" were defined inside a block B it could be referred to as B."+", but on application of the function we would have to use the prefix form rather than the infix form. For example:

J : = B."+" (C,D);

The linear elaboration of declarations in Ada causes difficulties with mutually recursive definitions. For sub-programs we can write a sub-program specification. This given in Example 8.14.

This overcomes the problem of requiring A to be declared when B

```
Level_1:
declare
  I: INTEGER := 32 ;
  J: INTEGER := 1 ;
begin

  .
  Level_2:
  declare
    I: INTEGER := J ;
    J: INTEGER := Level_1.J ;
  begin
    - - The names I and Level_2.I, J and Level_2.J
    - - refer to the same object respectively
    - - the outer objects can be referred to by the
    - - names Level_1.I, Level_1.J
  end Level_2 ;
end Level_1 ;
```

Example 8.11   Using redefined objects in blocks.

```
procedure Level_1 is
  I: INTEGER := 32 ;
  J: INTEGER := 1 ;
begin

  .
  procedure Level_2 is
    I: INTEGER := J ;
    J: INTEGER := Level_1.J ;
  begin
    - - The names I and Level_2.I, J and Level_2.J
    - - refer to the same object respectively
    - - the outer objects can be referred to by the
    - - names Level_1.I, Level_1.J
  end Level_2 ;
end Level_1 ;
```

Example 8.12   Using redefined objects in sub-programs.

```
function "+" (A,B: COMPLEX) return COMPLEX is
  I: INTEGER ;
begin
  .
  declare
    I: INTEGER := "+".I ;
  begin
    .
  end ;
end ;
```

Example 8.13   Using redefined objects in operators.

is elaborated and requiring B to be declared when A is elaborated. The use of specifications is more general than this, and we have already seen it used to specify sub-programs in packages that are defined in the package body.

Another mutually recursive definition can occur with **access** types. Consider Example 8.15. The elaboration of the incomplete type definition creates the type, thus allowing the recursive definition. One disadvantage of the partial definition of sub-programs can be seen in Example 8.16 which is obviously in error.

For sub-programs the scope of the parameter names is the same as

```
procedure A ( . . . ) ;   – – Declaration of A – –
procedure B ( . . . ) is   – – Declaration of B – –
begin
  .
  A ( . . . ) ;
  .
end B ;
procedure A ( . . . ) is   – – Body of A – –
begin
  .
  B ( . . . ) ;
  .
end A ;
```

Example 8.14   An example of mutually recursive procedures.

```
type CELL ; – – This is an incomplete type definition – –
type LINK is access CELL ;
type CELL is record
   Name: STRING (20) ;
   Addr: INTEGER ;
   Next: LINK ;
end record ;
```

Example 8.15   An incomplete type definition.

the scope of the sub-program name itself. This allows sub-programs to be called using named rather than positional parameters. Note, however, that the parameter name does not hide any name in the immediate declarative region and is unique in that it can only be used in the sub-program call from which it can be identified.

Packages are regarded as declarative regions in Ada. If there is a separate specification and body of a package, then both parts are considered to be the same declarative region. This means that names defined in the specification may not be redefined in the outermost level of the body. Of course, defining a body of a sub-program whose specification is given in the package specification is taken as the completion of the definition.

There are various ways in which the names declared in a package can be seen and hidden. The names declared in the package body are only in scope to the end of the package. For these the package acts like a block. Names declared in the private part of the specification are in scope for the private part and the package body. Names declared in the visible part of the package are in scope in the package and in the surrounding declarative region. Notice that if packages are nested then

```
function One return INTEGER ;
A: INTEGER:= One ;
function One return INTEGER is
begin
   return A ;
end One ;
```

Example 8.16   An erroneous set of declarations.

```
declare
    package Outer is
        package Inner is
            A: INTEGER ;
        end Inner ;
    end Outer ;
    C: INTEGER ;
begin
    C := Outer.Inner.A ;
end ;
```

Example 8.17   The visibility of names in packages.

the inner package names can be seen at two outer levels (see Example 8.17). To avoid the use of the dot notation we could have:

use Outer ; **use** Inner ;

or

use Outer,Outer.Inner ;

but not

use Outer,Inner ;

since the name Inner is not available without the dot notation until after the **use** clause declaring Outer.

Allowing the scope of names to extend beyond their immediate declarative region causes a problem of hiding names similar to those that occurred with nested scopes. With a **use** clause it is possible to cause two names which are the same, homographs in Ada's terminology, to appear at the same time. For example, two packages A and B may both have a name Day defined in them. By writing **use** A, B we have a possible conflict.

There is a simple rule in Ada, apart from using the **use** clause, which avoids this conflict. It is that a name is not made directly visible if it is within the immediate scope of a homograph. A consequence of this is that a **use** clause cannot hide a directly visible declaration. To access objects in the package that would have caused the conflict we must use the dot notation.

Example 8.18 explains which names are available with packages with conflicting names.

As we shall see later in the chapter, sub-program and enumeration literal overloading are exceptions to the above rules.

```
procedure Outer is
   package Weeks is
      Day: INTEGER ;
      A: REAL ;
      B: BOOLEAN ;
   end Weeks ;

   package Weekends is
      B: REAL ;
      Day: INTEGER ;
   end Weekends ;

   Day: BOOLEAN ;
   use Weeks,Weekends ;
begin
   - - Day means Outer.Day
   - - A means Weeks.A
   - - B is illegal we use Weeks.B or Weekends.B
end Outer ;
```

Example 8.18   Resolving name conflicts in packages.

The names of record fields are another instance where the scope of the name extends beyond its immediate scope. Consider Example 8.19. This is quite legal since the component name is always qualified by the object of the correct type. For the same reason these names are allowed in aggregates.

To complete the list of names whose scope extends beyond their immediate scope, we have:

- procedure parameters,
- an entry declaration,
- a generic parameter declaration,
- a discriminant specification.

Entry declarations are discussed in Chapter 9, generic parameters later in this chapter, and it is left to the reader to explore discriminant specifications.

8.2.2   Overloading

When writing a large software system it can become very tedious to invent new unique names for every object that is declared. The block structure of Ada helps with this and allows names to be reused without ambiguity. Similarly, component names in records may be reused.

```
declare
    type ONE is record
        Name: STRING ;
        Value: INTEGER ;
    end record ;

    type TWO is record
        Name: IDENT ;
        Value: BOOLEAN ;
    end record ;

    A: ONE ;
    B: TWO ;
    Value: INTEGER ;
begin
    .
    .
    .
    if B.Value then
        Value := A.Value ;
    end if ;
end ;
```

Example 8.19   The visibility of names in records.

Another place where it is tedious without some name-centred facilities is in the use of enumeration literals. Having to invent unique names for each enumeration literal in a given scope can distract the programmer, owing to the complexity of finding meaningful names.

To alleviate this problem Ada allows enumeration literals to be overloaded. That is, the same literal name can be used as long as there is no ambiguity about its use. For example:

```
type PRIMARY_COLOUR is (Red, Yellow, Blue) ;
type TRAFFIC_LIGHT is (Red, Amber, Green) ;

Light: TRAFFIC_LIGHT ;
Paint: PRIMARY_COLOUR ;
Light := Red ; Paint := Red ;
```

This is quite correct although the name Red is overloaded. The compiler can deduce from the context of both assignment clauses which Red is being referenced. If an ambiguity does arise then the literal can be qualified. Thus:

```
PRIMARY_COLOUR ' (Red)
```

would disambiguate the name Red.

It should be mentioned here that Ada really regards enumeration literals as zero-adic functions that return a value of the enumeration type. The literal yellow above could be regarded as being specified by

function Yellow **return** PRIMARY_COLOUR ;

Having said that, it will come as no surprise to the reader that sub-programs can also be overloaded. For example:

procedure Change (A: PRIMARY_COLOUR) ;

and

procedure Change (A: TRAFFIC_LIGHT) ;

could both be declared in the same scope. Since both the parameter types have literals with the same names, then calls using these names should be disambiguated by qualification.

Sub-programs can only overload others if their specifications are sufficiently different (do not conform is Ada's terminology). Thus a sub-program specification will hide an identical one in an outer scope and be illegal with one in the same scope. However, if the specifications are different then the inner sub-program will overlap the outer one. The same is true when the scope of names goes outwards with packages. The introduced name will either be overloaded or hidden.

For two sub-programs to conform they must have the same types and modes. Some variation is allowed in the parameter names and in the use of numeric literals as default parameters.

8.2.3   Renaming

The final name control mechanism in Ada is the **renames** clause. In general it is not a good idea to rename objects since this introduces aliases which are difficult to control. It is also not a good idea to use renaming to avoid typing long identifiers, since the use of the identifiers soon becomes meaningless. However, considerable efficiencies may be achieved by using renaming for partial evaluation. For example:

declare
    Harry: PERSON **renames** People (I).Son ;
begin
    Harry := Harry * Harry ;

A clever compiler could recognize such a declaration and use it to produce efficient object code.

Other legitimate uses of renaming are in resolving ambiguities without wishing to resort to the dot notation, and in dealing with names in the program library. Since operators cannot be library units they have to be given a name that is unique in the library. However, when they are retrieved from the library they may be renamed so that they can be used in infix form. For example:

function " + " (A,B: REAL) **return** COMPLEX **renames** Libraryplus ;

Another similar situation arises when we wish overloaded sub-programs to be separately compiled. The answer is to compile them with separate names, but rename them for overloaded use.

Finally it should be noticed that enumeration literals can be renamed as functions. Thus:

function Reddy **return** PRIMARY_COLOUR **renames** ' Red ' ;

is another way of disambiguating the literal Red.

8.3   Generics

Generics constitute another technique that the Ada programmer may use to control the size, and therefore the complexity, of the system being built. Generic sub-programs and packages are allowed in Ada and they act as a template from which particular instances of the sub-program or package may be formed. It often happens when writing a large piece of software that some of the components are similar. When this occurs it is usually possible to combine the two components into one that is parameterized. Ada provides a number of mechanisms for this, such as discriminated types and sub-programs. However, there is a difference between other types of parameterization and generics in Ada, in that with generics, the parameter substitution is performed at compile time.

The need for generics in Ada arises from the fact that not all the entities that can be described by the programmer are data types. In Chapter 6 we saw how types themselves are not data objects, since the language designers desired the safety of compile-time type checking. Program components that differ only in type cannot be combined into a sub-program which passes the type as a parameter, since types are not data objects and cannot passed as parameters.

One classic example of how generics are useful is in sorting procedures. In most languages two different procedures are required to sort an array of integers and an array of real numbers. Indeed, the situation is much worse than that since we require a different sort procedure for every different type.

To illustrate how Ada generics overcome this difficulty we shall use a selection sort procedure, whose complexity is of order $O(n^2)$. Consider Example 8.20. We have split this into small, separately compiled units for easy understanding. It would be very tedious to write down another procedure to perform Selectionsort on an array of things. The logic of the two would be the same. Instead we can write down a generic. Let us start with procedure Swap in Example 8.21. This is the declaration of the generic procedure General_swap which is compiled

```
procedure Swap (I, J: INTEGER ; A: in out INTEGER_ARRAY) is
  Temp: INTEGER := A (J) ;
begin
  A (J) := A (I) ;
  A (I) := Temp ;
end Swap ;

with Swap ;
procedure Selectionsort (A: in out INTEGER_ARRAY) is
  Bottom: INTEGER := INTEGER_ARRAY ' First ;
  Top : INTEGER := INTEGER_ARRAY ' Last ;
begin
  for I in Bottom..Top loop
    declare
      Min_index: INTEGER := I ;
    begin
      for J in I+1..Top loop
        if A (J) < A (Min_index) then
          Min_index := J ;
        end if ;
        Swap (I, Min_index, A) ;
      end loop ;
    end ;
  end loop ;
end Selectionsort ;

with Selectionsort ;
procedure Main is
  type INTEGER_ARRAY is array (INTEGER range <>) of INTEGER ;
  .
  .
  .
end Main ;
```

Example 8.20 The separate components of a sorting program.

separately as a library unit. To obtain a particular version of this
procedure we must instantiate the generic by substituting for all the
names declared between the reserved words **generic** and **procedure**. For
example:

```
procedure Swap is new
        General_swap (INTEGER, INTEGER, INTEGER_ARRAY) ;
```

would yield exactly the same procedure that we had in Selection_sort. Most
data types can be substituted in a generic instantiation, but types
themselves and, as we shall see later, sub-programs are by far the most

```
generic
  type ELEMENT is private ;
  type INDEX is (<>) ;
  type SWAP_ARRAY is array (INDEX) of ELEMENT ;
procedure General_swap (I, J: INDEX ; A: in out SWAP_ARRAY) is
  Temp: ELEMENT := A (J) ;
begin
  A (J) := A (I) ;
  A (I) := Temp ;
end General_swap ;
```

Example 8.21   The procedure General_swap.

useful. Before we pass on we should notice that generic instantiations may also be library units.

In the above generic we have three types that may be substituted. ELEMENT is a private type which means any type may be substituted for it. INDEX is a discrete type denoted by <> and SWAP_ARRAY is an array type mapping INDEXES to ELEMENTS. Other types that may be substituted are denoted by

```
type A is range <>     -- for an integer type
type B is digits <>    -- for a floating point type
type C is delta <>     -- for a fixed point type
type D is access E      -- for an access type
```

The list of names to be substituted in a generic are called the generic formal parameters. The actual parameters are the objects given in the instantiation. Like formal parameters the objects declared may have default values and be **in** or **in out**, but since most of the interesting cases are type substitution this will not concern us here.

The most important point about the generic parameter substitution is that it is performed at compile time. It is this fact that allows the type substitution to be performed and yet remain statically checked. Notice, however, that it is parameter substitution and not text substitution and thus any free variable of the generic is bound at its declaration and not its instantiation.

Let us return to Selection_sort. Since we have written Swap as a generic let us assume that it is in the library. We can now write the sort procedure (see Example 8.22). There are a number of points of interest here. First of all the procedure has been cleaned up so that it contains no references to particular types (like the literal 1 in the original). To do this the algorithm is changed slightly. The next point is that it customizes its own version of General_swap from the library. The

```
with General_swap ;
generic
  type ELEMENT is private ;
  type INDEX is (<>) ;
  type SORT_ARRAY is array (INDEX) of ELEMENT ;
  with function "<" (X, Y: ELEMENT) return BOOLEAN is <> ;
procedure General_selectionsort (A: in out SORT_ARRAY) is
  procedure Swap is new
        General_swap (ELEMENT, INDEX, SORT_ARRAY) ;
  Bottom: ELEMENT := SORT_ARRAY ' First ;
  Top : ELEMENT := SORT_ARRAY ' Last ;
begin
  for I in Bottom..Top loop
    declare
      Min_index: INDEX := I ;
      New_bottom: INDEX := INDEX ' Succ ' (I) ;
    begin
      for J in New_bottom..Top loop
        if A (J) < A (Min_index) then
          Min_index := J ;
        end if ;
        Swap (I, Min_index, A) ;
      end loop ;
    end ;
  end loop ;
end General_selectionsort ;
```

Example 8.22   The generic sorting procedure.

final and perhaps most interesting point is that the generic takes a function as a parameter. This is the only way of passing sub-programs as parameters in Ada since they are not allowed as parameters to sub-programs themselves. The above function has a default value denoted by <>, which means that if a function is not supplied then the one in scope at the point of declaration if any should be used. Now, assuming we have General_selectionsort in the library we could write a main program as shown in Example 8.23.

As an example of a generic package we shall use another classic example which has been described earlier in this book – that of the stack. A stack is characterized by its elements, its size, the operations Push and Pop and the overflow and underflow exceptions. This can be written as shown in Example 8.24.

```
with General_selectionsort ;
procedure Main is
   type INT_VECTOR is array (INTEGER) of INTEGER ;
   procedure INT_SORT is new General_selectionsort
                 (INTEGER,INTEGER,INT_VECTOR) ;
   -- This gives the original selection sort of integer arrays. However
   type THING is record
      X: INTEGER ;
      Y: STRING ;
   end record ;
   type THING_VECTOR is array (INTEGER) of THING ;
   function Lt (A,B: THING) return BOOLEAN is
   begin
      return A.Y = B.Y and A.X < B.X ;
   end Lt ;
   procedure Thing_sort is new General_selectionsort
          (THING, INTEGER, THING_VECTOR, Lt) ;
   -- gives the same sort algorithm with very different types
   -- and a < function
begin
   null ;
end Main ;
```

Example 8.23   The main sorting procedure.

It is left to the reader to write the body of the package. This could be instantiated by

```
package Int_stack is new
        General_stack (Size=>200, ELEMENT=>INTEGER) ;
```

```
generic
   Size: POSITIVE ;
   type ELEMENT is private ;
package General_stack is
   procedure Push (X: in ELEMENT) ;
   procedure Pop (X: out ELEMENT) ;
   Overflow,Underflow: exception ;
end General_stack ;
```

Example 8.24   A generic stacking package.

and used in the usual manner. Notice that each instantiation yields unique exceptions so that they can be distinguished. Of course we must use the dot notation here since the exception names cannot be overloaded.

There is a more subtle point about Ada generics that is well illustrated by the stack example. When we write the package body we have to give the stack a concrete representation. For example, we could use a linked list or an array to represent the stack. Now it may be that we desire different representation on different occasions. To do this in Ada we must write two different generics and instantiate them as appropriate. If the language allowed us to parameterize a generic package with another package then the generic stack could be written as one package.

8.3.1   The electronic mail system

The Mail_list package given earlier is a special case of a generalized list package which is defined in Example 8.25. This package could be instantiated for Mail_list by

```
package Mail_list is new
        General_list (ELEMENT => Mail_list.INSTANCE) ;
```

```
generic
    type ELEMENT is private ;
package General_list is
    type INSTANCE is private ;
    type ERROR_STATUS is (Ok, Error) ;
    procedure Head (List: INSTANCE ; M: out ELEMENT ;
                        Status: out ERROR_STATUS ) ;
    function Tail (List: INSTANCE) return INSTANCE ;
    function Add (List: INSTANCE ; Item: ELEMENT)
                return INSTANCE ;
    function Create return INSTANCE ;
    function Is_empty (List: INSTANCE) return BOOLEAN ;
private
    type LIST_ELEMENT ;
    type INSTANCE is access LIST_ELEMENT ;
end General_list ;
```

Example 8.25   A generic list package specification.

8.4 Summary

In this chapter we have discussed some problems associated with the construction of large software systems. These problems of scale arise when no one person can keep the complexity of the system under their intellectual control. Such systems are common and it is therefore important to provide the implementors and designers with tools to master this complexity.

There are many social and managerial problems associated with large systems. For example, if no one person totally understands the system then who acts as arbitrator in a dispute. We have not discussed these problems here, but have concentrated on the facilities of Ada for the technical management of this complexity. These are incremental system development, name space control and generics.

With incremental system development we have seen how to construct programs in both bottom-up and top-down manners. The Ada library may be considered as a depository for a set of software components which can be put together in the composition of systems. The library may also be used to contain fragments of systems in order to minimize recompilation when the system is altered.

The second aspect that we discussed in this chapter was name space management, with particular emphasis on the scope and visibility of names, overloading names and renaming objects. The control of names is of particular importance in programming in the large where there are large numbers of named objects available for use.

Finally, we discussed generics and how they may be used for generating sub-programs and packages. The technique allows the programmer to build a general tool and to specialize it for a particular purpose. This should greatly reduce the amount of duplicate code that is normally found in large systems.

8.5 Further reading

Le Verrand, D.,(1985). *Evaluating Ada*. Oxford: North Oxford Academic.

This book is a collection of critical reviews of Ada. In particular the sections on scope and visibility, generic units and separate compilation are of relevance to this chapter.

Chapter 9 **Parallel Programming**

A major advantage of the programming language Ada is that it allows the user to specify that different sections of code should be executed in parallel. Many of the activities that we wish to model are inherently parallel. For example, in a model of a supermarket there will be many customers and shop assistants working autonomously and in parallel. If we wish to capture the essential nature of this real-world activity then we require language primitives powerful enough to model it. It is interesting to note the correspondence between object-oriented programming and parallel programming. Indeed, the programming paradigm of Smalltalk (Goldberg and Robson, 1983) forces systems to be composed of objects executing in parallel. We shall see how this may be done in Ada later.

A second reason for parallelism is execution speed. There is a limit to the speed of sequential computers governed by the speed of switching and communication. Theoretically the limit is the speed of light, which travels about 1 foot in a nanosecond. To speed up a computer we can increase the switching and communication speed towards the speed of light, or reduce the distance to be travelled. Thus miniaturization will yield some increase in speed, as will increasing the speed of the components; but once the limit has been reached the only way to increase the speed of computers is to make them perform more than one activity at one time, that is, operate in parallel.

There has always been parallel operation in computer hardware. By fetching or storing a word in parallel instead of one bit at a time the speed of the store is increased. This computer efficiency can be further extended by duplicating arithmetic processors, I/O processors, registers and data highways where we know parallel activity may occur. The need for this type of parallel activity arises from the need for faster and faster computers as the complexity of problems solved using computational techniques is increased.

In recent years the availability of relatively inexpensive hardware has made it economically possible to build computer systems out of a large number of computer processors. This has yielded an environment in which the programmer may take advantage of the parallelism in the system and has led to extensive research into developing algorithms to harness it. Traditional applications of parallel programming such as operating systems have been joined by database management systems, large-scale scientific (vector) processing, real-time control systems, speech and vision systems, among others, as problems suitable for parallel solution. In many cases the expression of algorithms by using parallel techniques has led to a style of programming different from sequential programming.

Thus we see that there are two main reasons for studying parallel programming. The first is to model real-world activity, and the second is to increase the speed of our computations. In Chapter 10 we shall concentrate on the aspects of parallel programming relating to real time activity where speed is an essential property. Here we concentrate on other aspects of parallel programming, starting with some definitions.

A process, or a task in Ada's terminology, is the execution of a sequential program. A sequential program consists of a list of statements that are executed one after the other. It should be obvious that in the execution of a sequential process there is only one thread of control. That is, at any point in the execution there is only one instruction being executed.

A parallel program consists of two or more sequential programs that may be executed concurrently. Thus there will be more than one thread of control. At any point in the execution of the parallel program there will be one instruction being executed for each of the constituent sequential processes.

A multiprogramming system is one in which the illusion of parallel activity is provided by time multiplexing a very fast processor among the active processes. Each constituent sequential process does not use all the power of the processor on which it is executing, and the total effect is to give the impression that all processes have a less powerful processor to themselves. This kind of activity, although not true parallelism, is often used where the mismatch of the processor speed and the relatively slow needs of the processes is acceptable. For example, timesharing systems operate in this manner.

To obtain true parallel activity the underlying computer system must have more than one processor, and we shall make a distinction here between two different types of such systems. A multiprocessor system is one with many processors which share a common store, and a distributed system has many processors, possibly with their own store linked by a communication channel. The need to distinguish between the multiprocessor and distributed systems arises from the manner in which they may be efficiently programmed.

A multiprocessor system, as shown in Figure 9.1, is most efficient when we have a large amount of data that we wish to share among the processes. This is shown diagrammatically as a store, but could be a large database on a disk. There may be many processors in this type of

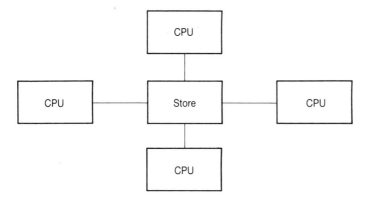

Figure 9.1   A multiprocessor system.

system, and thus the store and not the processors becomes a potential bottleneck in the system.

A distributed system, as shown in Figure 9.2, is most efficient when the need to communicate between modules is small. This removes the potential bottleneck on the store at the higher level of the application. That is, we can exploit the inherent higher level of parallelism in the application itself.

The rate at which a process executes depends on the type of system used and the speed of the processors. However, we would like to understand parallel computation in terms of the constituent sequential processes, and therefore the rate of execution of the sequential process should be unimportant in the understanding of the total system.

There are three major problems for the designer of a language in which we can express concurrent execution. They are:

1. How is concurrent execution and synchronization expressed?
2. How do processes communicate with each other?
3. How do processes avoid deadlock?

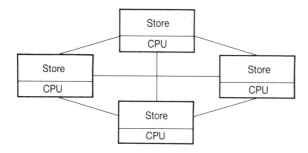

Figure 9.2   A distributed system.

We shall deal with each of these in the following sections. The flavour or style of the language depends on how the above problems are viewed. As we shall see, there are a number of tradeoffs in the design of the parallel constructs of Ada.

The aim of the chapter is to discuss the problems of parallel programming. We shall be looking at these in relation to Ada's facilities for parallelism. The topics covered include parallelism, specifying parallel computation, synchronization, communication, the rendezvous, producer–consumer problems, non-determinism, deadlock and task termination.

9.1   Expressing concurrent execution

One of the earliest forms of parallelism in programming languages is the coroutine of languages such as Simula (Birtwistle *et al.*, 1973), Bliss (Wulf *et al.*, 1971) and Modula-2 (Wirth, 1983). Each coroutine in a system can be viewed as a process. For example, in Figure 9.3, program A and coroutines B and C can be thought of as three processes. Program A initially calls coroutine B, which eventually resumes C.The transfer of control from one coroutine to the other via the **resume** statement is one-way, and B stops when C is active. This type of concurrency is adequate for programs that share a single processor but not for anything, else since the switching of processes is completely specified and not left to the implementation. The coroutines are synchronized by the **resume** statement.

A more general solution to parallelism may be found in languages such as PL/1 (IBM, 1972) and Mesa (Lampson and Reddell, 1980) which support variants of the **fork** and **join** statements (Conway 1963). A **fork** statement specifies that the named process should be activated in parallel with the current one. The **join** statement is used to synchronize the caller with the completion of the called process and may cause the caller to wait.

Program A	**Coroutine B**	**Coroutine C**
begin	.	.
.	.	.
call B	**resume C**	.
.	.	**resume B**
.	**return**	.
end	**end**	**end**

Figure 9.3   A set of coroutines.

Program A	**Program B**
begin	**begin**
.	.
fork B	.
.	.
join B	.
end	**end**

Figure 9.4   The **fork** and **join** statements.

When program A, in Figure 9.4, tries to execute the **join** statement it is suspended until program B executes its **end**. The fork and join primitives provide for dynamic process creation, including multiple activations of the same text, and some of the success of the UNIX (Ritchie and Thompson, 1974) system is due to their efficient implementation. There is one major drawback to these primitives. They are rather low-level and suffer from accidental or malicious misuse. Writing **fork** instead of **join** can cause immense damage to a system.

A safer language primitive is the cobegin–coend pair of Dijkstra (1968), Algol68 (van Wijngaarden *et al.*, 1969) and CSP (Hoare, 1978). It is this model on which the Ada task is based. Consider the problem of simulating the action of someone who likes to read the paper and eat breakfast in parallel. This may be done in Ada as shown in Example 9.1.

In this program the task Read_paper is executed in parallel with the main body of the procedure. The activation of the task occurs when the parent unit reaches the **begin** following the task declaration.

When a task is declared in a sub-program, block or task body it is said to depend on that parent unit. The synchronization of the tasks is such that the parent must wait for all of its dependent tasks to terminate before finishing itself. Thus in Example 9.1, if breakfast is eaten quickly the sub-program will still have to wait until the paper is read before returning.

In the general case a unit is said to be completed when it reaches its final **end** and will then be terminated when all its dependent tasks terminate. The task primitive thus retains the dynamic nature of the fork and join statements but with a greater degree of safety for the user.

9.2   Process communication

There are two main models of process communication in concurrent systems. In the shared-variable model the cooperating tasks share a common store through which they communicate. In the message-passing

```
procedure Breakfast is
   procedure Read_the_paper is
   begin
      null ;
   end Read_paper ;

   procedure Eat_the_breakfast is
   begin
      null ;
   end Eat_the_breakfast ;

   task Read_paper ;
   task body Read_paper is
   begin
      Read_the_paper ;
   end Read_paper ;
begin
   Eat_the_breakfast ;
end Breakfast ;
```

Example 9.1   Taking breakfast.

model processes communicate by sending messages to each other. The two models roughly correspond to the difference between a multi-processor system and a distributed system. In the multiprocessor system there is a common store shared among the processors, making it ideal for the shared variable model of communication. A distributed system is linked by a communications channel over which messages are sent. In both cases the communication must be synchronized in order to avoid information being lost or destroyed.

In the shared-variable model of process communication there are two types of synchronization required. A critical section is a sequence of statements which must appear indivisible. Processes must be mutually excluded from critical sections. For example, consider a set of railway points that administers the crossover of two tracks. In order to ensure that there are no collisions, trains must be mutually excluded from the shared points. This example illustrates the difficulty of detecting defective parallel programs. If the trains are not mutually excluded from the points they may run for years without a collision. When eventually they do collide no one can understand how a system that has run successfully for many years should suddenly go wrong. Worse still, a simulation of the system may not reveal these time-dependent bugs and thus the cost of detection and repair is always high.

A second type of synchronization is required when processes must be kept in step with each other. These types of processes are often called producer–consumer processes, because the synchronization must ensure that nothing is consumed before it is produced and that the producer does not overproduce.

In message-passing systems there seems to be little agreement by language designers over what are the appropriate primitives for the messages and their synchronization. However, all useful parallel programming systems have methods of programming critical sections and producer–consumer situations.

9.3 The Ada rendezvous

The designers of Ada have devised a method of process communication, which is loosely based on the language CSP, that provides facilities for communicating by all the methods described above. It is called the rendezvous.

Two tasks are said to rendezvous when the first calls an entry that is accepted by the second. Each task is a sequential process, has only one thread of control and therefore may be understood in terms of its sequential operation. When a task accepts an entry it executes a sequence of code on behalf of the calling task. This is sometimes referred to as remote procedure calling. There may be a time delay between the call of an entry and its acceptance. The protocol for synchronizing the two tasks is that when an entry is called the calling task is suspended until it receives the reply. This is called wait for reply. If the called task executes an **accept** statement before the entry is called, then it is also suspended until the entry is made. This is called wait for call. The protocol of 'wait for reply' by the sender and 'wait for call' by the receiver make up the rendezvous.

In its most degenerate form the rendezvous can be used to provide a critical section. Let us consider again the problem of trains sharing a set of points. If we regard the points as a critical section through which only one train may pass at a time, we could model it as a task with two entries, one to enter and one to leave it. The program in Example 9.2 shows how two trains may safely use the points.

The task Points loops forever, accepting the entries Enter and Leave in strict order. The trains must call the entries in that order. Notice that the rendezvous does not last for very long. Once the **accept** statement is executed the rendezvous is over and both tasks resume their independent activity.

This solution is equivalent to a semaphore solution to critical sections. It suffers from the same problems as the semaphore solution and again highlights the subtlety of parallel programming. The above

```
procedure Trains is
   task Points is
      entry Enter ;
      entry Leave ;
   end Points ;

   task body Points is
   begin
      loop
         accept Enter ;
         accept Leave ;
      end loop ;
   end Points ;

   task Train1 ;
   task body Train1 is
   begin
      Approach_points ;
      Points.Enter ;
      Cross_points ;
      Points.Leave ;
      Go_away_from_points ;
   end Train1 ;

   task Train2 ;
   task body Train2 is
   begin
      Approach_points ;
      Points.Enter ;
      Cross_points ;
      Points.Leave ;
      Go_away_from_points ;
   end Train2 ;
begin
   null ;
end Trains ;
```

Example 9.2   Trains crossing points.

solution is correct, but open to abuse. Suppose for example, the points
were not simple points, but a stretch of track 5 km long. A train driver
well acquainted with the timetables may know that he can safely enter
the critical section even though there is another train in it. The driver
knows that the first train is so far ahead that it will never be met in the
critical section. Thus, the driver reprograms the second train as shown

```
task body Train2 is
begin
    Approach_points ;
    Points.Leave ;        – – make the points believe
                          – – that the previous train has left
    Points.Enter ;
    Cross_points ;
    Go_away_from_points ;
end Train2 ;
```

Example 9.3   Reprogramming the second train.

in Example 9.3. In this way the second train gets into the critical section. However, if the train has left the points before the second one tries to enter, then the second train will be delayed. Worse still, one day the driver is not told of a timetable change which alters the direction of the first train. A collision occurs.

The point of the allegory is that, used in this way, the rendezvous is not safe from either accidental or deliberate misuse. We must develop better programming techniques to help us as we should always be suspicious of this inherent lack of safety. A second try at the problem is to force the trains to perform all their actions in crossing the points within the Points tasks. If there is any variation in the method used to cross the points the trains must identify themselves to the Cross_points procedure in order that the variations may be performed. In this solution (Example 9.4) the crossing of the points is made into an indivisible operation. The rendezvous lasts for a greater length of time in this example – that is for as long as it takes to execute the sequence code

```
accept Cross (Train: in TRAIN_TYPE) do
    Cross_points (Train) ;
end Cross ;
```

It is desirable to have short critical sections, since a property of parallel systems that has been observed in operating systems and database systems is that the amount of real parallelism is reduced by having long critical sections. This is because only one of the processes is active during the critical section instead of two or more. However, it is sometimes necessary to have long critical sections for safe sharing.

The parameter Train to the Cross entry obeys all the rules of parameter types for sub-programs. It is important to note that the parameter is evaluated before the rendezvous is made (in fact at the time of the call). This is not of interest here, but it is important when more elaborate parameters are involved.

```
procedure Trains is
  type TRAIN_TYPE is (One, Two) ;
  task Points is
    entry Cross (Train: in TRAIN_TYPE) ;
  end Points ;

  task body Points is
    procedure Cross_points (Train: in TRAIN_TYPE)
             is separate ;
  begin
    loop
      accept Cross (Train: in TRAIN_TYPE) do
        Cross_points (Train) ;
      end Cross ;
    end loop ;
  end Points ;

  task Train1 ;
  task body Train1 is
  begin
    Approach_points ;
    Points.Cross (One) ;
    Go_away_from_points ;
  end Train1 ;

  task Train2 ;
  task body Train2 is
  begin
    Approach_points ;
    Points.Cross (Two) ;
    Go_away_from_points ;
  end Train2 ;
begin
  null ;
  -- The main program waits until the dependent tasks terminate --
end Trains ;
```

Example 9.4   Safer points.

9.3.1   Producer–consumer problems

The Ada rendezvous may also be used to solve problems where processes must be kept in step with one another. The classic problem used to illustrate this is the producer–consumer problem. In this, a producer process produces items of a certain sort which are consumed by a consumer process. This might be programmed by Example 9.5.

```
procedure Producer_consumer is
   task Consumer is
      entry Put (A: in UNIT) ;
   end Consumer ;
   task body Consumer is
      Item: UNIT ;
   begin
      loop
         accept Put (A: in UNIT) do
            Item := A ;
         end Put ;
         - - consume item - -
      end loop ;
   end Consumer ;

   task Producer ;
   task body Producer is
      Item: UNIT ;
   begin
      loop
         Item := Prepare_item ;
         Consumer.Put (Item) ;
      end loop ;
   end Producer ;
begin
   null ;
end Producer_consumer ;
```

Example 9.5   The producer–consumer problem.

In this solution the producer process produces an item and then sends it to the consumer task which consumes it. While this solves the problem it is perhaps not the one we wish, since it hardly takes advantage of the parallelism inherent in the problem. Suppose, for example, the producer process runs on a computer that is ten times faster than the speed of the consumer processes' computer. That is, the producer can produce much faster than the consumer can consume. Since the solution given above forces the units to be produced and consumed at the same rate, then the producer is slowed down to the consumer's speed.

Such a data rate mismatch often occurs in computer systems. As an example consider a disk controller sending information to the CPU. The rate at which the disk controller gets information off the disk is usually several orders of magnitude slower than the rate at which the CPU can consume the data. The normal method of smoothing this data rate mismatch is to use a reusable first-in first-out buffer known as a ring buffer. The producer places data in the buffer when it is not full and the consumer takes units out of the buffer when it is not empty. The solution lies in making both the producer and consumer processes communicate with a third process which is the ring buffer. The producer and consumer tasks can be written as in Example 9.6.

The implementation of the ring buffer task ensures the strict order of the calling tasks. It stops the producer process when the buffer is full and resumes it when there is space, stops the consumer process when the buffer is empty, resuming it where there is a unit to be consumed. Mutual exclusion on the buffer is ensured by only one **accept** statement being executed at any one time in a task. In this example the reusable ring buffer has only one unit. In fact, for the producer and consumer to progress at different speeds it is necessary for the buffer to hold a number of units. This is organized as a reusable ring as in Figure 9.5.

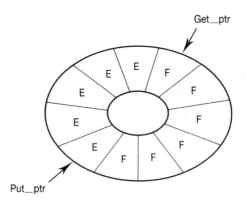

Figure 9.5 The ring buffer.

To solve the producer consumer speed mismatch we use three variables, Put_ptr to indicate the next location in which to place a unit, Get_ptr to indicate the next location in which to obtain a unit and Full_slots to indicate the number of locations that are full. When Put_ptr = Get_ptr the buffer is either completely full or empty. We can tell from the value of Full. When Full > zero we can consume units and when Full < size of buffer we can produce units. The task in Example 9.7 illustrates the method of counting the units.

It is a matter of simple arithmetic to convince oneself that this works. The cyclic counting is performed using the **mod** function of Ada and the conditions for accepting entries are placed in **if** statements. Notice that the critical sections are kept as short as possible to allow speedy resumption of the calling task. Each time around the loop, we either

```
procedure Producer_consumer is
   task Ring_buffer is
      entry Get (Item: out UNIT) ;
      entry Put (Item: in UNIT) ;
   end Ring_buffer ;

   task body Ring_buffer is
      Item: UNIT ;
   begin
      loop
         accept Put (A: in UNIT) do
            Item := A ;
         end Put ;
         accept Get (A: out UNIT) do
            A := Item ;
         end Get ;
      end loop ;
   end Ring_buffer ;

   task Producer ;
   task body Producer is
      Item: UNIT ;
   begin
      loop
         Item := Prepare_item ;
         Ring_buffer.Put (Item) ;
      end loop ;
   end Producer ;

   task Consumer ;
   task body Consumer is
      Item: UNIT ;
   begin
      loop
         Ring_buffer.Get (Item) ;
         - - consume item - -
      end loop ;
   end Consumer ;
begin
   null ;
end Producer_consumer ;
```

Example 9.6   The producer–consumer with a ring buffer.

```
task body Ring_buffer is
    No_of_units: constant := 500 ;
    Buffers: array (1..No_of_units) of UNIT ;
    Full_slots: INTEGER range 0..No_of_units := 0 ;
    Get_ptr, Put_ptr: INTEGER range 1..No_of_units := 1 ;
begin
    loop
        if Full_slots < No_of_units then
            accept Put (Item: in UNIT) do
                Buffers (Put_ptr) := Item ;
            end Put ;
            Put_ptr := Put_ptr mod No_of_units + 1 ;
            Full_slots := Full_slots + 1 ;
        end if ;
        if Full_slots > 0 then
            accept Get (Item: out UNIT) do
                Item := Buffers (Get_ptr) ;
            end Get ;
            Get_ptr := Get_ptr mod No_of_units + 1 ;
            Full_slots := Full_slots - 1 ;
        end if ;
    end loop ;
end Ring_buffer ;
```

Example 9.7   Counting the items in the ring buffer.

accept a Get or a Put or both, and clearly we have a solution. The updating of the ring buffer pointers can be done outside the critical section.

This solution again highlights the problems of discovering the nature of parallel algorithms. For although it works it does not work well. In fact it is a convoluted method of writing the first solution, since we must first accept a Put , setting Full_slots to one and therefore must then accept a Get, setting Full_slots to zero, and so on *ad infinitum*. However, we have done all the ring buffer calculation correctly, and if we could perform any number of either of the **if** statements in any order we would have a proper solution. For this we require the **select** statement.

9.4   Non-determinism

From the ring buffer problem we have seen that we require a mechanism for executing one statement out of many, not caring which it is as long as we do not get held up unnecessarily by doing it. This is generally called non-determinism and is provided in Ada by the **select** statement. For example:

```
select
   A ;
or
   B ;
or
   C ;
end select ;
```

will select one of A, B or C to execute, but only one. We are told that the Ada system will make an arbitrary choice when deciding which one is to be executed. The point is that the language implementor is free to choose and the programmer should not try to make use of a selection

---

```
task Counter is
   entry Add (N: in INTEGER) ;
   entry Subtract (N: in INTEGER) ;
   entry Inspect (N: out INTEGER) ;
end Counter ;
task body Counter is
   Total: INTEGER := 0 ;
begin
   loop
      select
         accept Add (N: in INTEGER) do
            Total := Total + N ;
         end Add ;
      or
         accept Subtract (N: in INTEGER) do
            Total := Total – N ;
         end Subtract ;
      or
         accept Inspect (N: out INTEGER) do
            N := Total ;
         end Inspect ;
      end select ;
   end loop ;
end Counter ;
```

Example 9.8   The select statement.

algorithm. Somehow the language implementor has to make the selection fair so that none of the options is ever ignored forever.

In Ada the choice of what A, B and C may be is strictly limited and is only intended for use with entry acceptances. To illustrate how it may be used consider a task that provides entries to add, subtract or inspect a value. Any number of tasks may request any number of adds, subtracts or inspects, in any order. A solution is shown in Example 9.8.

With the non-deterministic **select** one of the **accept** statements is executed each time around the loop. Since we do not care which one, the implementation should be free to decide. However, it would of course be a foolish implementation of Ada that chose one that had no entry waiting, and the language does indeed have a preferred method of choosing a **select** option. For each entry there is a queue of tasks trying to communicate with it. When an entry is accepted the queue is reduced by one. The queues are available to the implementor to make sensible decisions on how to implement the non-determinism. Incidentally, this is the same program as given in Example 7.3.

A variation on the above is to accept additions only when Total is less than 100_000 say. To do this we need to use a boolean

```
task body Counter is
   Total: INTEGER := 0 ;
begin
  loop
    select
      when Total < 100_000 =>
        accept Add (N: in INTEGER) do
          Total := Total + N ;
        end Add ;
    or
      accept Subtract (N: in INTEGER) do
        Total := Total - N ;
      end Subtract ;
    or
      accept Inspect (N: out INTEGER) do
        N := Total ;
      end Inspect ;
    end select ;
  end loop ;
end Counter ;
```

Example 9.9   The guarded select statement.

expression called a guard to protect the **accept** statement reprogramming the task as shown in Example 9.9. Every time the **select** statement is executed all the guards are evaluated. Those choices without guards are deemed to have true guards. Once the guards are evaluated the non-deterministic selection is made from the choices with true guards. If none of the guards is true the exception Program_error is raised. Since two of the choices have no guards in this case, the exception can never be raised.

There are a number of variations on the **select** statement that we will study in Chapter 10. For the present, let us return to the ring buffer problem. If we now replace the **if** statements by guarded select choices we get a correct solution to the producer–consumer problem. Example 9.10 is now a correct solution allowing both producer and consumer to proceed at their own own pace, but keeping up with a fixed number of iterations of each other.

```
task body Ring_buffer is
   No_of_units: constant := 500 ;
   Buffers: array (1..No_of_units) of UNIT ;
   Full_slots: INTEGER range 0..No_of_units := 0 ;
   Get_ptr, Put_ptr: INTEGER range 1..No_of_units := 1 ;
begin
   loop
      select
         when Full_slots < No_of_units =>
            accept Put (Item: in UNIT) do
               Buffers (Put_ptr) := Item ;
            end Put ;
            Put_ptr := Put_ptr mod No_of_units + 1 ;
            Full_slots := Full_slots + 1 ;
      or
         when Full_slots > 0 =>
            accept Get (Item: out UNIT) do
               Item := Buffers (Get_ptr) ;
            end Get ;
            Get_ptr := Get_ptr mod No_of_units + 1 ;
            Full_slots := Full_slots - 1 ;
      end select ;
   end loop ;
end Ring_buffer ;
```

Example 9.10 A correct ring buffer task.

9.5 Deadlock

In a system of multiple processes it is possible to have two processes
neither of which can continue until the other does. This situation is called
deadlock. Consider two processes P1 and P2 with two resources R1 and
R2. When executing, P1 requires R1, then R1 and R2, then R2 alone.
P2 requires R2 then R2 and R1 then R1 alone. Normally the processes
will obtain the resources they require without interfering with each other.
However, if P1 acquires R1 and at the same time P2 acquires R2, then
the system is deadlocked since neither P1 nor P2 can proceed. The Ada
tasks in Example 9.11 may deadlock.

Again the difficulty of finding errors in parallel programs may be
seen. If the two processes do not interfere with one another then the
program will work. The program may execute correctly for a long time
and then fail when the designer and writer are no longer available. This
means that great care has to be given to development of parallel systems.

```
procedure Deadlock is
  task Resource1 is
    entry Acquire ;
    entry Release ;
  end Resource1 ;
  task body Resource1 is
  begin
    loop
      accept Acquire ;
      accept Release ;
    end loop ;
  end Resource1 ;

  task Resource2 is
    entry Acquire ;
    entry Release ;
  end Resource2 ;
  task body Resource2 is
  begin
    loop
      accept Acquire ;
      accept Release ;
    end loop ;
  end Resource2 ;
```

(cont.)

Example 9.11   An example of possible deadlock.

In Example 9.11 it is relatively easy to spot the problem and correct it. Unfortunately the deadlock problem is more subtle than it first appears, and in the seminal paper on the subject Coffman *et al.* (1971) stated four conditions that must hold for deadlock to exist in a system. They are:

1. **Mutual exclusion condition.** Processes claim exclusive control over the resources they require.
2. **Partial allocation.** Processes hold resources already allocated to them while waiting for additional resources.
3. **Non-preemptive scheduling.** Resources cannot be removed from processes until the resources are used to completion.
4. **Circular Chain.** A circular chain of processes exists in which each process holds one or more resources that are requested by the next process in the chain.

```
task Process1 ;
task body Process1 is
begin
   loop
      Resource1.Acquire ;
      Resource2.Acquire ;
      Resource1.Release ;
      Resource2.Release ;
   end loop ;
end Process1 ;

task Process2 ;
task body Process2 is
begin
   loop
      Resource2.Acquire ;
      Resource1.Acquire ;
      Resource2.Release ;
      Resource1.Release ;
   end loop ;
end Process2 ;
begin
   null ;
end Deadlock ;
```

Example 9.11 (cont.)

There are a number of strategies that can be used in handling deadlock, depending on the situation. By ensuring that at least one of the above conditions does not hold then deadlock can be prevented in a system. Havender (1968) suggests the following separate strategies for denying deadlock:

1. Each process must request all its required resources at once and cannot proceed until all have been granted. This is non-partial allocation.

2. If a process holding certain resources is denied a further request, that process must release its original resources and if necessary request them again together with the original resources. This denies non-preemptive scheduling.

3. There should be imposition of a linear ordering of resource types on all processes; that is if a process has been allocated resources of a given type, it may subsequently request only those resources of types later in the ordering. This denies a circular wait.

Each of these strategies taken by itself will prevent deadlock, but at some cost. The first strategy makes processes state their total resource requirements before they start. Thus no process can claim resources that exceed the capacity of the system even if it does not require them all at once. This strategy is poor for such systems or where a process runs for a long time but makes use of the resources used for short periods. For example, a process may use ten resources in its execution. For the first 20 hours of execution it may require only one resource and for the last 10 seconds it may require all the others. The non-partial allocation strategy will reserve the ten resources for the full execution of the process, thereby causing the nine resources to be idle for long periods. This can seriously affect the efficiency of the total system.

The second strategy may also be costly if a process loses work by releasing its resources. It is also possible that, by unfair scheduling, a process may never terminate, always being chosen to give up its resources to prevent deadlock.

The third strategy, to prevent a circular chain, orders each of the resources. Processes whose dynamic request sequence does not have the same ordering as the static system sequence will be in difficulty here. They may predict all the resources required by the process and then when resource n is required it must request all the resources less than n in the ordering that it may require. This may again cause resources to be reserved unnecessarily.

Havender's list of strategies does not include one to prevent mutual exclusion on resources, as it is assumed that this is necessary for correct shared access to resources.

All of the above strategies are expensive and the question must be asked if it is worth it. If deadlock occurs infrequently then it is often considered a minor nuisance – rather like power supply failure – and not worth trying to prevent. In such cases, it is necessary to have a method of detecting that deadlock has arisen and a method of recovering from that deadlock. Techniques used by operating systems to detect deadlock usually assume the first three conditions hold and then try to find a circular chain. Methods involving resource allocation graphs are common. The method, however, depends on some process having a map of all the others' requests and itself not being involved in the deadlock. It is also not always clear that a system is deadlocked rather than taking a very long time to execute. Even if we could always easily detect deadlock, removing processes to break the deadlock could be painful if work is lost.

Where it is important that the system be highly reliable, then it is necessary to pay the rather high cost of preventing deadlock. Thus in designing a system of parallel processes we must design in an action for deadlock, whether it be prevention or detection and recovery. The decision will be based on the cost to the system.

9.6   Task termination

A task completes when it reaches its final **end** and may then terminate when all of its dependent tasks have terminated. Many of the tasks written for parallel programming systems are endless loops which never terminate. This means that it is impossible to terminate the parent unit. This is unfortunate if the parent unit decides that it no longer makes sense to continue. One method of resolving this difficulty would be to insist that in all of the sub-tasks there is an entry for just such a situation. Indeed, this is so frequently required that it is included as a special case in Ada.

In the ring buffer problem given above, the ring buffer task will exist forever and never terminate. If we assume the units were characters and that we were using the ring buffer to smooth the difference in speed between the input stream and the process consuming it, we can write the three tasks as in Example 9.12.

The producer and consumer tasks complete and terminate when they encounter an EOT character. To force the Ring_buffer to close down the **terminate** option must be selected. This is only done if the parent unit is completed and all the sibling and dependent tasks are either terminated or able to select their own terminate option. If this is the case the whole set of tasks terminates.

Unfortunately it is not safe to assume that all sibling and dependent tasks have been constructed correctly according to some good practice guidelines. In such cases, and in others such as partial deadlock,

```
procedure Smooth is
  task Ring_buffer is
    entry Get (Item: out CHARACTER) ;
    entry Put (Item: in CHARACTER) ;
  end Ring_buffer ;

  task body Ring_buffer is
    No_of_units: constant := 500 ;
    Buffers: array (1..No_of_units) of CHARACTER ;
    Full_slots: INTEGER range 0..No_of_units := 0 ;
    Get_ptr, Put_ptr: INTEGER range 1..No_of_units := 1 ;
  begin
    loop
      select
        when Full_slots < No_of_units =>
          accept Put (Item: in CHARACTER) do
            Buffers (Put_ptr) := Item ;
          end Put ;
          Put_ptr := Put_ptr mod No_of_units + 1 ;
          Full_slots := Full_slots + 1 ;
      or
        when Full_slots > 0 =>
          accept Get (Item: out CHARACTER) do
            Item := Buffers (Get_ptr) ;
          end Get ;
          Get_ptr := Get_ptr mod No_of_units + 1 ;
          Full_slots := Full_slots - 1 ;
      or
          terminate ;
        end select ;
      end loop ;
  end Ring_buffer ;

  task Producer ;
  task body Producer is
    Item: CHARACTER ;
  begin
    loop
      Item := Prepare_item ;
      Ring_buffer.Put (Item) ;
      exit when Item = ASCII.EOT ;
    end loop ;
  end Producer ;
```

(cont.)

Example 9.12   The ring buffer task with termination.

```
      task Consumer ;
      task body Consumer is
         Item: CHARACTER ;
      begin
         loop
            Ring_buffer.Get (Item) ;
            exit when Item = ASCII.EOT ;
            - - consume item - -
         end loop ;
      end Consumer ;
   begin
      null ;
   end Smooth ;
```

Example 9.12 (cont.)

it may be necessary to forcibly remove a number of processes. This may be done by the **abort** statement. For example:

   abort X, Y, Fork (2) ;

would abort the named processes. **abort** should be used with care as it can be very disruptive in a system. The cost of undoing the work of a process may be high in a transactional system and should be avoided whenever possible. If a task is aborted then so are its dependents.

In the producer–consumer example it would be possible to write the consumer processes as the main part of Smooth as in Example 9.13. The **terminate** solution is more elegant, however.

```
      Char: CHARACTER ;
   begin
      loop
         Ring_buffer.Get (Char) ;
         exit when Char = ASCII.EOT ;
         - - consume Char - -
      end loop ;
      abort Ring_buffer ;
   end Smooth ;
```

Example 9.13   The **abort** statement.

9.7 Tasks and objects

In Chapter 5 we studied object-oriented design and programming with special reference to the electronic mail system. The solution that we adopted there took no account of any possible parallelism in the system and consequently serviced one request at a time. Many problems, and in particular electronic mail systems, are inherently parallel in that many users may wish to perform activities at the same time. In the mail system, users may be sending and receiving mail simultaneously.

It is often the case when designing for parallel computation that a good starting point can be to use an object-oriented design and to make the objects execute in parallel. This is the preferred style of programming in the language Smalltalk, and we use it here to make the electronic mail system into one capable of parallel execution. To start we can write the main procedure in the form of a number of tasks (one for each user) as in Example 9.14.

The system is driven by the users generating requests from input and sending messages to the other tasks to perform the appropriate activity. The parallelism in the system depends on there being a task to service every terminal in the system. We can define other tasks inside the USER task. We could even make the other user activities, such as Mail_message and All_mail etc. into tasks for further parallelism, but will not for the present. Decomposition of the system in this manner roughly corresponds to the structure diagram of Figure 3.2, except that all the activities are performed in parallel. We can continue this decomposition into the various objects in the system, inventing new tasks for each of the objects to obtain the maximum parallelism. The structuring technique for tasks corresponds to object-oriented design since each of the tasks can be thought of as an object – that is an instance of an abstract data type – that runs concurrently. The operations are defined by the entries allowed on the task.

We shall now indulge in a little restructuring of the electronic mail system in order to make full use of parallelism. For example, some objects are shared by more than one task. The mailboxes themselves may be accessed by all the tasks and have therefore to supply the appropriate entry facilities for correct synchronization. Let us start by building the parallel mailbox by adapting the ring buffer task to yield the appropriate entries for the mailbox. We make the task a generic, so that it can be reused for many types of message. In Ada tasks are not allowed to be generics, but this can be easily overcome by hiding them in a package. Example 9.15 gives a suitable description of the ring buffer for a mailbox. Notice that we have changed the mailbox so that it can only put in or return one message at a time.

The mailbox package may be instantiated for the system by

```
with Mail_item ;
package Mailboxes is new Mailbox (
          MESSAGE => Mail_item.INSTANCE ;
          No_of_units => 200 ;
          Total_users => 10) ;
```

This yields a package that contains an array of tasks that are the concurrent mailboxes.

9.8 Summary

In this chapter we have introduced the concept of parallelism in Ada programs. The main issues are specifying parallel computation, synchronizing parallel tasks so that they may cooperate, communication between

---

```
procedure EM_system is
   task type USER is
      entry Get_Choice (Object: in MESSAGE) ;
   end USER ;

   Users: array (INTEGER range 1..Total_users) of USER ;

   task body USER is
   begin
      loop
         accept Get_Choice (Object: in MESSAGE) do
            Choice:= Object ;
         end Get_Choice ;

         case Choice is
            when Mail_message =>
               .
            when All_mail =>
               .
            when Help_message =>
               .
            when Profile =>
               .
         end case ;
      end loop ;
   end USER ;
end EM_system ;
```

Example 9.14   A concurrent electronic mail system.

```
with User ;
generic
  type MESSAGE is private ;
  No_of_units: NATURAL := 500 ;
  Total_users: INTEGER := 20 ;
package Mailbox_manager is
  function Get (Usr: User.ID) return MESSAGE ;
  procedure Put (Usr: User.ID ; Item: MESSAGE) ;
  function Is_empty (Usr: User.ID) return BOOLEAN ;
end Mailbox_manager ;
package body Mailbox_manager is
  task type Mailbox is
    entry Get (Item: out MESSAGE) ;
    entry Put (Item: in MESSAGE) ;
    entry Empty (Empt: out BOOLEAN ) ;
  end Mailbox ;

  Usr_mail: array (User.id) of Mailbox ;
  - - this is an array of tasks - -
  function Get (Usr: User.ID) return MESSAGE is
    Item: MESSAGE ;
  begin
    Usr_mail (Usr).Get (Item) ;
    return Item ;
  end Get ;

  procedure Put (Usr: User.ID ; Item: MESSAGE) is
  begin
    Usr_mail (Usr).Put (Item) ;
  end Put ;

  function Is_empty (Usr: User.ID) return BOOLEAN is
    Item: BOOLEAN ;
  begin
    Usr_mail (Usr).Empty (Item) ;
    return Item ;
  end Is_empty ;
```

(cont.)

Example 9.15   A generic concurrent mailbox.

tasks, non-determinism and deadlock. Ada provides tasks to allow for
the specification of parallel activity and the rendezvous for communication and synchronization of these tasks. We have not yet introduced all
the variants of the rendezvous, but have seen how to express non-

```
task body Mailbox is
    Buffers: array (1..No_of_units) of MESSAGE ;
    Full_slots: INTEGER range 0..No_of_units := 0 ;
    Get_ptr, Put_ptr: INTEGER range 1..No_of_units := 1 ;
begin
    loop
        select
            when Full_slots < No_of_units =>
                accept Put (Item: in MESSAGE) do
                    Buffers (Put_ptr) := Item ;
                end Put ;
                Put_ptr := Put_ptr mod No_of_units + 1 ;
                Full_slots := Full_slots + 1 ;
        or
            when Full_slots > 0 =>
                accept Get (Item: out MESSAGE) do
                    Item := Buffers (Get_ptr) ;
                end Get ;
                Get_ptr := Get_ptr mod No_of_units + 1 ;
                Full_slots := Full_slots - 1 ;
        or
            accept Empty (Empt: out BOOLEAN ) do
                Empt := Full_slots = 0 ;
            end Empty ;
        or
            terminate ;
        end select ;
    end loop ;
end Mailbox ;
end Mailbox_manager ;
```

Example 9.15 (cont.)

determinism and how to send messages to tasks, the latter mechanism being identical to the procedure parameter mechanism. Deadlock is such a specialized problem that it must be left to the particular application to determine how it is to be dealt with. Ada's facilities with task termination will help in this respect.

We have also looked at a method of structuring large programs to take advantage of parallelism and seen how this may be done in a method similar to object-oriented programming. In this the system is considered to consist of objects that operate concurrently.

9.9   Further reading

Coffman, E. G., Elphick, M. J. and Shoshani, A. (1971). 'System deadlocks' Computing Surveys, **3**,(2), 67–78.

> This seminal paper on system deadlocks explains the issues, problems and solutions to the deadlock problem. Every aspiring parallel programmer should be familiar with these concepts.

Peterson, J. L. and Silberschatz, A. (1985). *Operating Systems Concepts.* Reading, Mass: Addison-Wesley.

> Many of the problems that arise in parallel programming have been well-studied by operating system designers. A general overview of operating systems can be found in this book, with particular interest in Chapters 8, 9 and 10. 67–78.

Chapter 10 Real-time Programming

So far in this book we have discussed the various design issues of Ada that make it a general-purpose high-level language. These issues are readability, strong typing, programming in the large, name space control and data abstraction. In Chapter 9 we introduced the concept of tasking for the parallel execution of cooperating sequential processes. Ada was designed for the US Department of Defense (DoD) for use in developing embedded systems which, by their very nature, require facilities for parallel activity. An embedded computer system is one where the computer acts as the controlling device for some larger system. It may be a microprocessor in a dishwasher or a motor car or it may be a large number of computers cooperating to control a more complex entity such as an atomic power station or the blast furnaces in a steel mill. Historically, as discussed in Chapter 1, these activities (which for the DoD were mostly military) were programmed in a plethora of languages, giving rise to great difficulty in maintenance and enormous cost. By introducing a standard language such as Ada it is intended that the maintenance costs of embedded software will be greatly reduced. This will be achieved by better language design and the reusability of software components and of programmers.

There are a number of requirements for embedded systems that are not generally required for other types of computer software. The most important of these is reliability, where the total system is never allowed to fail even although parts of the system might. A good example of this is the world telephone system, where components of the system may develop faults without the total system crashing. Indeed, it is a requirement of the telephone system that sections of it may be taken out for repair while it is active.

While it may be possible to survive a total shutdown of the telephone system, there are situations (such as in aircraft control or atomic reactor control) where a lack of reliability is intolerable. One very daunting aspect of such systems is that they can never be tested to destruction without risking creating the disaster we are trying to avoid. Indeed, it is difficult to see how testing can be used to give any complete degree of confidence in the system. We would expect much greater care in their verification and validation. The study of reliable systems is beyond the scope of this book, but the reader is recommended to Randall (1978) for a discussion of the problems in this area.

As can be seen from the above discussion, embedded systems require specialized facilities. These are:

- the need to communicate with external devices
- the need to recover from component failure
- the need to meet some performance criteria.

The need to communicate with devices external to the computer in real-time gives rise to the interrupts of Ada, and the need to recover from component failure gives rise to the exceptions of Ada. Before we can introduce these concepts, however, we must first look at some other aspects of Ada such as scheduling of tasks, entry lists for rendezvous and the concept of time in the Ada environment.

The aim of this chapter is to look at the problems of real-time programming systems and how the various aspects of Ada may be used in programming them. We shall discuss resource scheduling in general and how task priorities, conditional, delayed and timed-out rendezvous in Ada may be used. Interrupt-driven systems are a necessary part of a real-time environment, as are exceptions and exception-driven programming.

10.1 Task priorities

An Ada program may consist of many tasks and it is simplest to think of each task as executing on its own individual processor. This ideal situation is often not realizable, since tasks may be created and terminated dynamically whereas the number of processors available to a given system is probably static at any one time. The allocation of tasks to processors is not within the control of the user, but is performed by the compilation system.

This method has a number of advantages. Principally, the addition and removal of processors from the system can be achieved with little disruption. Since the user does not know which processor the task is executing on, then executing it on a different processor should make little difference. Relieving the programmer of the burden of allocating tasks to processors provides a level of machine independence.

The main disadvantage of the system is that it is often necessary for the programmer to know that a certain algorithm is executed on a certain processor. Two computers, one in Tokyo and one in London, both running cooperating tasks would operate significantly differently with regard to local data if both tasks were executed on the London processor. This is because of the efficiency tradeoff of access to local and remote data. Similarly in the control of a power station, certain processors will be dedicated to specific tasks for the purposes of speed of response. The only mechanism for doing this in Ada is to compile the separate tasks with separate compilation systems and make the tasks communicate via interrupts. As we shall see later, this is not always satisfactory.

Given that there are not enough processors to execute all the tasks, the run-time system scheduler has to decide which task will be allocated a processor. In many timesharing systems, where there is often only one processor, the scheduling strategy used is called time slicing. Each task is allocated to a processor for a certain amount of time during which it may execute. It is then halted and the next task given the processor for the allocated amount of time, which is called a time slice. If ten tasks compete equally for the one processor then each task appears to execute on a processor running at one-tenth of the speed of the real processor. In reality, it is less than this since switching between processes takes some time.

A task in Ada may be in one of five states:

- *active*: allocated to a processor
- *ready*: waiting for a processor
- *blocked*: delayed, waiting for I/O or a rendezvous
- *completed*: waiting for dependent tasks to terminate
- *terminated*: no longer able to execute.

An active process will release a processor by exceeding its time slice or becoming blocked, completed or terminated. When the scheduler decides which task to allocate to a processor, it consults the list of ready tasks. In a round-robin system the list is circular and the next task on the list is given the processor. More sophisticated ordering of the ready list can be used to give different scheduling strategies (Coffman and Kleinrock, 1968). One such method is to order the list by priority. That is, each task is given a priority and the scheduler selects the ready process with the highest priority to allocate to the processor.

There are many ways of allocating priorities. The simplest method is to allocate a static, fixed priority to each task, but more sophisticated systems may involve the dynamic recalculation of priorities for tasks. This, of course, is not possible in Ada.

To allow priorities to be given to tasks Ada uses a **pragma**. For example:

```
task Ring_buffer is
    pragma PRIORITY (10) ;
    entry . . .
        .
        .
```

.
.

end Ring_buffer ;

The priority of the task is specified by a static expression of the subtype
PRIORITY, which itself is defined by

subtype PRIORITY **is** INTEGER **range** *implementation_defined* ;

The subtype PRIORITY is defined in the package SYSTEM. The main
program is also considered a task and may be given a priority by
specifying it in the outermost declarative section.

It is important to remember what we are doing here. The
specification of a priority is an aid to the scheduling system to help
it decide which task to run next. The higher the priority the more urgent
the task is considered. The only constraint of the use of priorities is given
by the LRM:

> If two tasks with different priorities are both eligible for execution
> and could sensibly be executed using the same physical processors
> and the same other processing resources, then it cannot be the case
> that the task with the lower priority is executing while the task with
> the higher priority is not.

Thus for tasks of the same priority or where the priority is not defined,
the scheduling order is not defined. The LRM does not make explicit
reference to pre-emption. However, from the above it is obvious that
pre-emption must take place when a task with a higher priority than the
executing one becomes ready. This strategy is known as highest priority
first.

The rules for task priorities during rendezvous are slightly different.
If both priorities of the tasks are defined, the maximum value is used
for the called task. If only one task has a defined priority, then at least
that priority is used for the rendezvous. If neither priority is defined, then
the priority of the rendezvous is undefined. This ensures that a high
priority task is not delayed because it is engaged in a rendezvous with a
low priority task. However, entry queues are serviced in a first-in first-out
manner and are not affected by priorities, and therefore a higher priority
task may be held up by a lower one if its call is later in the entry queue.
This may be overcome by programming using conditional entries, as we
shall see later. Note also that if the called task executes a **select** then the
priorities of the possible tasks are not taken into account when choosing
which branch to take.

Finally, priorities should never be used to synchronize tasks. It is not
guaranteed that the priorities will be used, and therefore they are
only an indication of which tasks are more urgent should the priorities
be taken into account. Synchronization should always be performed by
a rendezvous.

10.2 Select variations

In this section we discuss various facilities in Ada to enhance the **select** statement in order that it may be used for real-time programming. Different versions of the **select** statement are necessary since we may wish to establish communication in a number of different ways. The first is the conditional rendezvous.

10.2.1 Conditional rendezvous

One problem not yet covered is the situation where an entry is only accepted if it is pending. That is, the called task should not be delayed to wait for the call. An example of such a situation is where we would only answer the telephone if it was ringing. This could be programmed by:

```
select
    accept Telephone_call do
    .
    .
    .
else
    null ;
end select ;
```

In this conditional form of selective waiting, if no calls on any of the **accept** alternatives with open guards is pending, then the **else** option is executed. Thus in the above example, if there was not a telephone call pending then the **null** statement would be chosen for execution, avoiding a delay waiting for the telephone call. In the case of a conditional **select** statement, it is not an error to have all guards closed as the **else** option will then be executed.

To correspond to the problem of a task not being delayed by the caller, there is an Ada construct called a conditional entry call that ensures that the caller is not held up if the called entry is not ready to respond. As an example of a conditional entry call consider the plight of someone wishing to travel in the city. If a bus is available it is taken, otherwise a taxi is used. This may be programmed as follows:

```
select
    Bus.board ;
else
    Take_taxi ;
end select ;
```

In this, if the bus is not available for boarding a taxi is taken. This form of the **select** statement has exactly one unguarded entry call and an alternative sequence of code, and is unlike the general **select** statement in that there are only two possible courses of action.

The conditional call and conditional entry do not cover all the possible situations that may arise. For example, we may wish to wait five minutes for a bus before deciding the taxi is necessary. In general we may wish to make a call or an **accept** conditional on time. These are called timed-out entry calls and delayed accepts respectively in Ada, but before discussing these constructs we must introduce the concept of time.

10.2.2 Timed rendezvous

If two independent tasks use separate clocks there is an inherent difficulty in synchronizing these clocks. If they use the same clock then an outside observer may see the two tasks performing actions at different times when the tasks meant them to be simultaneous. This would happen where the time taken to receive a message from the clock is different for both tasks. The tasks would receive the same time signal at different times. In the age of satellite communication the 200 millisecond delay on sensitive electronic equipment may be important and should be catered for. The designers of Ada have ignored this problem for the present and given the Ada programmer a much cruder notion of time.

Indeed there are two notions of time, Ada – relative time and absolute time. The predefined type DURATION is a fixed point type (to avoid loss of accuracy) and is used to give relative time. For example, the Ada statement

delay 21.0 ;

suspends the task it is executing for at least 21 seconds. After 21 seconds the task becomes ready and will become active when the scheduler allocates it a processor. In any implementation it is guaranteed that DURATION ' small is not greater that 20 milliseconds and that we are allowed durations, both positive and negative, of up to 86 400 seconds (one day). Thus the limit of accuracy for time in an Ada program is 20 milliseconds, which is not be good enough for some applications.

A delay can be used in our telephone example such that it will look periodically to see if a call is pending. This is shown in Example 10.1. The task Accept_call will either accept a pending call or it will suspend itself for at least two seconds before trying to take the call again. This example will cause an incremental timing drift in that if Perform_other_action takes some time then the **select** statement may be executed at a gap considerably greater than two seconds. A solution to this will be given after we have discussed absolute time in Ada.

10.2.3 Absolute time

Absolute time is provided by the predefined package Calendar, whose specification is given in Example 10.2.

The function Clock returns the current absolute time, which may be

```
task Accept_call is
  entry Telephone_call ;
end Accept_call ;

task body Accept_call is
  Period: constant DURATION := 2.0 ;
begin
  loop
    select
      accept Telephone_call do
        .
      end Telephone_call ;
    else
      delay Period ;
      Perform_other_action ;
    end select ;
  end loop ;
end Accept_call ;
```

Example 10.1   A telephone call task with a delay.

decomposed into year, month, day and seconds by the appropriately
named functions, or all of these by the procedure Split. The function
Time_of will compose a TIME from its parts. The operations + and – are
defined to allow mixed arithmetic on TIME and DURATION and the
comparison operators $<, <=, >=, >$ are defined on TIME with the usual
meaning. The difference of two TIMES is a DURATION. The exception
Time_error can be raised by Time_of if the actual parameters do not form
a legal date and by "+" and "–" if the result goes out of range.

We can use the package Calendar to make timing more accurate. For
example:

```
loop    – – sound siren every 2 seconds – –
  delay 2.0 ;
  Sound_siren ;
end loop ;
```

is not quite as it appears at first sight and may not sound the siren every
two seconds. The problem is that we have not taken into account the
time taken to sound the siren. Inevitably we get a cumulative time drift.

This may be overcome by using a mixture of absolute time and
relative time as in Example 10.3. By using the absolute time we avoid
the cumulative drift by calculating differences on the absolute time. Of
course this will not work if Period is smaller than the time taken to
execute the rest of the loop. The solution is also vulnerable to the design

```
package Calendar is
   type TIME is private ;

   subtype YEAR_NUMBER is INTEGER range 1901..2099 ;
   subtype MONTH_NUMBER is INTEGER range 1..12 ;
   subtype DAY_NUMBER is INTEGER range 1..31 ;
   subtype DAY_DURATION is DURATION range 0.0..86_400.0 ;

   function Clock return TIME ;
   function Year (Date: TIME) return YEAR_NUMBER ;
   function Month (Date: TIME) return MONTH_NUMBER ;
   function Day (Date: TIME) return DAY_NUMBER ;
   function Seconds (Date: TIME) return DAY_DURATION ;

   procedure Split (Date: in TIME ;
                    Year: out YEAR_NUMBER ;
                    Month: out MONTH_NUMBER ;
                    Day: out DAY_NUMBER ;
                    Seconds: out DAY_DURATION) ;

   function Time_of (Year: YEAR_NUMBER ;
                     Month: MONTH_NUMBER ;
                     Day: DAY_NUMBER ;
                     Seconds: DAY_DURATION := 0.0) return TIME ;

   function "+" (Left: TIME ; Right: DURATION) return TIME ;
   function "+" (Left: DURATION ; Right: TIME) return TIME ;
   function "-" (Left: TIME ; Right: DURATION) return TIME ;
   function "-" (Left: TIME ; Right: TIME) return DURATION ;

   function "<" (Left, Right: TIME) return BOOLEAN ;
   function "<=" (Left, Right: TIME) return BOOLEAN ;
   function ">" (Left, Right: TIME) return BOOLEAN ;
   function ">=" (Left, Right: TIME) return BOOLEAN ;

   Time_error: exception ;
private
   -- implementation dependent --
end ;
```

Example 10.2 The package Calendar.

of the scheduler, which may not allocate a processor to the task within the time period.

We can also use time to delay a rendezvous. In our previous telephone call (Example 10.1) the task was delayed for a period of time before looking to see if a call was pending. We may, on the other

```
declare
  use Calendar ;
  Period: constant DURATION := 2.0 ;
  Next_time: TIME := Clock + Period ;
begin
  loop - - sound siren every 2 seconds - -
    delay Next_time - Clock ;
    Sound_siren ;
    Next_time := Next_time + Period ;
  end loop ;
end ;
```

Example 10.3   Overcoming incremental time drift.

hand, wish to wait for the call and take it as soon as it arrives instead of waiting for the full proscribed period. This could be programmed as in Example 10.4.

This example uses a delayed **accept**. If the **accept** statement can be executed within the period of the delay then it is. Otherwise the **or**

```
task Accept_call is
  entry Telephone_call ;
end Accept_call ;

task body Accept_call is
  Period: constant DURATION := 2.0 ;
begin
  loop
    select
      accept Telephone_call do
        .
      end Telephone_call ;
    or
      delay Period ;
      Perform_other_action ;
    end select ;
  end loop ;
end Accept_call ;
```

Example 10.4   The telephone call task with a delayed accept.

alternative is chosen. This solution should be compared with the previous one, in Example 10.1, to highlight the subtlety of timing. In the previous one, if the call was not pending immediately then the task was delayed before executing Perform_other_action. In this solution the **accept** can be executed at any time during the waiting period and Perform_other_action only executed if it is not.

For symmetry there is a timed-out entry call which, like the conditional entry, has only two alternatives. For example:

```
select
    Bus.board ;
or
    delay Period ;
    Take_taxi ;
end select ;
```

This allows us to take the bus if it is available in the period defined. Otherwise the taxi is used. This is again subtly different from

```
select
    Bus.board ;
else
    delay Period ;
    Take_taxi ;
end select ;
```

which, if the bus is not available, merely delays us before taking a taxi.

10.3 Resource scheduling

In real-time programming it is often the case that some activities are more urgent than others. We have some control over the relative priority of tasks by using the PRIORITY pragma, and as we shall see in the next section, by using interrupts. However, we have no control over the servicing of entry queues which are always handled in a first-in first-out basis. This can cause problems in a real-time situation where a resource required by a real-time activity is stuck on an entry queue waiting for a less urgent request to be satisfied. Such situations can only be avoided by explicit programming, and Ada provides the facility of a family of entries to help with this.

Consider the problem of a store controller which, since the store is connected to many processors, may accept high-, medium- or low-priority requests for service. Such a system might exist where the store is to be accessed by several processors and I/O devices. Normally I/O devices will request the store at high priority since they have difficulty in repeating requests. Processors would request priority according to the urgency of their task. The store takes an address, a data object and an

```
type PRIORITY is (High, Medium, Low) ;
task Store is
  entry Service (PRIORITY) (Add: ADDRESS ;
                            R_w: BOOLEAN ; D: in out DATA) ;
end Store ;

task body Store is
begin
  loop
    select
      accept Service (High) ( . . . ) do

      end Service ;
    else
      select
        accept Service (Medium) ( . . . ) do
          .
        end Service ;
      else
        select
          accept Service (Low) ( . . . ) do

          end Service ;
        else
          null ;
        end select ;
      end select ;
    end select ;
  end loop ;
end Store ;
```

Example 10.5   A store controller with a family of entries.

indication whether it is a 'read' or 'write' request as parameters. The task defined in Example 10.5 illustrates this situation.

The details of how the store performs the service are not important, only that it does it in the correct order – that is, highest priority first. For each entry in the discrete range defined there is a separate entry queue for each priority.

Another method of programming the store is to use the Count attribute which contains the number of tasks waiting in an entry queue. Example 10.6 uses this facility.

```
task body Store is
begin
  loop
    select
      accept Service (High) ( . . . ) do
        .
      end Service ;
    or
      when Service (High) ' Count = 0 =>
        accept Service (Medium) ( . . . ) do
          .
        end Service ;
    or
      when Service (High) ' Count = 0 => and
           Service (Medium) ' Count = 0 =>
        accept Service (Low) ( . . . ) do
          .
        end Service ;
    end select ;
  end loop ;
end Store ;
```

Example 10.6   A store controller using the count attribute.

This second solution is no more elegant than the first, or indeed a solution involving three separate entries. The main drawback for both of these solutions is that they are clearly awkward to code for a large number of entries since we have explicitly to write the code for each entry.

A better solution is shown in Example 10.7. In this, the loop will try the entries in the PRIORITY order. Once one entry is accepted and serviced the value P is set to the highest priority value in order that the correct servicing order may be resumed.

There are two main drawbacks to this solution. The first is that a busy form of waiting is employed to service the requests. That is, the task is continuously active, occupying a processor whether it has a request to service or not. The second drawback to the solution is that it is not easy to see how to introduce a **terminate** option into the task to allow for a graceful closedown.

The final solution of Example 10.8 overcomes all of these difficulties by first requesting the store for a particular entry and then performing the required action. The first rendezvous establishes the priority request and the second rendezvous performs the function.

```
task body Store is
   P: PRIORITY := PRIORITY ' First ;
begin
   loop
     select
        accept Service (P) ( . . . ) do

        end Service ;
        P := PRIORITY ' First ;
     else
        if P = PRIORITY ' Last then
           P := PRIORITY ' First ;
        else
           P := PRIORITY ' Succ (P) ;
        end if ;
     end select ;
   end loop ;
end Store ;
```

Example 10.7   A store controller using priorities.

The caller of this task must make two calls to perform the action required. For example:

```
Claim_store (Priority) ( . . . ) ;
Service (Priority) ( . . . ) ;
```

This works if every caller has its own priority. If not, it is trivial to alter the example to encode the user identification as part of the priority.

There are many problems where busy waiting and termination are not important. Our next example of an elevator controller is one such case where a processor is dedicated to nothing else, but servicing the requests for the elevator. The system will never terminate, except for complete breakdown, nor will it need to do anything else, but service requests, making busy waiting acceptable. It is also a good example of how requests may be serviced in a different order from that in which they are made. This is a typical example of an embedded system where the program is one component of the total.

To optimize the use of the elevator and to guarantee some sort of fairness in its use, the strategy used for controlling the elevator is to make it travel in one direction, up or down, for as long as it is necessary or possible. Thus at any floor the action the elevator may take is one of three:

1. It will move to the nearest floor in the direction it was travelling.

2. If not, it will reverse its direction and apply one.

3. If there are no requests it will stay where it is.

This is not the only way in which to control an elevator, but it is sufficient to illustrate the facilities of Ada for embedded systems.

Example 10.9 gives an initial solution to the elevator problem. In this solution we have a package called Elevator that allows the user to call the elevator at a given floor. The package body has a procedure Call_elevator to service the requests for the elevator and a task to manage the movement of the elevator. The procedure Call_elevator creates a rendezvous with the Elevator_manager task, which itself either accepts the rendezvous or moves the elevator. There is an entry for every floor and the task will only accept entries for the current one before moving.

```
type PRIORITY is (High, Medium, Low) ;
task Store is
   entry Service (PRIORITY) (Add: ADDRESS ;
                               R_w: BOOLEAN ; D: in out DATA) ;
   entry Claim_store (Request: PRIORITY) ;
end Store ;

task body Store is
   Level: PRIORITY ;
begin
   loop
     select
       accept Claim_store (Request: PRIORITY) do
          Level := Request ;
       end Claim_store ;
     or
       terminate ;
     end select ;
     select
       accept Service (Level) ( . . . ) do
          .
       end Service ;
     or
       terminate ;
     end select ;
   end loop ;
end Store ;
```

Example 10.8   A store controller with termination.

```
package Elevator is
    type FLOOR_NO is new INTEGER range 1..No_of_floors ;
    procedure Call_elevator (Floor: FLOOR_NO) ;
end Elevator ;

package body Elevator is
    task Elevator_manager is
        entry Move_to (FLOOR_NO) ;
    end Elevator_manager ;

    procedure Call_elevator (Floor: FLOOR_NO) is
    begin
        Elevator_manager.Move_to (Floor) ;
    end Call_elevator ;

    task body Elevator_manager is
        type DIRECTION is (Up, Down) ;
        Floor: FLOOR_NO := 1 ;
        Moving: DIRECTION := Up ;
        procedure Move_elevator (Floor: in out FLOOR_NO) is separate ;
    begin
        loop
            select
                accept Move_to (Floor) ;
            else
                Move_elevator (Floor) ;
            end select ;
        end loop ;
    end Elevator_manager ;
end Elevator ;
```

Example 10.9   An elevator simulation.

The actual movement of the elevator is performed by the procedure Move_elevator which is given in Example 10.10.

In procedure Move_elevator, if the Count attribute for this floor is not zero then the procedure returns. The reason for this is that the Count attribute may have changed between the **select** statement in Elevator_manager and the test in Move_elevator. If a call for this floor has come in during this time then it will be serviced before the elevator moves.

If the Count attribute is still zero then we apply the scheduling strategy outlined above. That is, we move in one direction until we can go no further or there are no more requests for this direction.

```
separate (Main.Elevator.Elevator_manager)
procedure Move_elevator (Floor: in out FLOOR_NO) is
   Next_floor: FLOOR_NO := Floor ;
begin
   loop
      if Move_to (Next_floor) ' Count /= 0 then
         Floor := Next_floor ;
         exit ;
      elsif Moving = Up then
         if Next_floor = FLOOR_NO ' Last then
            Moving := Down ;
            Next_floor := Floor ;
         else
            Next_floor := FLOOR_NO ' Succ (Next_floor) ;
         end if ;
      else
         if Next_floor = FLOOR_NO ' First then
            Moving := Up ;
            Next_floor := Floor ;
         else
            Next_floor := FLOOR_NO ' Pred (Next_floor) ;
         end if ;
      end if ;
   end loop ;
end Move_elevator ;
```

Example 10.10   Moving the elevator.

10.4   Interrupts

In real-time embedded systems it is essential to be able to respond very
quickly to certain stimuli. For example, a fire detection sensor may detect
a fire and wish the control system written in Ada to activate the
sprinklers. The input from the fire detection system is a rather specialized
form of input. First of all no general system could cope with predefining
all such possible inputs. Also, we wish the response to be rapid. For such
events Ada provides interrupts.

An interrupt acts like an entry call from a hardware task whose
priority is guaranteed to be greater than any task defined in the
program. The interrupt may be an ordinary entry call, a conditional entry
or timed entry depending on the type of interrupt and the implement-

ation. An interrupt that is lost if not immediately processed corresponds to a conditional entry.

The interrupt must have a method of associating a location or an address with an interrupt. When the interrupt at that address occurs the entry is called. The association between an address and an interrupt is done by a representation clause. For example:

```
task Fire_detector is
   entry Fire ;
   for Fire use at 16#40# ;
end Fire_detector ;
task body Fire_detector is
begin
   loop
      accept Fire do
         Activate_sprinklers ;
      end Fire ;
   end loop ;
end Fire_detector ;
```

Example 10.11 A fire detection interrupt.

In any real fire detection system there will be multiple detectors, multiple sprinklers and some criteria for calling the fire brigade service. Say we invent the rule that the fire brigade is called if two detectors are activated within 30 seconds of each other. Example 10.12 illustrates how this situation can be handled. This example can be extended to call in back-up fire services, etc.

10.5 Exceptions and errors

In the production of large-scale software engineering products, reliability is a major concern. When programs are used as the control mechanism in embedded systems the standard of the reliability required depends on the application. Allied to the problem of reliability is the one of recoverability. Depending on the application, the system may not recover at all, that is stop, or the system may have to be so robust that it must always make an attempt to recover from an exceptional circumstance. It is important that we clearly understand what we are trying to do here since it is so critical to our total understanding of system failure.

At each stage in the development of a large software product there are techniques, as we have seen, that should increase our faith in the correctness of the product. We do not have available, at present, proof systems that would allow us to prove this correctness. Even if we did, there would still be two drawbacks. First the proof system would only be able to show that the specification and the algorithms were equivalent. This is no mean feat and is worth achieving; but it does not show that the specification is an accurate statement of the problem. This is a limitation on all proof systems.

The second difficulty with proof systems is that they require checks to be placed in the programs to ensure that data-dependent operations are applied to data of the correct format. This means that we cannot statically check for every type of error in the system and must

```
type DETECTOR is new INTEGER range 1..No_of_detectors ;

task Fire_alarm is
    entry Fire_detection (This: DETECTOR) ;
    for Fire_detection use at 16#40# ;
end Fire_alarm ;

task body Fire_alarm is
    use Calendar ;
    Period: constant DURATION := 30.0 ;
    Detection_time: TIME := Clock ;
    No_of_detections: INTEGER := 0 ;
begin
    loop
        accept Fire_detection (This: DETECTOR) do
            Activate_sprinklers (This) ;
        end Fire_detection ;
        No_of_detections := No_of_detections + 1 ;
        if No_of_detections = 2
            and Detection_time < Clock + Period then
            Call_fire_brigade ;
            No_of_detections := 0 ;
        else
            No_of_detections := 1 ;
        endif ;
        Detection_time := Clock ;
    end loop ;
end Fire_alarm ;
```

Example 10.12   A fire alarm system.

allow the programmer the facility to recover from such an error if the system is to be robust. Before we go on to discuss the facilities for recovery in Ada, it is interesting to review Ada's classification of the types of errors that may occur. These are:

1. **Errors that must be detected at compile time by every Ada compiler.** Such errors are defined in the LRM and any program that contains such an error is not a legal Ada program. Type errors fall into this category. Of course any program free from this type of error may run, but still contain errors.

2. **Errors that must be detected at run time by the execution of an Ada program.** Errors in this category must raise an exception when detected by the run-time system. This allows the programmer to write an exception handler for the error in order to recover. Constraint errors fall into this category.

3. **Erroneous execution.** The language rules specify that some programs are in error, but does not guarantee to detect these errors – for example, an access to a deallocated object or more surprisingly the use of an undefined value. The effect of an erroneous execution is unpredictable.

4. **Incorrect order dependencies.** This applies to parts of the language where the order of evaluation is not defined by the language. The construct is in error if a different order of evaluation would give a different result.

Erroneous execution errors and incorrect order dependences are not guaranteed to be detected by the Ada system although, if it does, the exception Program_error may be raised. It is interesting to note that Ada does not guarantee to detect all errors, preferring to have the power of some constructs despite their unsafe nature. This places only a little more burden on the programmer, since the scope for writing incorrect programs is vast already. It is an interesting philosophy since, because we know that we cannot catch all errors, we had better be careful not to generate them!

10.5.1 Exceptions

There are a number of languages that allow exceptions to be handled, and consequently a number of variations on the theme. In general, the exception, which may be foreseen (such as a divide by zero) or unforeseen (such as storage overflow) is raised when the error is detected. When this happens, control is transferred to a handler which executes the recovery code for the exception. Once it has executed the recovery code, the handler returns to the program execution. The nature of this return has a number of variants itself. In general, if a program frame F has an exception E raised during its execution then the strategy of the handler may be:

1. **Termination**. F is considered to have terminated and the handler returns control to the unit enclosing the handler for E.

2. **Correction**. F is considered to be corrected and control is returned to immediately after where the exception was raised.

3. **Try again**. The results of F are deemed to be unsafe and so the actions are undone and F executed again.

4. **Clean up and terminate**. This is a variation of the first where the exception mechanism undoes all the actions of the program back to where the exception handler is executed. This technique is necessary in a transaction mechanism.

The strategy used in Ada is that of *termination*.

10.5.2   Ada exceptions

We have already discussed some aspects of exceptions in Chapter 7. Here we discuss them in more detail, starting with declarations. A name may be given to an exception by a declaration. For example:

> Overflow: **exception** ;

declares an exception called Overflow. The exception name can only be used in a **raise** statement, in a handler or in a renaming declaration. Each exception declaration declares a name for a different exception. The exception name is determined at compile time and is independent of how many times the declaration is elaborated. Hence if the declaration appears in a recursive sub-program the name denotes the same exception for all activations of the sub-program. However, if the exception declaration is contained in a generic unit each instantiation is performed at compile time and gives a different exception for each one.

There are five predefined exceptions in Ada. They are:

1. Constraint_error. This is raised when some constraint is violated.

2. Numeric_error. This is raised for an arithmetic error.

3. Program_error. This is raised when we encounter a control structure error.

4. Storage_error. This is raised when we run out of storage space.

5. Tasking_error. This is raised during intertask communication.

An exception may be suppressed by the pragma Suppress although this is a dangerous course of action for the programmer since the actions of the program are unpredictable when an exception that has been suppressed is raised.

An exception handler may be specified on a block, the body of a sub-program, package, task or generic unit, which are called frames for this purpose. In each case the general form of the frame is:

```
begin
    sequence_of_statements
exceptions
    exception_handler
    {exception_handler}
end
```

This is illustrated in Example 10.13.

An exception raised during the execution of a frame causes control to be transferred to the exception handler named for that exception. If there is no handler it may be handled by the **others** option, and if this does not apply the exception is propagated as we shall see later. An exception has no parameters and therefore cannot indicate where it was raised. The handler is in the same scope as the frame and therefore has access to the local variables or parameters, but it may not engage in any

```
declare
    Non_positive: exception ;
    function Square_root (N: REAL) return REAL is
    begin
        if N < 0.0 then
            raise Non_positive ;
        else
            Calculate_square_root ;
        end if ;
    exception
        when Non_positive =>
            Put ("Non positive parameter") ;
            return ;
        when others =>
            .
            .
            raise ;
    end Square_root ;
begin
    null ;
end ;
```

Example 10.13 A square root function with exceptions.

transfer of control between the frame and the handler via **goto** statements.

The handling of exceptions is performed dynamically rather than statically. That is, if an exception is propagated it is done so back along the dynamic calling sequence of the program. The handling also depends on whether the exception is raised in the declarative part, statement part or the exception handler itself.

If the exception E is raised in a frame F which has a handler for E, then control is passed to the handler for E in F. If, however, the exception E is raised in the declarative part of F, the exception handling part of F or the statement part of F which does not have a handler for E, then the propagation of the exception depends on the nature of F. If F is a block then E is propagated to the enclosing block, immediately after any task declarations and only after dependent tasks of F have been terminated. If F is a sub-program E is propagated to the point of call. If F is a package body or declaration or a task declaration, then the exception is propagated to the frame enclosing F. Finally, if F is a task body the task becomes completed and the exception Tasking_error is raised at the point of activation of the task.

The dynamic nature of the relationship between raising and handling exceptions means that exceptions may go out of scope before being propagated back to the handler. This is shown in Example 10.14. The exception E raised in F.A is propagated to C and then to F.B which handles it. E is out of scope when propagated to C, but comes back into scope in B. Exceptions are always eventually handled, even if it is by the Ada system at the outermost level.

10.5.3   Exception handling during task communication

When one task attempts a rendezvous with a task that has already completed or completes before accepting the rendezvous, then the exception Tasking_error is raised in the calling task at the point of call. If the calling task is aborted before the rendezvous is established, then the entry call is cancelled. If the rendezvous is in progress it is allowed to complete normally. In both cases no exception is raised in the called task.

If the rendezvous has been established and an exception is raised within the **accept** statement, but has no handler in its frame, the rendezvous is abandoned and the same exception is raised in the called task immediately after the **accept** statement and in the calling task at the point of the entry call. Also, if the called task is aborted during the rendezvous then the exception Tasking_error is raised in the calling task at the point of call. This covers all the possible cases for task communication and each situation should be taken into account when programming systems that are required to be reliable.

```
package F is
   procedure A ;
   procedure B ;
end F ;

procedure C is
begin
   F.A ;
end C ;

package body F is
   E: exception
   procedure A is
   begin
      .
      raise E ;
      .
   end A ;

   procedure B is
   begin
      .
      C ;
      .
   exception
      when E =>
      .
      .
   end B ;
begin
end F ;
```

Example 10.14   The scope of exceptions.

10.6 Summary

Ada is designed as a language for embedded systems, and although it is
a very useful general-purpose language its major application area is likely
to be embedded systems. Most such systems have some real-time needs
and it is important that Ada provides for these requirements. An aspect
of real-time embedded systems is that there are usually parts that can
never be tested without creating the situation they are supposed to be
reacting to. Allied to this is the fact that it is often impossible to recreate
the circumstances under which some program action was taken in

response to a real-time stimulus. This means that great care has to be taken in the design, construction and verification of such systems as the cost of correction during operation is likely to be very expensive.

The aspects of real-time programming that we have looked at in this chapter are resource scheduling and recovering from exceptions. The Ada facilities we explored were task priorities, conditional, delayed and timed-out rendezvous and exceptions.

10.7 Further reading

Coffman, E.G. and Kleinrock, L. (1968). 'Computer scheduling methods and their countermeasures' *AFIPS SJCC*. **32**,(11), 11–21.

> This paper contains a description of the problems of scheduling and how they may be overcome. The main emphasis is on operating systems, but the principles may be applied to other types of system.

Randall, B. (1978). 'Reliable computing systems' In *Operating Systems: An Advanced Course*. Berlin: Springer-Verlag, 282-392.

> This is a section of a book dedicated to reliability. It starts off by describing the problems of reliability and goes on to describe some solutions to the problem.

Chapter 11   Input and Output

Language designers have long recognized the difficulty in obtaining a clean model of input and output. The problem is that no sooner has a model been implemented when a new device is placed on the market that does not conform to that model. It is an unfortunate fact of life for the language designer that models of input and output are hardware dependent and must respond to changes in technology.

This has led to mixed reactions from language designers. For example in COBOL, FORTRAN, Pascal and Algol68 the language designers have, to a greater or lesser extent, built facilities for input and output into the language. In effect, they freeze the model, being convinced that it is sufficiently powerful for the application domain of the language. From time to time the language may be revised to provide a new standard and at this time any new device can be incorporated into the model or the model altered if necessary.

Another approach, first developed by Algol60, is to make no provision for input and output in the language at all. By this means, any model of I/O can be grafted on to the language, allowing it to adapt easily to new technologies or different applications. This appears at first sight to be a very sound concept, but it leads to great problems in the portability of systems and is often quoted as the main reason for the lack of widespread use of Algol60. As we shall see Ada follows Algol60's example, but tries to avoid the problems of portability by defining a standard system.

As with any programming language there are two fundamental questions to be answered with regard to I/O. They are:

1. What is the conceptual model of I/O?
2. How is it provided in the language?

On the second question the designers of Ada have made a great issue of having no special features for I/O in the language. The I/O system must therefore make use of the existing facilities for general programming already in the language. Any model of I/O can then be implemented without a great change to the language. The language designers also make a great issue of having no preferred model of I/O. This is, however, not quite true since the language supports a model of I/O as a standard package and this is further reinforced by the fact that the LRM has a chapter on I/O rather than leaving it to an appendix. It is this preferred model of I/O that we shall discuss for the rest of this chapter.

By using the package mechanism to encapsulate the operations for a standard I/O model, the designers of Ada have indicated how different models of I/O may be added to the language. To provide a new model of I/O in Ada it is sufficient to define a package with the required functionality.

In this chapter we look at the facilities of Ada for input and output. We discuss the standard I/O packages and show how I/O programming may be integrated with programming in the large. We also touch on the problems of portability with regard to I/O; a subject that is discussed more fully in Chapter 12.

11.1   Ada's conceptual model of I/O

The designers of Ada have taken a very conventional file-based view of input and output in their standard system. It allows communication with the user, communication with special low-level devices and communication with long-term storage devices. Correspondingly there are three levels in Ada's conceptual model of I/O. The file level provides for the long-term storage of data, the text level for user communication and the device level for I/O with physical devices. The different sections of the I/O system are supported by standard packages.

With the file level of I/O the user is presented with the notion of external and internal files. External files are real files that depend on the implementation. They are referred to in programs by file names which are strings in the language. Internal files are abstract entities in the program that are used to specify a particular file. A mapping mechanism is therefore necessary between external and internal files in order that long-term storage may be achieved. Files may be organized as sequential files or as direct-access files, depending on the requirements of the user. A sequential file has the property that the objects may be accessed one after the other in order. Direct-access files have the properties of a one-dimensional array in that the objects in the file may be randomly accessed. The generic packages Sequential_io and Direct_io support sequential and direct files respectively. Since they are generic packages they may be instantiated to yield files of any particular type. However, it should be noted that the effect of input and output for **access** types is implementation dependent.

Text-level I/O is provided by the package Text_io and is used for user communication. The organization of text is purely sequential – the text is considered as characters which are made up into lines which themselves are made up into pages. This allows structure to be placed on the text. Files are available at this level, but only sequential files.

The package Low_level_io provides the facilities for the device level. At this level, control or data can be sent or received from a device. The details are implementation dependent.

11.1.1 File management

Files exist for direct I/O, sequential I/O and text I/O. In each of the I/O packages a number of attributes concerned with file management are defined. As has already been mentioned, Ada has the notion of external and internal files. Both states of a file are available to the programmer, who may set up the association between an external and internal file and may also manipulate the attributes of a file.

The I/O primitives of Ada can be split into three categories: those which yield the attributes of the files, those which manipulate the association between external and internal files, and those associated with manipulating the elements of the file. An external file is identified by two parameters, its name and its form. The meaning of these two strings is implementation dependent and so may include aspects particular to some file system. For example, in UNIX we could use a full path name such as

"/USR/BIN/COMMAND"

for the name and a string such as

"RWE"

to represent the form which, in the UNIX case, is the file protection mode.

Each file also has a mode that is defined by the enumeration type FILE_MODE in each of the packages. For direct files this type is

type FILE_MODE **is** (In_file, Inout_file, Out_file) ;

The enumerations correspond to files that can be 'read only', 'read/write' and 'write only'. The mode of the file can be reset during use.

For sequential files and text files the file mode type is defined by

type FILE_MODE **is** (In_file, Out_file) ;

which means that these files may be 'read only' or 'write only'. These attributes may be found by the following functions:

function Mode (File: **in** FILE_TYPE) **return** FILE_MODE ;
function Name (File: **in** FILE_TYPE) **return** STRING ;
function Form (File: **in** FILE_TYPE) **return** STRING ;

The association between external and internal files may be set up by the procedures Create and Open. The user is also allowed to close the file, delete the file if possible, reset the file to the start (changing mode if desired) and to test if the file is open. The facilities are provided by the following procedures and function:

```
procedure Create (File: in out FILE_TYPE ; Mode: in FILE_MODE ;
        Name: in STRING ; Form: in STRING) ;
procedure Open (File: in out FILE_TYPE ; Mode: in FILE_MODE ;
        Name: in STRING ; Form: in STRING) ;
procedure Close (File: in out FILE_TYPE) ;
procedure Delete (File: in out FILE_TYPE) ;
procedure Reset (File: in out FILE_TYPE ; Mode: in FILE_MODE) ;
procedure Reset (File: in out FILE_TYPE) ;

function Is_open (File: in FILE_TYPE) return BOOLEAN ;
```

The functions of the third category to manipulate the elements of a file depend on the type of I/O involved. However, each style of I/O provides facilities to read from a file, write to a file and test for the end of file. These are provided by the following:

```
procedure Read (File: in FILE_TYPE ; Item: out ELEMENT_TYPE) ;
procedure Write (File: in FILE_TYPE ; Item: in ELEMENT_TYPE) ;
function End_of_file (File: in FILE_TYPE) return BOOLEAN ;
```

These sub-programs taken together constitute the file manipulation facilities of Ada.

11.2 Binary I/O

Binary files consist of binary data. That is, the form of the data is the same in both main store and file. This means that format conversion is not necessary between main store and file and leads to efficient input and output.

For the storage of data between the activation of programs, Ada provides sequential files and direct-access files. A sequential file is one where the data may be accessed in order one after the other. A direct-access file is one where the data may be accessed randomly. Both kinds have many features in common and, in general, programs that will work for sequential files will also work for direct-access files.

11.2.1 Sequential I/O

The sequential I/O package is defined in the LRM. The package is generic and it may therefore be instantiated with any appropriate type. For example, we may have files of integers, booleans or some complex record type. It should be noted, however, that the generic formal parameter is **private** and therefore limited types such as tasks are not allowed as elements of files. The input and output of **access** types is also implementation dependent and may even not be implemented since it involves conversion of addresses from internal to external form.

In sequential I/O the Read operation reads the next item in the file. An exception will be raised if the file is not an In_file, if there are no more elements in the file or if the item in the file is not of the correct type. The Write operation writes an element to the end of the file. An exception will be raised if the file is not an Out_file or if the capacity of the file is exceeded. For an In_file the user can test for the end of the file.

The procedure shown in Example 11.1 copies the contents of an integer file. The names of the source and destination files are given as parameters to the procedure.

```
procedure Copy_integer_sequential_file
              (Source, Destination: STRING) is
    package Integer_sequential_io is new Sequential_io (INTEGER) ;
    use Integer_sequential_io ;
    Source_file, Destination_file: FILE_TYPE ;
    Item: INTEGER ;
begin
    Open (Source_file, In_file, Source) ;
    Create (Destination_file, Out_file, Destination) ;
    while not End_of_file (Source_file) loop
        Read (Source_file, Item) ;
        Write (Destination_file, Item) ;
    end loop ;
    Close (Source_file) ; Close (Destination_file) ;
end Copy_integer_sequential_file ;
```

Example 11.1   A procedure to copy sequential files of integers.

For the moment we shall ignore the problem of exceptions being raised during the execution of the procedure. Instead we concentrate on making the procedure adaptable to any type of sequential file, since it would be a major disadvantage to have to write a copy procedure for every different type of sequential file. We can write this generalized copy procedure by using a generic to abstract over the file element type. Example 11.2 does this.

Thus we now have a generalized procedure for copying sequential files.

```
generic
  type ELEMENT is private ;
procedure Copy_any_sequential_file (Source, Destination: STRING) is
  package Any_sequential_io is new Sequential_io (ELEMENT) ;
  use Any_sequential_io ;
  Source_file, Destination_file: FILE_TYPE ;
  Item: ELEMENT ;
begin
  Open (Source_file, In_file, Source) ;
  Create (Destination_file, Out_file, Destination) ;
  while not End_of_file (Source_file) loop
    Read (Source_file, Item) ;
    Write (Destination_file, Item) ;
  end loop ;
  Close (Source_file) ; Close (Destination_file) ;
end Copy_any_sequential_file ;
```

Example 11.2   A generic sequential file copy.

11.2.2   Direct I/O

A direct-access file can be viewed as a linear array of objects of the same type that can be accessed in random or sequential order. Each element in the file has an index of type COUNT, an implementation-defined positive integer type. Associated with each internal file is a current index which is used to specify the element to read or write. The Read and Write procedures may set the current index before performing their action and both automatically increment it after their task is performed. The current index may be set and interrogated independently of the Read and Write procedures.

With direct-access files it is possible to write beyond the current end of file. This will result in the intermediate elements being undefined, assuming that the capacity of the external file has not been exceeded. The function Size may be used to determine the capacity of the external file to avoid reading or writing beyond the physical end of file.

We may use the sequential copy procedure, given above, to copy direct files since the abstractions used in the procedure (Open, Create, Close, Read, Write, End_of_file) are common to both sequential and direct files. We have, of course, to alter the name of the package to be instantiated inside the copy procedure to obtain the correct file type. The procedure shown in Example 11.3 can be used to copy direct files.

In the copy example, we first abstracted over the type of elements in the file. It would now be sensible to abstract over the abstract

```
generic
   type ELEMENT is private ;
procedure Copy_any_direct_file (Source, Destination: STRING) is
   package Any_direct_io is new Direct_io (ELEMENT) ;
   use Any_direct_io ;
   Source_file, Destination_file: FILE_TYPE ;
   Item: ELEMENT ;
begin
   Open (Source_file, In_file, Source) ;
   Create (Destination_file, Out_file, Destination) ;
   while not End_of_file (Source_file) loop
      Read (Source_file, Item) ;
      Write (Destination_file, Item) ;
   end loop ;
   Close (Source_file) ; Close (Destination_file) ;
end Copy_any_direct_file ;
```

Example 11.3   A generic direct-access file copy.

structure of the file, yielding one generic procedure that could be instantiated for either direct or sequential files – or indeed any data structure with the required set of procedures and functions. Unfortunately this turns out to be non-trivial and long winded in Ada. We offer Example 11.4 which may be used to yield an integer sequential file copy by:

```
package Integer_sequential_io is new Sequential_io (INTEGER) ;
use Integer_sequential_io ;
procedure Integer_sequential_copy is new
      Copy (INTEGER, FILE_TYPE, FILE_MODE) ;
```

The above solution is somewhat unsatisfactory, since the abstract data structure is always a limited type and the parameter passing modes of some of the procedures may make substitution difficult, or at best inefficient. For example, if the data structure is a stack with the following:

```
procedure Pop (S: in out STACK; Item: in ELEMENT) ;
procedure Push (S: in out STACK; Item: out ELEMENT) ;
```

then Pop and Push could not be directly substituted for Read and Write respectively because of the mode of the first parameter. A further layer of procedures is necessary to solve this.

This example again highlights a problem with generics that we have commented on in several places in this book. It is, that we cannot easily parameterize a generic with another package. The problem stems

```
generic
   type ELEMENT is private ;
   type F_TYPE is limited private ;
   type F_MODE is private ;
   with procedure F_Create (File: in out F_TYPE ;
               Mode: in FILE_MODE ;
               Name: in STRING ;
               Form: in STRING) is Create ;
   with procedure F_Open (File: in out F_TYPE ;
               Mode: in FILE_MODE ;
               Name: in STRING ;
               Form: in STRING) is Open ;
   with procedure F_Close (File: in out F_TYPE) is Close ;
   with procedure F_Read (File: in F_TYPE ;
               Item: out ELEMENT_TYPE) is Read ;
   with procedure F_Write (File: in F_TYPE ;
               Item: in ELEMENT_TYPE) is Write ;
   with function F_End_of_file (File: in F_TYPE)
               return BOOLEAN is End_of_file ;
procedure Copy (Source, Destination: STRING) is
   Source_file, Destination_file: F_TYPE ;
   Item: ELEMENT ;
begin
   F_Open (Source_file, F_MODE ' (In_file), Source) ;
   F_Create (Destination_file, F_MODE ' (Out_file), Destination) ;
   while not F_End_of_file (Source_file) loop
      F_Read (Source_file, Item) ;
      F_Write (Destination_file, Item) ;
   end loop ;
   F_Close (Source_file) ; F_Close (Destination_file) ;
end Copy_any_direct_file ;
```

Example 11.4   A generic file copy.

from the fact that packages are not data objects themselves, but even so this could be overcome by some syntax.

11.3   Text I/O

The package Text_io is provided in Ada for user communication. Two procedures Put and Get in various overloaded forms provide the method of sending and receiving information to and from the user. The procedure Put has the general form

```
procedure Put (File: FILE_TYPE ; Item: in T) ;
procedure Put (Item: in T) ;
```

The procedure Put converts the binary form of Item to a sequence of characters and then writes the characters to the file. The procedure Get also has two forms defined by

```
procedure Get (File: FILE_TYPE ; Item: out T) ;
procedure Get (Item: out T) ;
```

Procedure Get performs the reverse operation to Put. That is, it reads a sequence of characters corresponding to a value of type T and then converts it to the binary form of Item.

The procedures Put and Get are overloaded for the types of character, string, numeric (integer, fixed-point and floating-point) and enumeration. The package Text_io yields the generic packages Integer_io, Fixed_io, Float_io and Enumeration_io which must be instantiated to the particular type in order to yield the correct versions of Put and Get. For example, integer to text I/O could use:

```
with Text_io ;
package Integer_text_io is new Text_io.Integer_io (INTEGER) ;
```

One instance of each package is required for each distinct type involved in text I/O.

11.3.1 Text file structure

A text file is made up of a sequence of pages followed by an end of file symbol. A page is a sequence of lines followed by an end of line or an end of file symbol. A line is a sequence of characters followed by an end of line, page or file symbol. Each character in a line occupies one column. Although text files are strictly sequential some structure can be placed in them by splitting the file into pages, lines and columns. There are facilities to find and set the page and line lengths, to find and set the column and line number, to test for the end of line, page and file and finally to write a new line or page symbol on output and skip a line or page on input. The precise details of each of these operations is given in the LRM, but as an example of their use we give a program to copy text files (Example 11.5).

11.3.2 Text file manipulation

The operations available for sequential files defined by the package Sequential_io are also defined in the Text_io package. These are Create, Open, Close, Delete, Reset, Mode, Name, Form and Is_open. With text I/O

```
with Text_io ; use Text_io ;
procedure Copy_text is
    Char: CHARACTER ;
begin
    while not End_of_file loop
        if End_of_line then
            Skip_line ; New_line ;
        elsif End_of_page then
            Skip_page ; New_page ;
        else
            Get (Char) ; Put (Char) ;
        end if ;
    end loop ;
end Copy_text ;
```

Example 11.5   A copy text procedure.

there is a notion of a default input and output file. Most of the procedures and functions in the Text_io package that have file parameters are defined twice. For example:

```
function New_page (File: FILE_TYPE) ;
function New_page ;
```

The second version assumes the default output file since New_page is an output operation. For input operations the abbreviated form will assume the default input file.

When a program is started, the default input file is set to the standard input for the system and the default file to the standard output. The user can set the default input and output to other files if required using the procedures Set_input and Set_output respectively. In order to keep control of the files used in this manner the user can also find out the current default and standard, input and output files.

11.4   Device I/O

To control physical devices in Ada the package Low_level_io is used. The package supplies a procedure to send data to a device and a procedure to receive data from a device. The types of devices and the types of data that are available depend on the particular implementation. However, to add a new device or data format it is sufficient to provide an overloaded implementation of the two procedures. The package is defined by:

```
package Low_level_io is
    - -declarations of the possible types of device and data - -
    - -declarations of the overloaded procedures for these types - -
    procedure Send_control (Device: DEVICE_TYPE ;
            Data: in out DATA_TYPE) ;
    procedure Receive_control (Device: DEVICE_TYPE ;
            Data: in out DATA_TYPE) ;
end Low_level_io ;
```

As we have mentioned before, the I/O facilities of Ada use a very conventional file-based model. The emergence of new types of devices, such as graphics workstations with bit-map raster graphics and mouse interrupts, pose a problem for the Ada applications programmer. The problem is that the power of the workstation that we wish to have for large software engineering problems cannot easily be coded in Ada. Nor, as discussed in Chapter 2, is the type of the device discussed in the APSE requirements, with the result that no APSE support can be relied on.

In the following examples we propose a solution to the problem of implementing workstation facilities in Ada by using device I/O and interrupts in a special package. The system is based on the graphics facilities of PS-algol (Morrison *et al.*, 1986). We shall start with a task to control the mouse, which for our purposes has four coloured, buttons. The task can receive an interrupt from the mouse when a button is depressed or accept a rendezvous from the user to find out the colour of the last, button that was pressed. In real workstations, the mouse task will be a little more complicated than this as we shall also wish to know the position of the mouse. However, in the interest of clarity we do not clutter the example with detail. Example 11.6 contains the mouse task.

The second part of implementing the workstation is to build a package of graphics operations for the device. This we do by defining a raster type and the operations on the rasters which are Xor, Copy, Nand, Not, Nor, Xnor, Ror and Rand. Example 11.7 does this.

Each raster procedure sends a record to the device which contains the particular raster operation and the raster itself. Again the raster instructions in a real system will be more complicated than this, but the example illustrates how the system may be implemented. The procedure body of Send_control may be written with code statements.

11.5   Exceptions

All three of the standard I/O packages, Sequential_io, Direct_io and Text_io, name the package Io_exceptions in their context clause. The package Io_exceptions contains the definitions of all the exceptions that

```
type MOUSE_BUTTON is (Red, White, Green, Blue) ;
task Mouse is
   entry Pressed (Button: in MOUSE_BUTTON) ;
   entry Which_button (Button: out MOUSE_BUTTON) ;
   for Pressed use at 12#45# ;
end Mouse ;
task body Mouse is
   Last_button_pressed: MOUSE_BUTTON ;
begin
   loop
      select
         accept Pressed (Button: in MOUSE_BUTTON) do
            Last_button_pressed := Button ;
         end Pressed ;
      or
         accept Which_button (Button: out MOUSE_BUTTON) do
            Button := Last_button_pressed ;
         end Which_button ;
      or
         terminate ;
      end select ;
   end loop ;
end Mouse ;
```

Example 11.6   The mouse task.

can be raised by the I/O system. It is defined by:

```
package Io_exceptions is
   Status_error: exception ;
   Mode_error: exception ;
   Name_error: exception ;
   Use_error: exception ;
   Device_error: exception ;
   End_error: exception ;
   Data_error: exception ;
   Layout_error: exception ;
end Io_exceptions ;
```

The package Io_exceptions does not require a body as it only contains declarations. The details of how each exception may be raised is given in the LRM. The order of the declarations in the package is important, for if two exceptions can be raised at the same time only the earlier one in the declaration list is raised.

```
package Workstation is
  type MOUSE_BUTTON is (Red, White, Green, Blue) ;

  task Mouse is
    entry Pressed (Button: in MOUSE_BUTTON) ;
    entry Which_button (Button: out MOUSE_BUTTON) ;
    for Pressed use at 12#45# ;
  end Mouse ;

  type RASTER is array (NATURAL) of BOOLEAN ;

  procedure Xor (A: RASTER) ;
  procedure Copy (A: RASTER) ;
  procedure Nand (A: RASTER) ;
  procedure Not (A: RASTER) ;
  procedure Xnor (A: RASTER) ;
  procedure Xnor (A: RASTER) ;
  procedure Ror (A: RASTER) ;
  procedure Rand (A: RASTER) ;
end Workstation ;

package body Workstation is
  task body Mouse is
    - - See Example 11.6 - -
  end Mouse ;

  type RASTER_OP is (Xor_code, Copy_code, Nand_code,
      Not_code, Nor_code, Xno_coder, Ror_code, Rand_code) ;
  type DATA_TYPE is record
    A: RASTER_OP ;
    B: RASTER ;
  end record ;

  procedure Xor (A: RASTER) is
    Station: device_type ;
    Data: DATA_TYPE := (Xor_code, A) ;
  begin
    Send_control (Station, Data) ;
  end Xor ;
    .
    .
    .
begin
    .
end Workstation ;
```

Example 11.7   The workstation package.

```
declare
    package Integer_sequential_io is new Sequential_io (INTEGER) ;
    use Integer_sequential_io ;
    procedure Integer_sequential_copy is new
        Copy (INTEGER, FILE_TYPE, FILE_MODE) ;
begin
    Copy ("MYFILE", "MYFILE_COPY") ;
exception
    when Name_error =>
        Copy ("MYFILE", "") ;
    when others =>
        raise ;
end ;
```

Example 11.8   A use of I/O exceptions.

By placing the definition of the exceptions in a separate package rather than in the three packages themselves, the problem of defining new exceptions on each instantiation of a standard package is avoided. Thus programming to catch an I/O exception is made easier.

To illustrate I/O exceptions, we shall assume that when using our Copy procedure, a Name error in the destination file name may arise. In this case, we wish to create a temporary copy of the file. This is achieved by Example 11.8. Notice that the shortened version of the exception name is available from the instantiation of the package Sequential_io. All other exceptions are propogated.

11.6   Input and output in large systems

The main difficulty in I/O programming with any programming language is portability, a subject covered fully in Chapter 12 where we make a number of suggestions for increasing the portability of Ada programs. Text I/O for certain classes of device is likely to be standard throughout most implementations of Ada and provides little in the way of portability problems. On the other hand, the Send_Control procedure and Mouse task in the workstation example are likely to cause major problems of portability, and we should always aim to program so that these difficulties are kept to a minimum. We can do this by containing the I/O parts of a system to well-defined areas and abstracting over them using packages and sub-programs so that the I/O facilities are only explicitly programmed in one section. The abstractions are available everywhere else in the system.

We can as far as possible collect all the system dependencies into one part of the system so that reimplementation involves that module being tailored to the new system. The UNIX system makes extensive use of this technique by collecting system dependencies into a configuration file which has to be tailored to a particular environment. This also allows for dynamic system configuration, a subject mentioned in Chapter 3.

The I/O facilities of Ada may be used to extend the size of the main store of a target computer. For example, if we invent the right abstractions, there is no reason why some data object should not be kept in a direct-access file rather than an array. If the array is very large there may not be enough space to fit it into main store, and the obvious solution is to place it on disk. We can keep it on file without losing any of the power of programming, only of execution speed.

As an example of this we shall take the class Sequence given in Example 5.13 and implement it as a direct-access file instead of an array. The package specification remains the same and is given again in Example 11.9.

The package body can be written as a layer of sub-programs that hide the implementation of the sequence as a direct-access file. This is shown in Example 11.10.

By using this technique of programming we can extend the store to use files. This should only be done where speed is not essential, but space

```
generic
    type ANY_TYPE is private ;
package Sequence is
    - -Put adds an item to the end of the sequence
    procedure Put (Val: ANY_TYPE) ;
    - -Get returns an item from the sequence at the position referenced
    - -by some notional sequence pointer
    procedure Get (Val: in out ANY_TYPE) ;
    - -Reset sets the notional sequence pointer to refer to the beginning
    - -of the sequence
    procedure Reset ;
    - -AtEnd determines if the sequence pointer refers to the last
    - -sequence member
    function AtEnd return BOOLEAN ;
    - -IsEmpty determines if the sequence has any members
    function IsEmpty return BOOLEAN ;
end Sequence ;
```

Example 11.9   The class Sequence.

```
with Direct_io
package body Sequence is
   package Seq is new Direct_io (ANY_TYPE) ;

   Seq_file: Seq.FILE_TYPE ;

   procedure Put (Val: ANY_TYPE) is
   begin
      Seq.Write (Seq_file, Val) ;
   end Put ;

   procedure Get (Val: in out ANY_TYPE) is
   begin
      Seq.Read (Seq_file, Val) ;
   end Get ;

   procedure Reset is
   begin
      Seq.Reset (Seq_file) ;
   end Reset ;

   function AtEnd return BOOLEAN is
   begin
      return Seq.End_of_file ;
   end AtEnd ;

   function IsEmpty return BOOLEAN is
   begin
      return Seq.Size = 0 ;
   end AtEnd ;
begin
   Create (Seq_file, Inout_file, " ") ;
end Sequence ;
```

Example 11.10   The class Sequence with a file implementation.

is. The technique can also be used for the long term storage of such data structures between activations of programs. A word of caution, however. Since I/O is not defined on **access** types and some other types, then the technique is some way short of orthogonal persistence (Atkinson *et al.* 1983).

11.7   Summary

The designers of Ada have taken a very conventional file-based view of input and output in their standard packages. It allows communication with the user, communication with long-term storage devices and communication with low-level devices. The facilities have been provided without adding any new features to the language, utilizing instead the existing package structure.

Whether the I/O design of Ada constitutes a success or not is a matter of opinion; however, we do feel that the designers have missed an opportunity by not being radical enough in their thoughts on I/O. The facilities provided, while comprehensive, do not always solve all the users' problems. For example, there is no provision for the growing use of graphics and sound in user communication. A more serious problem is that the facilities constitute a major investment in understanding by the programmer. In a typical database application the user has to master over 100 names in the various packages. The lack of orthogonality of the system with regard to **limited private** types and the lack of I/O on **access** types contribute to this complexity.

This last point requires some clarification. To output a complete tree or graph structure takes a considerable amount of code to break it down to its components so that it contains no **access** variables. On reading the data structure back in, the reverse process is required. Such complexity increases life cycle costs.

11.8 Further reading

Le Verrand, D., (1985). *Evaluating Ada*. Oxford: North Oxford Academic.

> This book critically examines the various aspects of Ada. Many of the sections are worth reading and the section on I/O is particularly good, pointing out the strengths and weaknesses of Ada's I/O system.

Chapter 12 Portability and Reuse

The principal objective in developing Ada was to reduce the cost of software maintenance after the software was delivered. In addition, reliable programs should be easier and cheaper to develop using Ada rather than other lower-level programming languages. Recall our earlier observation that large software systems are long-lived entities and many of the costs of system maintenence are incurred in partial system reimplementation so that it will execute on new target hardware. Given that a typical life for a large system might be 12–15 years and that computers become obsolete in 4–5 years, it is clear that moving the system from one target machine to another is probably inevitable at least once in its lifetime.

A key requirement for Ada was that it should be a standard language which was independent of any particular computer. Thus an Ada program developed for system P (say) should, in principle, execute without change on system R. In practice, this is unlikely unless systems P and R are very similar indeed. It is virtually impossible to hide all machine and operating system details completely for all programs, and although a standard language like Ada reduces portability problems it does not eliminate them completely. In this chapter, we look at portability problems that can arise when Ada is used for large systems development, and at how these can be minimized.

The chapter is also concerned with a topic that is related to portability, namely software reusability. Software reuse is a 'motherhood principle' in that it is accepted as worth while by almost all software developers; yet, in reality, it is only rarely practised in a systematic way. The reasons for this are discussed later in the chapter. It is clear that the extensive reuse of software is likely to reduce software costs during the design and implementation phase (the software need not be written) and during the validation phases (the software has already been checked). It was a design aim of Ada that the language should encourage software reuse, and we examine how Ada constructs such as generic packages may be used to build reusable components.

12.1 Program portability

In principle, any program written in a high-level programming language, like Pascal, ought to be portable. Given that a language compiler is available on all target machines, a Pascal program should compile and run on all of these systems. In practice, for all except trivial programs which have little interaction with their environment, this is unlikely to be the case.

There are a number of reasons for this unfortunate fact:

1. Programming languages are usually defined and implemented before a standard for the language specification has been adopted. This means that the language implementors often make changes to the language design to adapt it to particular hardware, to interface it to a particular operating system or to correct language design defects. However, different versions of the language implementation are normally incompatible as the implementors make different changes to each version. There is thus no single, standard version of the language. Although there are national standard bodies (such as the British Standards Institution and the American National Standards Institute) who establish language standards, this standardization is usually applied to a mature language. Unfortunately, it is then often too late to ensure that the standard is generally accepted as a great deal of investment may have been made in programs written in non-standard versions of the language.

2. Features of the target machine architecture may be reflected in the high-level language implementation. With modern machine architectures, this is most apparent in number representations where different machines have different real number precisions. The problem arises, to a lesser extent, with the range of the allowed integers where the upper integer limit on 16-bit machines is 32 767 and is 2 147 483 647 on 32-bit computers.

3. Features of the target machine operating system may be reflected in the high-level language implementation. This is particularly likely in the area of input/output constructs and file handling, which are poorly defined in most programming languages. This has often resulted in arbitrary, non-portable extensions to fit a language to a particular operating system.

4. Real-time embedded computer systems usually interact directly with the system hardware. If no language facilities for this are provided, this involves linking sections of assembly code with the high-level language. Apart from the inherent non-portability of assembly code, the linkage mechanisms that have been adopted for different languages are often totally different.

Ada was designed with these problems in mind. In the following sections, we look at each of them in turn and examine how well Ada has avoided portability problems in these areas.

12.1.1 Language standardization

From the outset, it was intended that a standard version of Ada should be established and that the proliferation of language extensions that has occurred with Pascal, say, should not be repeated in Ada implementations. Indeed, the name 'Ada' has been trademarked and a programming language that does not conform to the Ada standard may not be sold as 'Ada'.

An ANSI (American National Standards Institute) standard for Ada was established in 1983 and will be subject to periodic revisions as deficiencies in the language become apparent and are corrected. These revisions will be infrequent because of the cost of standard development and because of the need to protect investment in existing Ada programs.

The first version of Ada was published in 1979 and a period of four years is a remarkably short time to develop a programming language standard. However, for most programming languages, a compiler can be written in much less than four years and it might have been expected that Ada compilers would have come into existence, been used and hence established a *de facto* Ada standard. This did not actually happen for two reasons:

- The defence organizations in the USA and Europe who are, by far, the largest purchasers of Ada programs did not admit Ada as a recognized language until a standard had been established. This meant that there was little benefit to be gained by 'quick and dirty' Ada implementations.

- Ada is a large and complex language and compilers for the language are expensive and difficult to write. Indeed, at the time of writing this book, only a few Ada compilers are of a high standard in that they translate the full version of Ada and produce compact and efficient object code. The complexity of the language precluded a large number of early language implementations before the language standard was developed.

Conformance with the Ada language standard is checked by a complex suite of validation procedures, intended to make sure that an Ada compiler will compile only standard Ada programs, will not compile a superset of Ada and has implemented all standard Ada facilities. Unless an Ada compiler passes this validation, it may not be used for the development of US DoD or UK MoD systems. In addition, Ada implementations must be revalidated if the compiler is changed and are subject to periodic revalidation as the validation suite is improved and updated.

Whilst the notion of a validation suite that checks conformance with a language standard is an attractive one, it is not practically possible to develop a set of validation programs that unequivocally checks that a superset of a language has not been implemented. Whilst it is possible to check that all language features are recognized by a compiler, there are an infinite number of possible language supersets and it is impossible to check for every possible extra which might be added to a language. Furthermore, it is quite unneccesary. If a contract requires that programs be written in standard Ada this is a requirement for that particular system. Should the compiler handle some Ada superset, this is of no interest to the system purchaser as long as these additional features are not used.

A further problem with certifying that an Ada compiler is 'valid' is that this implies that the compiler has reached some minimal standard of quality. In fact, the validation process implies no such thing. A valid Ada compiler may be very slow to compile programs, may produce bulky and inefficient object code, is not guaranteed to be robust, may be incorrect and may produce object code that is not a correct translation of the Ada source program. It is quite impractical to test compiler correctness because of the immense number of possible interactions within the compiler, and so validation must not be taken as a universal stamp of compiler quality.

It is perhaps appropriate to discuss the general question of Ada standardization and whether the early establishment of a standard is likely to lead to the cost savings which it implies. It is undoubtedly the case that systems developed in Ada will use a language that conforms to the standard and that portability problems due to non-standard language implementations will not exist. However, the danger with establishing a standard before a language has been widely used is that it may result in poorly designed language features becoming impossible to avoid. Ada has been extensively evaluated and, although there are some language features that are poorly designed (variant records are an example, proper Algol68-like type unions would be much better), the design of standard Ada is a reasonable one.

A more serious problem, which is universal in subjects like computing where technological change is very rapid, is that the establishment of a standard freezes development. Whatever is standardized may become technologically obsolete by the time the standard is agreed. This is perhaps most apparent in the standardization of the Graphical Kernel System (GKS) which is effectively a standard for vector graphics operations. Almost as soon as that standard was accepted, raster graphics systems (which GKS does not properly support) became widely used and are likely to be the most common graphics devices for the foreseeable future.

This seems likely to occur with Ada to some extent. Ada is, in essence, a language designed for writing programs to run on traditional, sequential Von Neumann machines. Its support for parallelism (tasking) is such that the user must make the decision on how a problem may be implemented using parallel processing, which may or may not be mapped on to multiprocessor systems. At the time of writing, there is a great deal of research going on into machine architectures that are inherent parallel processors, and it seems likely that such parallel systems will become widely used in the 1990s. It is not clear how Ada can take advantage of these.

12.1.2   Operating system dependencies

Ada is principally intended for embedded system programming and it is envisaged that the development of Ada programs will take place on some host machine in the context of an Ada Program Support Environment. These programs will execute on a target machine which may be the same machine as the host system, but more commonly will be a separate computer. This host-target mode of development means that two levels of portability problem can arise. These occur in the following circumstances:

1. When the original host system is replaced and the program must be ported to a new host. Here, the problems are not in the portability of the Ada application program, but in the portability of its associated development system, which may include special-purpose development tools.

2. When it is necessary to retarget the system to some new target machine. Here, the portability of the application system is of direct interest.

The first of these problems was recognized by the Department of Defense, and so an associated portable development environment (the APSE) was also specified. In principle, this means that there should be few problems of host portability. Given that a program is developed in the context of an APSE and that all support tools are written in Ada, it should be possible to rehost the system on to any other host machine which also supports an APSE. In practice, however, life is never so simple.

As we discussed in Chapter 2, serious thinking on the APSE did not start until late on in the Ada language design programme. The initial APSE requirements only laid out the principal APSE facilities and did not specify, in detail, the interfaces to the Kernel-APSE which should be expected by the APSE designer. As a result, a good deal of APSE work was carried out using incompatible kernel systems, and it is only now that a standard APSE interface (the CAIS interface), designed by the KIT/KITIA working group, is starting to emerge.

Given the difficulty of APSE implementation and the fact that this was an almost completely new application area, a delay was perhaps inevitable. Indeed, even with standard KAPSE interfaces implementing an APSE is a very difficult task and we are unlikely to see effective, portable APSEs before the early 1990s. As a result, a great deal of Ada program development will occur outside the context of an APSE, either under an operating system such as UNIX or in the context of a non-portable support environment provided by Ada compiler vendors. Clearly, then, host independence is important in Ada systems development.

When a validated Ada compiler is used for system development, there should be no portability problems caused by compiler incompatibilities if another host system with a different Ada compiler is used for systems development. Any problems that ensue are likely to be in the software tools used to support application software development. For many large systems, the effort involved in support tool development is comparable to the effort expended in system development, so the importance of tool portability should not be underestimated.

Here, we shall discuss how the underlying host machine operating system can affect portability. While host machine architecture incompatibilities can cause problems, these are unlikely to be serious as it will usually be the case that comparable types of computer are used for Ada systems development. Machine architecture problems will be covered later when target portability is considered. Notice that operating system portability problems also arise when target systems run different operating systems, although it will often be the case that the target operating system is actually part of the embedded Ada system.

A number of different operating system incompatibilities can arise between different Ada host systems. Probably the most significant of these are problems caused by different filing system organizations and problems caused by different operating system command languages. Let us address the latter of these problems first as it is, perhaps, the most intractable.

The operating system command language provides a means of specifying what programs are to be run, in what order these programs are to be run and which system files are to be associated with the program executions. Typically, program development operations invoke more than a single tool – a file may first be preprocessed by some macro-processing system, compiled, and then linked with several program libraries. Whilst this might be invoked by a single command (like the UNIX cc command), it is perhaps more logical to invoke these tools via a command language procedure. Indeed, one of the strengths of the UNIX operating system is the ease of constructing command language procedures that allow tools to be invoked in sequence and information to be passed from tool to tool.

In general, when a toolset is ported from one host system to another which uses a different command language, it is necessary to rewrite all command language procedures. There is no common command language. The role of the command language with respect to the operating system is comparable to that of assembly language *vis-à-vis* machine architecture, so there is no simple way of writing portable command language procedures.

Dependencies on the filing system of the host's operating system probably cause most of the common problems that arise when attempting to port a high-level language program from one operating system to another. The filing system incompatibilities which arise fall into a number of categories:

1. **File name incompatibilities**. Different systems have different conventions for file names and, in particular, different systems place different restrictions on the length of file names.

2. **File system structure incompatibilities**. Some systems make use of a hierarchical organization whereas others use a 'flat directory' organization.

3. **File typing incompatibilities**. Some systems associate a distinct type (binary, FORTRAN-text, etc.) with each system file, whereas other systems simply consider all files to be files of characters.

4. **File limits incompatibilities**. Systems have different limits on the maximum size of files, the number of open files allowed by any one program at any one time, the number of characters in a file record, etc.

5. **File access control incompatibilities**. Some systems keep a list of allowed users, others associate more general access permissions with a file.

6. **File access primitive incompatibilities**. Different systems use different ways of opening, closing, reading and writing a file. However, this should not be a serious problem if tools are developed using Ada, as the file access primitives are concealed in the Ada I/O packages and only standard Ada I/O facilities should be used.

Fortunately, many of the problems caused by incompatible file systems can be circumvented if they are anticipated. Guidelines for portability can be developed. Some guidelines that we believe should always be followed when developing Ada programs under an operating system rather than an APSE are as follows:

1. *Avoid the use of long filenames*. Although these are very useful for descriptive purposes, they can cause problems if the system is ported

to a machine that has a limit on the length of file names. A good rule of thumb is to use file names whose length is 12 characters or less. Few systems have file-name length limits less than 12.

2. *Always use 'flat' file names.* In systems with a hierarchical organization, the names of files may reflect this hierarchy or may simply be names in the 'current' directory. It is always advisable to use the latter option and to bind a 'path name' to this when the program is executed or loaded. This means that porting to a flat directory system is straightforward. Indeed, this guideline should be followed even when the system is only intended to run on systems with a hierarchical file organization. If a hierarchical path name is embedded in a program, this can cause problems when porting to a system that uses different conventions for hierarchy naming.

3. *Avoid 'typed' files whenever possible.* Most systems allow files to be represented as simple character files and this is the most general-purpose organization. Unfortunately, it is not always possible to adopt this convention as some systems use 'moded' tools (such as compilers). This means that the software tools expect files of a particular type as input and produce files of a particular type as output.

4. *Conceal file access control primitives in separate routines.* This is straightforward in Ada systems where the normal way of providing I/O primitives is via an I/O package.

5. *Avoid keeping files open when this is not strictly necessary.* There is usually a limit on the number of open files. There are no real precautions that can be taken against arbitrary limits such as maximum file size, etc. Fortunately, these are unlikely to cause many difficulties on systems powerful enough to be used for Ada development.

A further portability problem that may occur when interactive systems are being developed is that of interacting with different types of user terminal. There is a multiplicity of terminal types available and, although there are some *de facto* standards (such as the DEC VT100 terminal), these are often based on obsolete systems and do not allow the full power of some modern intelligent systems to be utilized. This is a problem even when the underlying computer and operating system are unchanged.

Perhaps the most effective solution to this problem is that adopted by some versions of the UNIX system. This system keeps a file of terminal capabilities and provides a procedural interface to this file. All interaction with a user's terminal is carried out via this procedural interface, and the application program may ignore details of the particular terminal capability. However, this is an expensive solution which imposes a further portability problem, in that the terminal capability table and associated access procedures must be ported when systems using that table are moved from machine to machine. The problem is compounded by the availability of personal workstations which make extensive use of graphics and menus. There is little or no standardization in this area, and attempting to keep a 'capability file' is almost impossible because of the extensive differences between these systems.

It is to be hoped that most of the portability problems caused by operating system dependencies will be resolved when APSEs come into widespread use. Until then, the most effective approach to avoiding these problems appears to be to standardize on some widely used operating system as a development system and require that that operating system should be available if the development is ported to some other computer. At the time of writing, the most widely available operating system (excluding personal computer systems) is UNIX and, as we discussed in Chapter 2, this system is reasonably well-suited to program development. Unfortunately, there are almost as many variants of UNIX as there are manufacturers, although a standard seems likely to emerge in the near future.

12.1.3 Machine architecture dependencies

Assuming a host-target mode of development, the portability of an application program is not affected by dependencies on the operating system of the host computer, although the problems described may arise if the target machine is run under the control of an operating system. However, in embedded systems applications, the target machine is a 'bare machine' which has only a primitive operating system (sometimes called the executive) and this operating system is supplied as part of the embedded application system. As a result, the major portability problems are not caused by operating system dependencies, but by dependencies on the machine architecture of the target machine.

In principle, a vast range of computer architectures ranging from primitive 8-bit microprocessors to powerful multiprocessor mainframe systems might be target machines for systems that have been developed in Ada. One approach to target system portability is to define a virtual target system with minimum attributes. Programs are written to operate on such a virtual target system and machine architecture dependencies are eliminated. Porting the program simply involves mapping the virtual machine capabilities on to the capabilities of the real target machine. Such a target system is set out (in part) by Nissen and Wallis (1984) in a discussion on portable Ada programs. Their suggested target machine attributes are as follows:

1. The target machine should have at least 16 bits available to represent the Ada type INTEGER.

2. The target machine should have at least 32-bit accuracy for Ada fixed-point types.

3. The target machine should have at least 6 decimal digits available for the Ada type FLOAT.

4. The target machine should have at least 10 decimal digits available for programmer-defined floating-point types.

5. At least 80 character positions per line should be available for text output display.

Whilst some very primitive 8-bit microprocessor systems may not meet these requirements, such systems are now obsolete and, by the time Ada comes into widespread use, it is very unlikely that there will be a requirement to use such systems as target machines for Ada applications.

In practice, an abstract machine approach to target independence is often unrealistic. Each application has its own requirements in terms of efficiency, integrity, security and accuracy, and it is necessary to chose a target system which best allows these requirements to be met. A universal target machine would not actually be very useful as there would be only a few applications for which it was suitable. Because of application demands, it is inevitable that particular target machine characteristics are used, and this is likely to lead to portability problems if the software is moved to some other target system.

Rather than list the constructs of Ada which might lead to target machine dependencies (Nissen and Wallis provide such a list), we consider some of the problems that arise owing to machine architecture dependencies and suggest how the Ada program developer can minimize these problems by making use of packages to encapsulate non-portable parts of a program.

The most obvious machine dependency likely to arise is a consequence of different target machines having different word lengths. The maximum and minimum value of integer and fixed-point numbers is likely to be dependent on word lengths as is the accuracy of floating-point numbers. Whilst adopting a set of minimal requirements reduces portability problems in this area, such an approach may be undesirable as it may lead to unnecessary complications when numbers outside the minimal ranges are to be manipulated. Furthermore, it is usually unrealistic to standardize on such minimal requirements as it is unlikely to be necessary to port to a system whose word length is less than that of the original target system.

Consider the following example. An Ada application program is used to count the number of alpha particles emitted from a radioactive source. The information is passed through a detector and, at periodic intervals, the counter value is saved in a database and the counter is cleared. The minimum number of alpha particles in a given time is zero and the maximum number of particles expected is 20 000 000. On a target machine which has a 32-bit architecture this range may be represented as an integer, whereas machines which have a 16-bit architecture must represent the large integer range in some other way. If the most likely target system is a 32-bit machine, it seems sensible to make the most effective use possible of the machine's capabilities rather than artificially adopt some other scheme for representing this range of integers. However, the possibility that the program may be ported to a machine with a shorter word size should be taken into account by implementing the counter as an abstract data type rather than as an integer. A specification for a package implementing such an abstract data type might be written as shown in Example 12.1.

Notice how this package has been specified as a generic package with the range of values to be handled by the counter specified as formal object parameters. The package may then be instantiated for any particular range, not just the built-in range of 0 to 20 000 000. The body

```
with TEXT_IO ;
    -- The values below are not generic parameters
    -- because their ultimate representation might not be numeric
    -- Counter_minimum: NATURAL := 0 ;
    -- Counter_maximum: NATURAL := 20_000_000 ;
package Alpha is

    -- Implements an alpha particle counter so as to localize representation
    -- dependencies.
    -- In order to port to a different architecture with a lesser range of
    -- integers the representation of COUNTER and the body of the
    -- procedures that act on it should be changed.
    -- Needs the I/O package TEXT_IO.

    type COUNTER is private ;
    function Increment (C: COUNTER) return COUNTER ; --adds 1
    function Clear return COUNTER ; --sets to 0
    procedure Write (C: COUNTER ; Output: TEXT_IO.FILE_TYPE) ;
    procedure Initialize (C: out COUNTER; Filename: STRING) ;
private
    --On a 32-bit computer. Expected range is as in header comment
    type COUNTER is new NATURAL ;
end Alpha;
```

Example 12.1 The specification of an alpha particle counter.

for this package as it might be implemented on a 32-bit computer is shown as Example 12.2.

If it becomes necessary to port this system to some machine where the range of integers is less than that of a 32-bit system (say a 16-bit machine), all architectural dependencies are encapsulated in the package and only the private part of the package and the package body must be rewritten.

```
with TEXT_IO ;
package body Alpha is

    Output: TEXT_IO.FILE_TYPE ;
    Counter_minimum: constant COUNTER := 0 ;

    function Increment (C: COUNTER) return COUNTER is
    begin
        return C + 1 ;
    end Increment ;

    function Clear return COUNTER is
    begin
        return Counter_minimum ;
    end Clear ;

    procedure Write (C: COUNTER ; Output: TEXT_IO.FILE_TYPE ) is
        S: STRING (1..100) ;
        function Convert_counter (C: COUNTER) return STRING is
            begin
                - - Converts counter to string value for I/O
                - - not defined here
                return "The string value" ;
            end Convert_counter ;
    begin
        S := Convert_counter (C) ;
        TEXT_IO.Put (Output, S) ;
    end Write ;

    procedure Initialize (C: out COUNTER ; Filename: STRING )
    begin
        C := Counter_minimum ;
        TEXT_IO.Open (Output, TEXT_IO.OUT_FILE, Filename, " ") ;
    end Initialize ;
end Alpha ;
```

Example 12.2 Package body for Alpha on a 32-bit machine.

For example, a machine with a 16-bit word length can represent integers from –32 768 to 32 767. Therefore, one possible represent-ation of COUNTER is as a pair with the first element holding the number of thousands and the second element holding a value between 0 and 999. In Ada, this would be implemented as a record and the private part of the package Alpha would become:

```
type COUNTER is record
    Thousands: NATURAL ;
    Units: NATURAL ;
end COUNTER ;
```

The package body would be rewritten as shown in Example 12.3. For brevity, we have excluded the definition of the procedure Write as this is only slightly changed.

It is a good general rule to implement all representation-dependent objects as abstract data types. This localizes the code that has to be changed when the system is ported to a new target, yet still allows advantage to be taken of features of the machine architecture to improve program performance, integrity, etc.

Let us turn now to a portability problem which is characteristic of real-time systems – namely timing dependencies. Typically, real-time embedded systems are made up of a number of cooperating sequential processes which execute concurrently and which interact with each other via a rendezvous or via message passing. Each process has a particular priority which may be allocated by the compiler or which may be set up by the system developer using the priority pragma. Processes may execute on a single processor under the control of a scheduler, on a multiprocessor system made up of a number of closely coupled processors, or on a distributed system made up of several processors connected via a communications network. In principle at least, the Ada tasking mechanism allows systems to be written that are independent of the number of processors used for execution.

Given that all target configurations were made up of identically fast processors with a processor for each task, portability, as far as tasking was concerned, would be no problem. The performance of all algorithms and the timing of process interactions would be identical in all cases. An algorithm whose performance was satisfactory on one target configuration would perform in the same way on all other targets. In practice, of course, target configurations are quite different in terms of processing speed, and this can result in significant portability problems.

For example, say some process is used as part of the control system, made up of four processes, for a radiation detection system. It is required to interrogate a sensor 1000 times per second to determine if a radioactive input has been detected, and the results of this interrogation are placed on a queue for processing by some other consumer process. The requirement that the process should examine the sensor 1000 times

```
with TEXT_IO ;
package body Alpha is

   Output: TEXT_IO.FILE_TYPE ;
   Counter_minimum: constant NATURAL := 0 ;

   function Increment (C: COUNTER) return COUNTER is
      Count: COUNTER ;
   begin
      Count.Units := C.Units + 1 ;
      if Count.Units = 1000 then
         Count.Thousands := C.Thousands + 1 ;
         Count.Units := 0 ;
      else
         Count.Thousands := C.Thousands ;
      end if ;
      return Count ;
   end Increment ;

   function Clear return COUNTER is
      C: COUNTER ;
   begin
      - -assumes Counter_minimum is less than 1000
      C.Thousands := 0 ;
      C.Units := Counter_minimum ;
      return C ;
   end Clear ;

   procedure Write (C: COUNTER ; F: FILE_TYPE ) is
   begin
      ...
   end Write ;

   procedure Initialize (C: out COUNTER ; Filename: STRING)
   begin
      C.Thousands := 0 ;
      C.Units := Counter_minimum ;
      TEXT_IO.Open (Output, TEXT_IO.OUT_FILE, Filename, " ") ;
   end Initialize ;
end Alpha ;
```

Example 12.3   Package body for Alpha on a 16-bit machine.

per second implies that it must be scheduled every millisecond and that its execution time must be less than a millisecond. Assume the initial implementation of this process executed on a dedicated 4 MIP target processor and the algorithms used involved executing 2000 machine instructions. This meets the requirements as the process is constantly scheduled and its execution time is 0.5 milliseconds.

Now assume that a low-cost version of this system is to be built using a single processor to execute all four processes. Assume that the speed of this processor is 8 MIP so that, in effect, each process has its own 2 MIP processor. However, when several processes share a single processor, there is some scheduling overhead as these processes are stopped and started, so that the effective speed of each 'virtual processor' is less than 2 MIP. Given that the above process involves executing 2000 instructions, this means that the requirement for 1000 process executions per second cannot be met. The process is not portable and must be recoded to use a more efficient algorithm if it is to execute properly on the new target system.

The requirements for embedded real-time systems are often such that it is essential that the execution time for processes must be minimized in a target environment that is constrained by costs, power consumption or physical size. This means that a target configuration must be chosen which is less then ideal and the deficiencies compensated for by expending effort on developing very efficient software to drive the target machine. The above example illustrates that this may require the recoding of the system using different algorithms if the software is ported to a new target. This may be an inevitable penalty of the system's efficiency requirements and, apart from following the good design principles of high coherence and loose coupling, there are no programming techniques to minimize such recoding costs.

When developing real-time systems that are intended to be portable, it is essential to avoid using particular characteristics of a target machine implementation to enhance efficiency. For example, say there are a number of producer processes (A, B and C) and a consumer process D. The action taken by D depends on which of the producer processes was resposible for its input. A well-engineered implementation of this scheme would be for the producer processes A, B and C to tag their output with their name and place it on a queue for subsequent processing by D. Such a scheme is not dependent on characteristics such as scheduling of processes or process execution speed.

Now assume that the initial implementation of this system is on a single processor target system and the scheduler is such that it runs the processes in the order A, D, B, D, C, D, A, D, etc. If A, B and C are always guaranteed to produce an input, a more efficient implementation of the system might be to use a single shared variable for process communication rather than a queue, and for A, B and C simply to place their output in that variable. Knowledge of the scheduling system may be used by D to work out whether its input arises from A, B or C. Such a scheme may meet the efficiency requirements of the application and may perform satisfactorily.

However, porting such an implementation to another target configuration can be very costly. Say the new target configuration is a multiprocessor system so that A, B, C and D are always scheduled on their own processor. This means that a single shared variable is not adequate for process communication as each producer process operates in parallel and must lock out other producer processes until its output has been consumed. The benefits of multiprocessor operation are lost! Also, the asynchronous operation of the producer processes means that it is no longer possible for D to use scheduling information to determine the source of its input.

Details of how target configuration dependencies affecting real-time systems may be avoided are given in Nissen and Wallis (1984). The following is a summary of their conclusions:

1. Do not make assumptions about the order of activation of task objects declared in the same list.

2. Do not make assumptions about queue configurations resulting from several tasks making entries in the queue. That is, do not assume that entries will always be made in the same order if the system is moved to a new target configuration.

3. Avoid side effects in selective wait guard evaluation and do not make assumptions about order of guard evaluation.

4. Do not use the priority pragma to enforce synchronization.

5. Do not assume that a task which is aborted will actually terminate within a particular time interval.

6. Avoid the use of shared variables.

A general approach to real-time systems construction which simplifies system maintenance as well as making the system more portable is to develop a system design without taking efficiency considerations into account. This design may then have a number of variants tailored to particular target machines with efficiency compromises documented in each variant. In general, these will probably affect less than 10 per cent of the system code. This can be rewritten from the original design when the system is moved to a new target configuration.

In most embedded systems, it is necessary to make use of representation clauses to interface the Ada programming system to the underlying hardware. These are inherently non-portable and code which includes such clauses will have to be rewritten when the system is moved to a new target configuration. Similarly, if machine code segments are inserted in an Ada program in order to gain efficiency, these are non-portable and must be rewritten. As far as possible, the use of such machine-dependent features should be avoided.

In order to localize essential machine-dependent features of a program, use should again be made of packages. A machine-independent specification should be presented to other parts of the system with the machine-dependent constructs localized in the package body. Particular care must be taken with machine code segments that the registers set up by the compiler are not corrupted by the machine code execution. This is liable to be a particular problem if different versions of the compiler (which may have different conventions) are used for system compilation.

12.1.4 Compiler dependencies

In principle, there should be no need to include information on compiler dependencies in a discussion of portability as all compilers should process the language in the same way. Unfortunately, this is never the case and it is very important to avoid the use of constructs that are implementation dependent. In this section, we look at features that can cause portability problems because of compiler differences – namely default variable initialization, side effects in expressions, and mixed-language programming.

The Ada language reference manual is quite clear that an attempt to access an uninitialized variable which is of some scalar type is erroneous. This has the implication that the predefined exception PROGRAM_ERROR should be raised if an undefined variable is accessed, but the language standard is specific that this is not mandatory. In practice, the detection of undefined values can be difficult so it is likely that some implementations of Ada will assign some default initial value to all declared variables. Portability problems arise if deliberate or accidental use is made of this default value.

For example, say the default value for objects of type INTEGER is zero and the following code is written to sum the elements of an array:

```
Sum: INTEGER ;
The _array: INTEGER_ARRAY ; – –assume this type declared elsewhere
for I in The_array ' RANGE loop
   Sum := Sum + The_array (I) ;
end loop ;
```

If the variable Sum is initialized to zero then this code will execute correctly. However, say the code is ported to another system whose default initialization value is –1 (on a two's complement machine, this involves setting all bits in a word). The above code will no longer execute correctly, but if the sum of the array elements is large; the error in the computed value will be small and may not be immediately detected. Indeed, the error may only become obvious long after the system port is complete and cause serious problems for maintenance programmers.

As we have already discussed, it is a good general rule to initialize all declared variables or, if this is inconvenient, to comment them with details of when they will be initialized. This ensures that the accidental omission of initialization may be readily detected and that deliberate use of default initialization is eliminated.

As a general programming principle, side effects should be avoided. This means that functions used in expressions should not modify non-local variables. The principal reason for this is that side effects make programs much harder to understand because modification of the system's global environment is not explicit. Another important reason is that side effects may make the value of expressions dependent on the order of evaluation of sub-expressions. This is illustrated by the program fragment shown in Example 12.4.

```
type INT_ARRAY is array (1..10) of INTEGER ;
The_array: INT_ARRAY ; – –initialized using Tacky
J: INTEGER := 1 ;

function Tacky ( A: INTEGER) return INTEGER is
   B: INTEGER := A + 1 ;
begin
   J := J + 1 ; – –J keeps track of the number of calls
   return B;
end Tacky ;

begin
   while J < 11 loop
      The_array (J) := J + Tacky (J) ;
      – – J is incremented in Tacky
   end loop ;
end ;
```

Example 12.4   A function with side effects.

If sub-expressions in an expression are evaluated from left to right, this fragment would result in The_array having the value (3, 5, 7, 9, 11, 13, 15, 17, 19, 21). However, if the sub-expressions are evaluated from right to left (this is quite permissable according to the Ada standard), The_array would be set up as (4, 6, 8, 10, 12, 14, 16, 18, 20, 22).

This unsubtle example illustrates that the order of evaluation of an expression can affect its value and side effects may cause problems in both expression evaluation and in the evaluation of sub-program parameters. The ability to write functions with side effects was included in Ada because they simplify some operations on certain abstract data types (updating a stack pointer, for example). However, we believe that their inclusion is a defect in Ada's design and that they should never be used because of their detrimental effect on system maintainability and portability.

An immense amount of useful software is written in languages other than Ada and it is desirable that systems written in Ada should be able to make use of this software if appropriate to do so. Thus, the designers of Ada have included the predefined pragma INTERFACE which allows sub-programs written in other languages to be called from Ada programs. This is an inherently non-portable construct for the following reasons:

- The sub-programs called may be part of a local program library that cannot be readily ported to a new target system.

- There is no specified set of languages which must be supported by all Ada compilers. This means that one compiler might allow access to JOVIAL procedures, but this is not permitted by some other compiler.

- The calling conventions for different languages will almost certainly differ from machine to machine and these may be reflected in the Ada program. Thus particular implementations may place different restrictions on how linkage is made to external sub-programs written in some other language.

If a principal requirement is that programs should be portable, the use of sub-programs in some other language should be avoided. However, economic considerations sometimes make this an unattractive option and it is clearly a decision for software management to decide on the tradeoff between software portability and software reuse.

12.2   Software reusability

As we suggested above, there is an immense volume of software in existence and it is clearly desirable to make use of this software in building new systems wherever possible. In practice, however, formalized, effective software reuse is limited to a few application domains (such as mathematical software) and, in most software development organizations, software reuse is limited and informal. Whilst the notion of reusable software components has been around for a long time, the reality is that the widespread use of existing components is unusual in most large embedded software systems. There are several reasons for this:

1. Apart from specialized routines, such as numerical algorithms, it is

very difficult indeed to describe the function of a software component in a precise way. This has hindered the creation of catalogues of software routines for reuse, which has meant that determining the existence of useful components can be very difficult indeed.

2. Building software components that are readily reusable requires considerable thought and effort, and a reusable component is almost always more expensive to construct than a non-reusable component with the same function. While project managers and software engineers are assessed by their results on a particular project, there is little incentive to create reusable components.

3. The sale of reusable routines is likely to lead to loss of future business for the contractor.

4. Components are often not reusable directly, but require some adaptation to interface them with an existing system. This means that the source code of the components must be available, and many companies are unwilling to release their source code. There is unlikely to be a large market for object code components.

The economic arguments for software reuse are unassailable. If a software component is reused rather than rewritten effort is saved in the design and implementation of that component. Perhaps more importantly, reusable components are inherently more reliable than new components because they have been exposed to a greater degree of validation simply because they are exercised in more than one system. It has been suggested (Boehm, 1984) that very significant increases in productivity will only come about when software is effectively reused.

Furthermore, the existence of a large library of reusable components will simplify the problem of producing low-cost system prototypes. Components will be selected from the library and 'bolted together' to form a prototype system which may then be used to refine the software requirements. Arriving at a definitive set of requirements is one of the most difficult problems in large system construction. Given a prototype, however, users are able to establish their requirements by experiment rather than hypothetical analysis, and are thus less likely to make errors in the system requirements specification.

It was one of the objectives of the Ada development to ensure that language features did not hinder the reuse of software and, indeed, wherever possible should encourage the production of reusable software components. To some extent this has been achieved in that Ada packages are sometimes a convenient encapsulation for reusable components. In this section, we shall look at the classes of reusable software components and examine how the Ada package may be used to build reusable components.

We do not discuss details of Ada programming for reuse. It goes without saying that a component that is intended for reuse should be written in such a way that it is understandable and adaptable. These are characteristics we have tried to stress throughout the book, and by using the style guidelines set out in Chapter 7 and the design principles of information hiding, coherence and loose coupling, the developed components should be readily adapted for reuse.

12.3 Reusable component classes

The notion of a software component comparable to a hardware component is a useful one, but it is important to realize that it is a general idea rather than a reference to a particular software unit. Components can be very large (operating systems for example) or very small (type declarations) and might be represented in software systems as processes, packages, procedures or object declarations.

In fact, there are three classes of component which might be reused in software systems:

1. Generalized components that are sufficiently adaptable to be used in a variety of applications. An example of such a component might be a database management system that is used in conjunction with different applications. Generalized components are usually large and multifunctional and it is often cost-effective to constrain application software design in order to reuse such components.

2. Primitive components that carry out a single clearly defined function which may be required by a number of different applications. An example of such a component is a function to compute the square root of a number – this could clearly be used in a wide variety of numerical applications.

3. Subsystems dedicated to a particular task, but composed of several rather than a single function. Examples include abstract data types such as a list data type and a polar navigation subsystem which provides all necessary navigation functions.

Let us now consider the characteristics of each of these classes of component.

12.3.1 Generalized component reuse

Generalized components are large-scale application systems such as operating systems, database management systems, word processing systems, etc. It is almost always cost effective to reuse such systems if they are suitable for a particular application because of the amount of work involved in reimplementing the facilities they provide. Indeed, it is often cost effective to modify system requirements in order to reuse such components. Of course, the disadvantage is that their development is normally outside the control of the developers of the application system that uses the component. This has three consequences:

- The application system developers are unable to make changes to the component. In some circumstances, a small inexpensive change to a system can have a critical effect and the inability to make that change may mean that reuse is impossible.

- The cost of the reusable component is outside the control of the application system developers. Thus, buyers of the application system must also buy (and pay for the maintenance of) the reused component.

- The portability of the application is constrained by the portability of the reused component.

These disadvantages often preclude the reuse of large-scale components whose development is outside the control of the application system developers. Nevertheless, because of the cost saving gained, reuse should be considered wherever possible.

12.3.2 Function reuse

The reuse of individual functions and procedures is probably the most widely practised form of reuse. This is particularly true for functions in particular application areas (such as mathematical computation) where large function libraries are commercially available and widely used. However, unless the application being developed can make use of a large part of a function library, the cost saving from reusing primitive function components is less than that gained from using larger components. However, because of the specialized nature of many functions (optimized series computation, say), the cost savings from reuse of primitive function components can be significant.

Again, the development of function components is often outside the control of the application developers, but, in this case, this is less critical. The individual functions are usually sufficiently inexpensive to implement, so that inappropriate functions may be rewritten as part of the application software.

12.3.3 Subsystem reuse

Subsystem reuse is only usually practicable when the source code of the subsystem is available to the application developers. Generally, the subsystem must be adapted in some way to make it suitable for use with a particular application. This type of reuse offers large cost savings as such subsystems usually make up large parts of an application. However, these cost savings must be traded off against the cost of adapting the component and, possibly, altering its structure in such a way that maintenance becomes more expensive. The Ada package construct is particularly suitable for defining subsystems that may be reused, and this is the topic of the following section.

One of the problems in attempting to reuse subsystems is that it is sometimes the case that the component which is most useful for an application is actually implemented as a sub-component of a subsystem. If the design of that subsystem is not well-layered, it may not be clear that the sub-component actually exists. Sometimes detailed application knowledge is necessary to work out that subsystem X with function Y must include some component P as P is an intrinsic sub-function of Y.

To take a fairly trivial example, say the required component is one that produces a list of all of the unique words in a piece of text. Assume that the source code of a spelling checker subsystem is available – this almost certainly includes the required function, but that may not be obvious without foreknowledge of what is involved in spelling checker programs.

The solution of such problems requires that the cataloguing of software components be carried out in an intelligent and thorough way and that catalogue retrieval software should exist to retrieve sub-components. Some work on this topic is reported in Davies (1986).

12.4   Building reusable components from Ada packages

We have already looked at the Ada package construct in some detail elsewhere in this book. Probably more than any other, it is the feature of Ada which makes the language suited to the construction of large software systems. Using packages, we can write abstractions over declarations, set up abstract data types, develop and compile sections of program code independently and encapsulate machine-dependencies. In addition, the package also appears to be a suitable base form for reusable software components.

Generic packages, in particular, can be used to construct generalized abstract data types that may be instantiated using different types. Thus, a single generic package may be reused in many ways. For example, consider the generic package in Example 12.5 which is a generalization of the MAIL_LIST abstract data type introduced as part of the electronic mail system discussed in earlier chapters. This package may be instantiated for various types. For example:

```
package Integer_linked is new Linked (ELEMENT => INTEGER) ;
package String_linked is new Linked (ELEMENT => STRING) ;
```

```
generic
    type ELEMENT is private ;
package Linked is
    type LIST is private ;
    type STATUS is (Ok, Error) ;
    function Create return LIST ;
    function Add (L: LIST ; E: ELEMENT) return LIST ;
    procedure Head (L: LIST ; Value: in out ELEMENT ;
                        Result: in out STATUS) ;
    function Tail (L: LIST) return LIST ;
    function Is_empty (L: LIST) return BOOLEAN ;
private
    type LIST_ELEM ;
    type LIST is access LIST_ELEM ;
end Linked ;
```

Example 12.5   A generic package to implement lists.

The linked list package need only be written once and may then be reused for any appropriate type by instantiating it using that type. This works well as long as the operations on linked lists that are required by a user are those set out in the package – should the user require different operations, he or she must take a copy of the source code of the generic package and modify it to provide the required operations.

There are two disadvantages that are a result of forcing the user to modify the source code of a package:

- It is very difficult to transmit details of subsequent changes to the package to all users who have made their own modifications. It may be even more difficult for users to assess the impact of these modifications on their own version of the package.

- A proliferation of similiar, but slightly different packages is likely to be created. It is very difficult for a user to decide which of these is most appropriate to his or her needs.

In order to minimize the need for end-user adaptation, it is important to define the operations on abstract data types to be as complete and as general as possible. Naturally, for any particular instance, this increases the package development cost, but, within an organization, this may be traded off against savings from subsequent reuse. The above example illustrates that simply picking an application package and making it generic does not necessarily create a reusable software component. In a report on Ada and software reuse, Braun and Goodenough (1985) set out the classes of operation that should be provided to define a complete abstract data type. These are:

- creation;
- termination (if appropriate);
- conversion;
- state inquiry;
- state change;
- input/output representation.

Creation involves both creating and initializing an object. Termination is a means of making the object inaccessible for the remainder of its scope. Conversion allows for the change of representation from one type to another. State inquiry functions allow the user to determine the state of the object, state change functions allow that state to be changed, and input/output representations are primarily useful for application debugging purposes.

Thus, a more complete definition of an abstract data type list which incorporates the above classes of operation is as shown in Example 12.6.

Notice the important change that has been made if the package is to be reused. As well as dramatically increasing its functionality, all functions are now implemented as procedures and an explicit error level indicator is returned by each procedure. Procedures are used rather than functions because the type of ELEMENT may be limited private and assignment may not be defined. In this case, it would be impossible to assign the results of functions which returned ELEMENT. An extra procedure called Explain_error has been added to convert the error level to a meaningful error message.

This package definition is clearly much larger and more generalized than the previous definition of Linked, but it is by no means clear that it will necessarily provide the operation required by a particular application. For example, one required state inquiry function might be a function to check if there are duplicate list members, and this has not been provided here. The definition of interfaces to packages is essentially arbitrary as functions may be added almost indefinitely. Actually, there is usually a small set of primitive functions out of which all others may be constructed given that parts of the structure may be copied and named.

However, structure copying involves significant overhead and this is likely to preclude reuse of a component, particularly in embedded systems. Thus, a reasonable criterion for interface design is to include operations that would require structure copying if implemented in terms of more primitive operations.

12.4.1   Exception handling

One extremely difficult problem which faces the designer of reusable software components is how to handle exceptions that arise in the course of component execution. Applications are so diverse that it is unlikely that any single technique will be appropriate for all applications that reuse a component. Two extreme approaches may be taken and (obviously) combinations of these may be used. The extreme approaches are:

1. Do not attempt to handle exceptions. Publish the exception names in the definition of the component interface and force all exceptions to be handled by the calling program. All exceptions are propagated on detection.

2. Make arbitrary decisions on exception handling and publish these as part of the component documentation. If users do not like this arbitrary approach, they must adapt the component accordingly.

One important guideline that should be followed in component interface design is to define state inquiry functions which can be used to detect if a state change function is likely to cause an exception. For example, the functions above that modify the list according to whether an element is present might cause an exception to be raised if the list does not contain that element. Before calling such functions, the user might be advised to call the function 'Contains' to check that the element is present in the list.

An alternative approach is to implement an exception handler as a sub-program call and to pass the sub-program that handles the exception as a generic formal sub-program. Thus, it is up to the user to decide how he or she wishes to handle particular exceptions and to provide the appropriate sub-program when the generic package is instantiated. Thus, the header of the package Linked might be augmented as shown in Example 12.7. Here, two generic procedure parameters have been included so that the user may provide his or her own exception handling procedures. Notice that a default exception handler (Empty_list_handler and Missing_element_handler) has been provided in each case.

The same technique of providing generic sub-program parameters may also be used in situations where different interface operations require quite different implementations depending on the generic parameter type. For example, each type really requires its own print operation, so it is reasonable to expect a user to provide a print routine when the package is instantiated. Thus, the package header (leaving out

```ada
with TEXT_IO ;
generic
  type ELEMENT is private ;
  type ELEMENT_ARRAY is private ;
package Linked is
  type LIST is limited private ;
  type STATUS is range 1..10 ;
  --creation
  procedure Create (Error_level: out STATUS) ;
  -- termination not appropriate for this abstraction
  -- Conversion to and from arrays
  procedure Array_to_list (A: ELEMENT_ARRAY ; Outlist: out LIST ;
                Error_level: out STATUS ) ;
  procedure List_to_array (L: LIST; Outarray: in out
                                        ELEMENT_ARRAY;
                Error_level: out STATUS ) ;
  -- state inquiry
  procedure Is_empty (L: LIST; Result: out BOOLEAN ;
                Error_level: out STATUS ) ;
  procedure Size_of (L: LIST ; Size: out NATURAL ;
                Error_level: out STATUS ) ;
  procedure Contains (E: ELEMENT; Result: out BOOLEAN ;
                Error_level: out STATUS ) ;
  procedure Head (L: LIST; E: in out ELEMENT ;
                Error_level: out STATUS ) ;
  procedure Tail ( Outlist: in out LIST ;
                Error_level: out STATUS ) ;
  -- state change procedures
  -- Append adds an element to the end of the list
  procedure Append ( E: ELEMENT; Outlist: in out LIST ;
                Error_level: out STATUS ) ;
  -- Add adds an element to the front of the list
  procedure Add ( E: ELEMENT; Outlist: in out LIST ;
                Error_level: out STATUS ) ;
  -- Add_before adds an element before element which matches E
  procedure Add_before ( E: ELEMENT ; Outlist: in out LIST ;
                Error_level: out STATUS ) ;
  -- Add_after adds an element after element E
  procedure Add_after ( E: ELEMENT; Outlist: in out LIST ;
                Error_level: out STATUS ) ;
  -- Replace replaces the element matching E1 with E2
```

(cont.)

Example 12.6   A linked list package tailored for reuse.

```
procedure Replace ( E1, E2: ELEMENT; Outlist: in out LIST ;
                Error_level: out STATUS ) ;
-- Clear deletes all members of a list
procedure Clear ( Outlist: in out LIST ;
                Error_level: out STATUS ) ;
-- Prune removes the last element from the list
procedure Prune ( Outlist: in out LIST ;
                Error_level: out STATUS ) ;
-- Prune_to deletes the list up to and including the element
-- which matches E
procedure Prune_to ( E: ELEMENT; Outlist: in out LIST ;
                Error_level: out STATUS ) ;
-- Prune_from deletes list after element matching E
procedure Prune_from( E: ELEMENT; Outlist: in out LIST ;
                Error_level: out STATUS ) ;
-- Remove deletes the element which matches E
procedure Remove ( E: ELEMENT; Outlist: in out LIST ;
                Error_level: out STATUS ) ;
-- Remove_before and Remove_after delete the element before and
-- after E respectively
procedure Remove_before ( E: ELEMENT; Outlist: in out LIST ;
                Error_level: out STATUS ) ;
procedure Remove_after ( E: ELEMENT; Outlist: in out LIST ;
                Error_level: out STATUS ) ;
-- I/O procedures
-- The problem here is that some kinds of element may not have a
-- printed representation and that conversion for file I/O may be
-- impossible for some types of element. In general, these procedures
-- may not operate for access types, but must trap incorrect use
procedure Print_list (L: LIST;
                Error_level: out STATUS ) ;
procedure Save_list (F: TEXT_IO.FILE_TYPE ; L: LIST;
                Error_level: out STATUS ) ;
procedure Restore_list (F: TEXT_IO.FILE_TYPE ; Outlist: out LIST ;
                Error_level: out STATUS ) ;
procedure Explain_error (Level: STATUS ; Message: out STRING) ;
private
    type LIST_ELEM;
    type LIST is access LIST_ELEM ;
end Linked ;
```

Example 12.6 (cont.)

the exception handlers) would be as follows:

```
generic
    type ELEMENT is private ;
    type ELEMENT_ARRAY is private ;
    with procedure Print_element (E: ELEMENT) ;
package
    ...
```

Notice that, in this case, no default print routine has been provided. This must be supplied by the user on instantiation.

Another problem which sometimes arises, particularly in exception handling, is that of unwanted generality. Clearly, a reusable component should cater for all exceptional conditions that might arise during its use, but, for any particular application, it may not be possible for some of these exceptions to arise. Thus, the user of the component has to accept the additional overhead of checking for exceptions that cannot possibly occur.

This problem can be circumvented, to some extent, by tailoring the component with generic boolean parameters which allow exception checking to be switched off. For example, say a particular application making use of the package Linked always checked for itself that a list contained an element before calling a state change function. In-built exception checking could be controlled by a boolean called Existence_check which was instantiated with the package. This would be included in the package header as follows:

```
generic
    type ELEMENT is private ;
    type ELEMENT_ARRAY is private ;
    Existence_check: BOOLEAN := TRUE ;
package Linked
    ...
```

In order to turn off checking, Existence_check should be instantiated

```
generic
    type ELEMENT is private ;
    type ELEMENT_ARRAY is private ;
    with procedure Handle_empty_list is
            Empty_list_handler ;
    with procedure Handle_missing_element is
            Missing_element_handler ;
package Linked is
    ...
```

Example 12.7   Exception handlers as generic parameters.

to false when the generic package is instantiated. This means that the code will contain a section headed **if False then...** and a good optimizing compiler will be able to remove that code entirely from the generated object code.

The fact that generalized components imply additional overheads (particularly space overheads) can cause serious problems in embedded systems that must operate under tight memory constraints. For example, say the above list abstract data type was used. It is unlikely that all of the defined operations would be required, but most linkers would include the entire package of functions and not just those used in the program.

Ideally, an intelligent linker would operate simply by including those functions that are needed. However, an approach which the user may take is to make use of the pragma INLINE to tell the compiler that inline code for the function may be generated. This means that an optimizing compiler can perform optimization across function calls and can recognise (perhaps) that the package functions are never called and may be removed from the object code. Braun and Goodenough (1985) discuss in detail how pragmas may be utilized to assist compiler optimization.

This short discussion on reuse illustrates many of the problems which can arise when designing reusable components and, at present, it is impossible to provide a set of definite guidelines which guarantee reusability. This whole topic is currently the subject of a great deal of research and it is to be hoped that a discipline of reuse will emerge in the next few years.

12.5 Summary

Ada was designed with portability in mind and a standard language was established at an early stage in the development process. This means that Ada programs are likely to be fairly portable, but two classes of machine dependency are unavoidable.

These are dependency on the machine architecture of the target computer and dependency on the operating system of the host system used for program development. This latter class of dependency should be minimized when APSEs are widely available, but is likely to be a problem for the next few years. Machine architecture problems are basically the result of different data representations in different machines, and we have demonstrated how use of packages and abstract data types can localize dependencies and minimize the changes required when programs are moved from one architecture to another.

Potential portability problems can arise in programs which use tasks. These are a result of different processing speeds, which can result in situations where programs that meet their performance requirements on one system cannot be ported successfully to a machine with a slower processor. We have presented a number of guidelines to minimize these problems, but, in essence, they cannot be altogether avoided.

The final part of the portability discussion looked at compiler dependencies. Although the Ada language has been standardized there are some unspecified compiler actions, such as the order of expression evaluation. We have suggested programming techniques that do not make assumptions about particular compiler characteristics.

Software reuse is desirable from an economic point of view, but very difficult in practice. We have identified different classes of software component and suggested the economic benefits of reusing components from each of these classes.

Ada was designed with software reuse as an objective and the generic facilities of the language mean that general-purpose components can be defined and instantiated for particular requirements. However, it is by no means easy to construct a component that is truly reusable without a great deal of additional effort.

12.6 Further reading

Nissen, J. and Wallis, P. (1984). *Portability and Style in Ada*. Cambridge: Cambridge University Press.

> This is one of a set of books on Ada published by CUP. It presents a set of sensible style guidelines and discusses in detail general portability problems that can arise in Ada programs.

IEEE Transactions in Software Engineering. **SE-10**, (5) 1984.

> This special issue contains several papers on software reuse which provide an effective summary of the state of the art.

Braun, C.L. and Goodenough, J. B. (1985). *Ada Reusability Guidelines*. SofTech Report 3285-2-208/2 for the USAF, Electronic Systems Division.

> This report is essential reading for the serious student of Ada and software reuse. It presents an in-depth look at the problems of reusing Ada and offers some tentative solutions to these problems. We hope that this report will be published in a more generally available form in future and, because of its importance, include it here as suggested reading.

Appendix   Examples and Exercises

In this appendix we present a number of examples and exercises intended to help the reader using this book for self-study, and the instructor using the book to support a course in Ada software development. The examples are of three types: design examples which concern large system design, project examples which are suggestions for individual projects using Ada, and programming examples which are relatively short exercises intended to reinforce material discussed in the book.

A.1   Design examples

The examples in this section are broad outline descriptions of large real-time software systems which could, conceivably, be built using the techniques described in this book. It is obviously not intended that readers should build such systems; but we believe that it is instructive to develop these at an architectural level and to continue the design in more detail for selected parts of the system. We have made use of these examples in a software engineering course to illustrate requirements specification and software design techniques, and student group projects may be set up to produce requirements and design documents for these systems.

Some of the examples here are of real-time systems and the problem with trying to present examples of these systems is that many are very application-dependent. Understanding the system requires an understanding of its domain. In that respect, we have chosen fairly general examples which are necessarily simplified, but which should be understandable to all readers.

Example 1   A command and control system for a gas supply utility

A computer system is required to support the emergency response system of a regional gas supply utility. The utility's emergency response system is geared to responding to reports of gas leakages and a large number of vehicles are deployed at various sites throughout the region. When a telephone message reporting a gas leak is received, the location is recorded and one or more of these vehicles is sent to investigate the problem. On arrival at the site, the vehicle reports its position to the controller.

It is assumed that all domestic gas customers have a standard gas supply, but industrial customers may have one of a number of different types of gas-fuelled equipment. The gas supply utility maintains a database of which customers use what equipment. If an emergency call is received from an industrial customer, the control system interrogates this database and transmits details of the equipment type to the emergency vehicles that have been routed to the reported leak.

The support computer system is intended to provide the following:

1. a continually updated display showing the current locations of all emergency vehicles;
2. a record of all reported incidents, the time these were reported, the time action was initiated and the time that the emergency was cleared;
3. assistance to schedulers suggesting which vehicles should be diverted to handle incidents (Note that the system does not make a decision on this – it merely offers the human scheduler information on which vehicles are most likely to provide the quickest response to an incident);
4. communication facilities with the customer database so that information on industrial supplies may be sent to the emergency vehicles.

Example 2   A weather data collection system

A software system is required to collect and collate meteorological information gathered from a network of automatic, computer-controlled weather stations. To simplify processing, to reduce communications costs and to allow local forecasts to be provided, the weather station network is structured so that each weather station reports to an area computer, which collates local information and, periodically, transmits the information to the central meteorological computer system for final processing and long-term storage. Figure A.1 shows how this network might be organized.

Each local weather station collects the following information:

Air temperature	Every second
Ground temperature	Every second
Wind speed	Every second
Wind direction	Every minute
Rainfall	Hourly or since last collection.
Relative humidity	Every second

| Barometric pressure | Every second |
| Visibility | Every second |

Information is collated at the weather station and is transmitted hourly to the local area computer using a dial-up link. The following information is transmitted:

Air temperature	Mean, minimum, maximum
Ground temperature	Mean, minimum, maximum
Wind speed	Mean, minimum, maximum
Wind direction	Observed average direction
Rainfall	Measured amount.
Relative humidity	Mean, minimum, maximum
Barometeric pressure	Mean, minimum, maximum
Visibility	Mean, minimum, maximum
Precipitation	Raining/snowing or not

If the designated area station is unavailable, the weather station tries up to three other stations to make its report. If all of these attempts are unsuccessful, it tries to dial-up the central meteorological office system to report failure. If a weather station does not call in within 3 minutes of its designated time, the local computer attempts to call that station. If this fails, a failure report is sent to the central meteorological office machine.

Each local station collects the information from all of its associated weather stations and, using that information, produces a sequence of

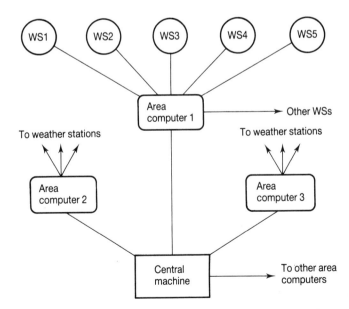

Figure A.1   A weather station computer network.

charts/maps summarizing the information. When complete, these are transmitted in digital form for further processing by the central machine. In addition, the raw information is stored and, once per day, all weather station information is saved on a tape. This tape is sent to the central meteorological office weekly.

Example 3   A fire alarm monitoring system

A software system is to be built to control the heat and smoke sensors, the fire alarms and the fire fighting systems in a large building. The building is made up of a number of areas and each area is equipped with three sensors. If, in any one area, two out of the three sensors indicate a fire, the fire alarm sequence set out below should be activated.

1. Signal alarm in building control centre. Illuminate the area where fire is detected on a building map panel. Wait for a response.

2. If a response is received which acknowledges that the alarm is positive, then continue with the actions as set out below. If the response indicates that the alarm is negative, reset the sensors and the alarm system. If the response indicates that the sensors are faulty, isolate them from the system. If no response is received within 30 seconds, assume a positive response and continue as set out below.

3. If the sensors indicate a problem within three *sensitive areas*, automatically shut down the electrical equipment in these sensitive areas. Continuously monitor the spread of the fire using the sensor alarms and activate equipment shutdown as necessary.

4. Activate an auto-dial call to the fire brigade detailing the area of the building where the problem was detected.

5. Activate fire alarms throughout the building. Illuminate direction signs to the fire doors. Automatically, route exits away from area where the fire is indicated.

6. If the fire is in a sensitive area equipped with carbon dioxide flooding equipment, activate an alarm indicating that carbon dioxide flooding will be activated.

7. Wait 30 seconds, then activate carbon dioxide flooding in the area where fire is indicated.

Example 4   An automated banking system

The operation of a bank account is a potential application for an Ada program. Typical operations on a bank account are:

- open the account;
- close the account;

- deposit money;
- withdraw money;
- calculate bank charges;
- issue a statement of the account.

All these are very straightforward operations. Design an Ada program which would allow such a banking system to be set up. Note that if automated teller machines are used, it is necessary to check the validity of access to the account and allow for multiple simultaneous access to the account. Some form of Reader–Writers protocol is required for this.

As an extension to this banking system, design a program to control the operation of an automated teller machine that communicates with your banking system. You should study your local system and copy it. As a word of warning there are a number of design issues in Auto Teller systems that are not immediately obvious. For example, systems usually make the user remove their card before issuing money to ensure cards are not left in the machine. So be careful in your design.

A.2 Project examples

The examples in this section are of systems that could conceivably be built by students using Ada in a term or semester project. We have avoided suggesting real-time system projects because of the specialized hardware requirements which may be involved. In general, all of the projects are open-ended and the facilities suggested are intended simply as a starting point – many enhancements to the projects here might be provided.

Example 1   An Ada program browser

The aim of a program browser is to give the user the capability of examining Ada programs as structured objects rather than simply as linear text. Thus the program browser has built-in knowledge of Ada syntax and (perhaps) local standards for Ada programs. The system interacts with the browser, specifying the type or instance of information of interest, and this is then displayed.

For example, using the browser the user should be able to identify a name and then specify that the declaration and all uses of that name (along with local contexts) should be displayed. It should also be possible to 'compress' the display so that only declarations are shown, only procedure headings are displayed, package and procedure body listings are suppressed.

There is a virtually unlimited set of facilities which may be added to the browser. It may be implemented on a simple character terminal,

but a more effective implementation would make use of a bit-mapped
workstation equipped with a mouse or other pointing device. To use the
browser, the programmer would simply point at names or types of
interest, and then select the class of display from a function menu.

Example 2   A generalized re-usable display and menu management system

More and more applications are now menu-driven rather than command-
driven and it is the aim of this project to produce an Ada system that
allows a generalized menu-management system to be constructed. This
system must operate on a range of devices, from simple character
terminals to bit-mapped workstations which provide a good deal of
support for menu-display. The addition of new device types should
require as little effort as is practicable.

Some of the facilities to be offered by this system are:

1. the ability to define the strings representing menu items and the
   associated Ada procedures that should be invoked when that item is
   selected;
2. the ability to handle dynamic menus which change during the
   execution of an application;
3. the ability to define the names of Ada procedures which are invoked
   whenever a particular menu item is chosen;
4. an inbuilt help system which allows the user to provide help frames
   associated with menu items;
5. the ability to define where on the user's display menus should be
   presented and the styles in which individual items are displayed (for
   example, the user may specify that a particular string is to be
   displayed in bold text, and this must be translated to whatever
   hardware facilities are offered by the device);
6. an associated message system which allows the user to specify where
   messages from applications are displayed and the form in which these
   are displayed.

This project requires the definition of a simple language to describe
menus and displays or, if a workstation is available, the displays may
be built interactively and recorded by the system. This system might be
constructed either as one or more generic packages or as a program
generator which outputs an Ada menu manager package.

Example 3   A software components catalogue

If we are to practise effective software reuse, there is a need for retrieval
systems for software components. The aim of this project is to build a

components cataloguing system that allows details of software components to be recorded in a database and these details to be retrieved by potential component users. The system must be structured in such a way that it takes less time to find a component than to write that component afresh.

It is suggested that a forms-based interface should be devised for both component cataloguing and retrieval (query languages take time to learn and are not popular with casual users) and that keywords are used to classify and retrieve individual components. If a bit-mapped workstation is available, the user interface facilities on this machine should be used.

Example 4 A structure editor for software engineering documents

In large software engineering projects it is normal for a document standard to be established and for all project documents to conform to that standard. It is often the case that the standard is very detailed and ensuring exact conformance is a time-consuming task. The aim of this project is to produce a structured document editor that makes use of a document description and uses this to drive the editing system. Thus, this project consists of defining a notation for describing document structure, constructing an analyser for this notation and generating tables to drive the document editor.

The document editor should be a WYSIWYG editor which incorporates simple text processing capabilities, but need not have full word processing capabilities. The initial versions of this system should assume that documents are text-only, but later additions might include the facility to deal with program source code, forms and diagrams.

Example 5 A group diary and time management system

Simple electronic diaries where users may record appointments and be reminded of these automatically are now relatively common. The objective of this project is to develop an enhanced version of such a diary which, as well as providing simple recording and reminder facilities for individuals, may be used for scheduling group meetings and activities. Thus, if a group meeting is to be scheduled (say), the system must be able to interrogate all members' diaries to see when they are available, find a suitable slot, make the appointment and electronically mail group members that the meeting has been scheduled. A variety of such facilities may be incorporated and we leave it to the system designer to choose exactly what should be supported.

A possible extension of this project is to introduce the notion of cancellable meetings so that diaries may be automatically reorganized to make members available for group meetings or to manage a member's time more effectively. For example, if an individual is involved in technical work, the diary might be optimized so that as many uninterrupted periods as possible are scheduled. Again we leave it to the imagination of the system designer to devise appropriate optimization facilities.

Example 6   An airline reservation database

An airline reservation system contains as part of the total system a database with information on each flight. This information may itself contain data such as the number of passengers, number of free seats, the allocated seats, the names and ticket numbers of the passengers, the number of seats sold and not yet checked in, etc. In designing such a system the programmer must take into account various stages of flight information; for example:

- ticket sales from multiple sites with a fixed waiting period for vendors
- check-in and seat allocation from multiple sites.

Write a system that will handle both the database and point-of-access tasks. Be careful about locking the database during update.

A.3   Programming exercises

This section is made up of a number of relatively short programming, specification and design exercises. These are intended to supplement the material in the book. They may be developed to any appropriate level of detail from a high-level design through to a full implementation.

1. A queue is a data structure whereby items are added at one end and removed from the other end. It is generally implemented as a cyclic entity so that the front and back of the queue progress through the data structure.
    This exercise is to define and implement a queue as an Ada package. The operations, which should be defined using an algebraic approach, are:

Create	bring the queue into existence
AddItem	add an item to the queue
RemoveItem	take an item from the queue
IsFull	report true if the queue is full, false otherwise
IsEmpty	report true if the queue is empty, false otherwise

2. A structured graphics system is to be built which uses the primitives of line, rectangle, and curve to allow users to create simple line diagrams. Suggest specifications for the data types line, rectangle and

curve. Invent a sensible set of operations on these data types to build the specification.

1. Using the specification of the graphics system types, design an Ada package called GRAPHICS_TYPES which provides these types and their associated operations to graphics system builders.

2. Bit-mapped graphics workstations usually incorporate a window management system whereby a window is considered as a system object. Define a set of operations on windows such as Move, Resize, Close, etc. and construct an algebraic specification for these.

3. Devise an object-oriented model of your favourite operating system. For example, a UNIX model might include directory objects, file objects, document objects, C-program objects etc. Design Ada packages to represent these objects and to generate the appropriate operating system commands.

4. Design an Ada package which provides a 'soft' keyboard. That is, it should be possible for the user to define which ASCII codes are generated by particular keyboard operations and the package should convert the keyboard character generated to that specified by the user.

5. Design an Ada package which can be connected to a modem to provide auto-dialling of telephone numbers. The user must be able to specify the number to be dialled and an associated identifier. Input of that identifier then causes the auto-dial.

6. Design an Ada program which may be used to drive colour display screens made up of rectangles of different colours and of arbitrary size. Assume that overlapping of rectangles is handled so that the user may specify which rectangle is considered the foreground and which the background colour. Develop both functional and object-oriented designs for this system.

7. Design and implement a procedure to merge two ordered sequential files of any type. Use this program to sort a sequential file.
   Care must be taken here to parameterize the procedure correctly as a generic. A '<' operator over the element type must be used as must scratch files in the second part.

8. Design a hash implementation of a symbol table that will allow the user to customize the system for a particular hashing algorithm and record type.

9. One of the languages that Ada is designed to replace is FORTRAN, which allows fixed format I/O – that is, the reading and writing of records split up into fields without separators. This is achieved by format statements that specify the shape of the data fields in the record and their type. A read or write statement which uses the format will transfer data of the correct shape. For example

10 FORMAT (I5, 10A2, 2F8.2, A2, 2F8.3)

will specify the shape of one integer of 5 fields, 10 alphanumerics of 2 fields, 2 floating-point numbers, one alphanumeric, and finally 2 floating-point numbers.

Design an Ada package using Text I/O that will simulate the above format, ignoring errors. The package should contain read and write procedures.

As a second part, take account of format errors in output when the object does not fit the format.

As a third part, make the package dependent on the format – that is, be parameterized by it.

10. Write a procedure that will perform a matrix multiplication. This should be generic to allow for any type of matrix and should raise exceptions if error conditions are found.

11. A common situation in parallel programming is where a resource, which is shared by a number of processes, has to be synchronized for update and reading. Typically, if we are updating the resource we do not wish anyone reading it at the same time. However, if we are reading it does not matter how many others are also reading. This problem, like most in parallel programming, is more subtle than at first meets the eye. For example, we wish to ensure that updates do eventually get done.

12. A very famous example in parallel programming is that of the dining philosophers – due to E. W. Dijkstra. These philosophers either eat or think. Thinking is little problem since it is conducted in the mental plane. Eating, however, poses more of a problem, especially since the food available is a special spaghetti that requires two forks. There are five philosophers, five place settings and five forks arranged as

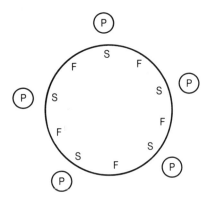

Figure A.2   The dining philosophers.

shown in Figure A.2. Note that S stands for spaghetti, F for forks and P for philosophers.

Write a program to simulate the lives of the philosophers. Once you have solved the problem you should ask yourself what is significant about the number five in this example. Notice that the philosophers are analogous to processes in an operating system and the forks are resources.

15. Ada does not have a SET data constructor. Write a generic package that would provide appropriate operations for sets of any types.

16. Simulate a vending machine that will take any number of coins and a selection of the goods required and then issue the goods and the appropriate change.

Bibliography

Abbott, R. (1983). 'Program design by informal English description' *Communications of the ACM*, **26**, (11), 882–894.

Abrial, J., (1980). *The Specification Language Z: Syntax and Semantics*. Oxford: University Programming Research Group.

Alderson, A., Bott, M. F. B. and Falla, M. E. (1985). 'An overview of the ECLIPSE architecture' In *Integrated Project Support Environments*, ed. J. McDermid. London: Peter Peregrinus.

Atkinson, M. P., Bailey, P. J., Cockshott, W. P., Chisholm, K. J. and Morrison, R. (1983). 'An approach to persistent programming' *Computer Journal*, **26**, (4), 360–365.

Bell, T. E., Dixler, D. C. and Dyer, M. E. (1977). 'An extendable approach to computer-aided software requirements engineering' *IEEE Transactions on Software Engineering*, **SE-3**, (1), 49–60.

Birtwistle, G. M., Dahl, O. J., Myrhaug, B. and Nygaard, K. (1973). *SIMULA BEGIN*. Auerbach.

Boehm, B. W. (1975). 'The high cost of software' In *Practical Strategies for Developing Large Software System*, ed. E. Horowitz. Reading, Mass.: Addison-Wesley.

Boehm, B. W. (1979). 'Software engineering: R & D trend and defense needs' In *Research Directions in Software Technology*. ed. P. Wegner. Cambridge, Mass.: MIT Press.

Boehm, B. W. (1981). *Software Engineering Economics*. Englewood Cliffs, N. J.: Prentice-Hall.

Boehm, B. W. (1984). 'A software development environment for improving productivity' *IEEE Computer*, **17, (6)**.

Booch, G. (1983). *Software Engineering with Ada*. Menlo Park, Calif: Benjamin Cummings.

Bourne, S. R. (1978). 'The UNIX shell', *Bell Systems Technical Journal*, **57**, (6), 1971–1990.

Brachman, R. J. (1983). 'What is-a is and is-a isn't' *IEEE Computer*, **16**.

Braun, C. L. and Goodenough, J. B. (1985). *Ada Reusability Guidelines*. SofTech Report 3285-2-208/2, USAF.

Brooks, F. P. (1975). *The Mythical Man-Month*. Reading, Mass.: Addison-Wesley.

Burstall, R. and Lampson, B. (1984). 'A kernal language for abstract data types and modules'. In *Lecture Notes in Computer Science*, Vol. 173. Springer-Verlag.

Campbell, R. H. and Haberman, A. N. (1974). 'The specification of process synchronization by path expressions, In *Lecture Notes in Computer Science*, Vol. 16, Springer-Verlag.

Campbell, R. H. (1986). 'SAGA: A project to automate the management of software production systems'. In *Software Engineering Environments*, ed. I. Sommerville. London: Peter Peregrinus.

Cardelli, L. (1984). 'A semantics of multiple inheritence' In *Lecture Notes in Computer Science*, Vol. 173. Springer-Verlag, 51–67.

Cherry, L. and MacDonald, N. H. (1983). 'The UNIX Writer's Workbench software', *BYTE*, **8**, (10), 241–52.

Coffman, E. G., Elphick, M. J. and Shoshani, A. (1971). 'System deadlocks' *Computing Surveys*, **3**, (2), 67–78.

Coffman, E. G. and Kleinrock, L. (1968). 'Computer scheduling methods and their countermeasures' *AFIPS SJCC*, **32** (11), 11–21.

Constantine, L. L., Myers, G. and Stevens, W. (1974). 'Structured design' *IBM Systems Journal*, **13**, (2), 115–319.

Constantine, L. L. and Yourdon, E. (1979). *Structured Design*. Englewood Cliffs, N. J.: Prentice-Hall.

Conway, M. (1963). 'A multiprocessor system design.' *AFIPS FJCC*, **27**, 139-146.

Dahl, O. J., Dijkstra, E. W. and Hoare, C.A.R. (1972). *Structured Programming*. New York: Academic Press.

Davies, R. (1986). *Intelligent Information Systems – Progress and Prospects*. Chichester: Ellis Horwood.

DeMarco, T. (1978). *Structured Analysis and System Specification*. New York: Yourdon Press.

Dijkstra, E. W. (1968a). 'A constructive approach to the problem of program correctness'. *BIT*, **8**, 174–186.

Dijkstra, E. W. (1968b). 'Cooperating sequential processes' In *Programming Languages* (editor F. Genuys). London: Academic Press, 43–112.

Dolotta, T. A., Haight, R. C. and Mashey, J. R. (1978). 'The programmer's workbench' *Bell Systems Technical Journal*, **57**, (6), 2177–2200.

Downes, V. A. and Goldsack, S. (1982). *Programming Embedded Systems in Ada*. London: Prentice-Hall.

Gladden, G. R. (1982). 'Stop the life cycle, I want to get off' *ACM Sigplan Notices*, **7** (2), 35–39.

Goguen, J. A., Thatcher, J. and Wagner, E. G. (1977). 'Initial algebra semantics and continuous algebras' *JACM*, **24** (1), 68–95.

Goldberg, A. (1984). *Smalltalk-80: the Interactive Programming Environment.* Reading, Mass.: Addison-Wesley.

Goldberg, A. and Robson, D. (1983). *Smalltalk-80: the Language and its Implementation.* Reading, Mass.: Addison-Wesley.

Guttag, J. (1977). 'Abstract data types and the development of data structures' *Communications of the ACM*, **20**, (6), 396–405.

Gunn, H. I. E. and Morrison, R. (1979). 'On the implementation of constants' *Information Processing Letters*, **9** (1), 1–4.

Hall, J. A., Hitchcock, P. and Took, R. (1985). 'An overview of the ASPECT architecture' In *Integrated Project Support Environments*, ed. J. McDermid. London: Peter Peregrinus.

Havender, J. W. (1968). 'Avoiding deadlocks in multitasking systems' *IBM Systems Journal*, **7** (2), 74–84.

Heninger, K. L. (1980). 'Specifying software requirements for complex systems: new techniques and their applications' *IEEE Transactions on Software Engineering*, **SE-6** (1), 2–13.

Hill, A. (1983). 'Towards an Ada-based specification and design language' *Ada UK News*, **4** (4), 16–35.

Hoare, C. A. R. (1974). 'Monitors: an operating system structuring concept' *Communications of the ACM*, **17** (10), 549–557.

Hoare, C. A. R. (1978). 'Communicating sequential processes' *Communications of the ACM*, **21** (8), 666–677.

Hoare, C. A. R. (1981). 'The Emperor's old clothes' *Communications of the ACM*, **21**(8), 667–677.

IBM Corporation, (1972). *System/360 PL/1 Language Reference Manual.* Form GC28-8201-4.

Ivie, E. L. (1977). 'The programmer's workbench – a machine for software development' *Communications of the ACM*, **20** (10), 746–53.

Iverson, K. E. (1962). *A Programming Language.* John Wiley.

Jackson, M. A. (1975). *Principles of Program Design.* London: Academic Press.

Jackson, M. A. (1982). *System Development.* Englewood Cliffs, N.J.: Prentice-Hall.

Jones, A. K. and Liskov, B. (1978). 'A language extension for expressing constraints on data access' *Communications of the ACM*, **21** (5), 358–367.

Jones, C. B. (1980). *Software Development–Rigourous Approach.* Englewood Cliffs, N. J.: Prentice-Hall.

Jones, T. C. (1978). 'Measuring programming quality and productivity'*IBM Systems Journal*, **17** (1), 39–63.

Kernighan, B. W. and Mashey, J. R. (1979). 'The UNIX programming environment' *Software – Practice and Experience*, **9** (1).

Kernighan, B. W. and Ritchie, D. M. (1979). *The C Programming Language*. Englewood Cliffs, N. J.: Prentice-Hall.

Kreig-Bruckner, B. and Luckham, D. C. (1980). 'Anna: Towards a language for annotating Ada programs' *ACM Sigplan Notices*, **15** (11), 128–138.

Krieg-Bruckner, B., Luckham. D. C., von Henke, F. W. and Owe, O. (1984). *'Anna – Preliminary Reference Manual*. Computer Systems Laboratory, Stanford University.

Lampson, B. W. and Reddell, H. E. (1980). 'Experience with processes and monitors in Mesa' *Communications of the ACM*, **23** (2), 105 – 117.

Le Verrand, D. (1985). *Evaluating Ada*. Oxford: North-Holland Press.

Lientz, B. P. and Swanson, E. B. (1980). *Software Maintenance Management*. Reading, Mass.: Addison-Wesley.

Lindley, L. M. (1983). 'Ada program design language survey update' *ACM Ada Letters*, **4** (1), 61–63.

Linger, R. C., Mills, H. D. and Witt, B. I. (1979). *Structured Programming – Theory and Practice*. Reading, Mass.: Addison-Wesley.

Liskov, B. and Berzins, V. (1979). 'An appraisal of program specification's In *Research Directions in Software Technology*. ed. P. Wegner. Cambridge, Mass.: MIT Press.

Liskov, B. H., Synder, A., Atkinson, R. and Schiffert, C. (1977). 'Abstraction mechanisms in CLU' *Communications of the ACM*, **20** (8), 564–576.

Liskov, B. and Zilles, S. (1974). 'Programming with Abstract Data Types' *ACM Sigplan Notices*, **9** (4), 50–59.

Liskov, B. and Zilles, S. (1979). 'Programming with abstract data types' *ACM Sigplan Notices*, **9** (4), 50–59.

London, R. L. and Robinson, L. (1979). 'The role of verification tools and techniques' In *Software Development Tools*, eds. W. E. Riddle and R. E. Fairley. New York: Springer-Verlag.

McCracken, D. D. and Jackson, M. A. (1982). 'Life cycle concept considered harmful' *ACM Sigplan Notices*, **7** (2), 29–32.

Milner, R. (1979). 'A theory of type polymorphism in programming' *JACM*, **26** (4), 792–818.

Milner, R. (1983). *A Proposal for Standard ML*. Technical Report CSR-157-83, University of Edinburgh.

Morris, J. H. (1973). 'Protection in programming languages' *Communications of the ACM*, **16** (1), 15-21.

Morrison, R. (1979). *S-Algol Language Reference Manual*. University of St Andrews, CS/79/1.

Morrison, R. (1982). 'Low cost computer graphics for micro computers' *Software - Practice and Experience*, **12** (8), 767–776.

Morrison, R., Brown, A. L., Dearle, A. and Atkinson, M. P. (1986). 'An integrated graphics programming environment' *Computer Graphics Forum* **5** (2), 147–157.

Nissen, J. and Wallis, P. (1984). *Portability and Style in Ada*. Cambridge: Cambridge University Press.

Parnas, D. L. (1972a). 'A technique for software module specification with examples' *Communications of the ACM*, **15** (5), 330-336.

Parnas, D. (1972b). 'On the criteria to be used in decomposing systems into modules' *Communications of the ACM*, **15** (2), 1053–1058.

Parnas, D. (1979). 'Specifications: formal and informal' In *Research Directions in Software Technology*, ed. P. Wegner. Cambridge, Mass.: MIT Press.

Peterson, J. L. and Silberschatz, A. (1985). *Operating system concepts*. Wokingham: Addison-Wesley, 2nd edn.

Randall, B. (1978). 'Reliable computer systems' In *Operating Systems: an Advanced Course*. Berlin: Springer-Verlag, 282–392.

Ritchie, D. M. and Thompson, K. (1974). 'The UNIX timesharing system' *Communications of the ACM*, **17** (7), 365–375.

Ritchie, D. M. and Thomson, K. (1978). 'The UNIX time-sharing system' *Bell Systems Technical Journal*, **57** (6), 1991–2020.

Robson, D. (1981). 'Object-oriented software systems' *BYTE*, **6**, (8), 74–79.

Rochkind, M. J. (1975). 'The source code control system' *IEEE Transactions on Software Engineering*, **SE-1** (4), 255–265.

Rosenberg, D. (1985). 'PRISM – Productivity improvement for software engineers and managers' *Proceedings of the Eighth International Conference on Software Engineering*, London, 2–7.

Sommerville, I. and Smith, D. J. (1984). 'An electronic secretary' *Software – Practice and Experience*, **14** (9), 817–825.

Sommerville, I., Smith, D. J. and Welland, R. C. (1985). 'Computer-aided software design' *Proceedings of the Eighth European ACM Conference*, Florence.

Standish, T. A. (1981). 'ARCTURUS. An advanced highly integrated programming environment.' In *Software Engineering Environments*, ed. H. Hunke. North-Holland: Amsterdam.

Stenning, V. (1986). 'An Introduction to ISTAR' In *Software Engineering Environments*, ed. I. Sommerville. London: Peter Peregrinus.

Stephens, M. and Whitehead, K. (1985). 'The Analyst – a workstation for analysis and design' *Proceedings of the Eighth International Conference on Software Engineering*, London, 364–371.

Strachey, C. (1967). *Fundamental Concepts in Programming Languages*. Oxford: Oxford University Press.

Stucki, L. G. and Walker, H. D. (1981). 'Concepts and prototypes of ARGUS' In *Software Engineering Environments*, ed. H. Hunke. North-Holland: Amsterdam.

Taylor, W. J. (1983). 'Ada as a design language' *Ada UK News*, **4** (1), 43–46.

Teichrow, D. and Hershey, E. A. (1977). 'PSL/PSA: A computer-aided technique for structured documentation and analysis of information systems' *IEEE Transactions on Software Engineering*, **SE-3** (1), 41–48.

Teitelbaum, T. and Reps, T. (1981). 'The Cornell Program Synthesiser' *Communications of the ACM*, **24** (9), 563–573.

Teitleman, W. and Masinter, L. (1984). 'The InterLisp programming environment' In *Integrated Programming Environments*, ed. D. R. Barstow, H. E. Shrobe and E. Sandewall, New York: McGraw-Hill.

Van Leer, P. (1976). 'Top-down development using a program design language' *IBM Systems Journal*, **15** (2), 155–170.

Van Wijngaarden, A. *et al.* (1969). 'Report on the algorithmic language Algol 68' *Numerische Mathematik*, **14** (1), 79–218.

Warnier-Orr, J. D. (1977). *Logical Construction of Programs* New York: Van Nostrand Reinhold.

Wegner, P. (1982). 'Capital-intensive software technology' *IEEE Software*, **1** (3), 7–45.

Willis, R. R. (1981). 'AIDES: Computer-aided design of software systems' In *Software Engineering Environments*, ed. H. Hunke. North-Holland: Amsterdam

Wirth, N. (1971). 'Program development by stepwise refinement' *Communications of the ACM*, **14** (4), 221–227.

Wirth, N. (1976). *Systematic Programming: an Introduction*. Englewood Cliffs, N. J.: Prentice-Hall.

Wirth, N. (1983). *Programming in Modula-2*. Berlin: Springer-Verlag, 2nd edn.

Wulf, W. A., Russel, D. B. and Haberman, A. N. (1971). 'Bliss: a language for systems programming' *Communications of the ACM*, **14** (12), 780–790.

Wulf, W. A., Goos, G., Evans, A. and Butler, K. J. (eds.) (1983). *Diana: an Intermediate Language for Ada*. Berlin: Springer-Verlag.

Youll, D. P. (1983). 'Experience with Ada as a PDL' *Ada UK News*, **4** (1), 47–51.

Zilles, S. (1974). *Algebraic Specification of Abstract Data Types*. Progress Report 11, Project MAC, Cambridge, Mass.: MIT Press.

Index